CAPTAIN MAC

WAR HERO, MY HERO

By Jerry Wiley

Captian Mac
War Hero, My Hero

For information please contact
Jerry D. Wiley, 26115 Cedarwood Lane, Shell Knob, MO 65747.

Library of Congress Control Cataloging-in-Publication Data is Avaliable

ISBN: 978-1-60725-547-5

Cover design by Sheila Wiley and Heidi Lowe

Printed in the United States of America
By Litho Printers & Bindery
Cassville, MO 65625

*T*his book does not serve as an all-encompassing his-tory of Captain Robert Brown McHolland, of World War II, or of any particular unit. It is strictly a biographical documentary of the life of Captain Robert Brown McHolland as compiled by an admiring neph-ew, Jerry D. Wiley. The book has been constructed from interviews with family and friends of Captain McHolland, letters written by Captain McHolland while in service during World War II, his Official Per-sonnel File, his Individual Deceased Personnel File, re-cords of the Grand Lodge of Missouri, and his official transcript from Missouri State University. In addition, the author drew freely from his unit's Battle History of the Third Battalion, 358th Infantry, a brief history of the 358th Infantry, Peragimus, "We Accomplish.", Hobert Winebrenner and Mike McCoy's Bootprints: An Infantryman's Walk through World War II, John Colby's War from the Ground Up: The 90th Division in World War II, and the World War II Experiences of Emmett T. Boyd Captain USA Ret. The book may contain unintentional errors in dates, locations or other details. The author has made every effort to ensure the accuracy and completeness of information contained in this book and assumes no responsibility for errors, inac-curacies, omissions, or other inconsistencies herein. The author offers his regrets if there are any slights of people, places or organizations. If they occur, they are entirely unintentional.

Dedication

…. *to the memory of Captain Robert Brown McHolland, his family and friends, and to the men, women and families who gave so much in defense of our precious freedom in World War II. May their service to and sacrifices for our country never be forgotten … to Thomas Earl Hill, Jr., who equally shares with me the most profound admiration and respect for our Uncle Bob … and to his namesakes: Robert Stanley Wiley, Robert Edward McHolland, and Robert Maurice Wiley.*

Acknowledgements

Thanks to my wonderful wife, Sheila, for her patience, understanding, and loving encouragement. Completion of this tribute could not have been possible without her constant and unyielding love and support.

Thanks to my fantastic aunt, Mary Lea McHolland Brown, who kept the scrapbook of Uncle Bob's letters, newspaper articles, pictures, and other useful information and unselfishly shared it with me. She also endured many more hours of answering my many questions about Uncle Bob and the early years of his life. Thanks to her husband, my uncle Travis Brown, and to his brother, John Brown, for sharing their memories of Uncle Bob. They were particularly helpful in providing information about his college and teaching years.

Thanks to Edwin Dean, a war hero and an original Darby's Ranger, for information, pictures, and insight about his good friend.

Thanks to my cousin, Tom Hill, for always being there to listen and to share the least bit of information about our hero.

Thanks to Inez Inmon Bowman, childhood friend of Uncle Bob and close friend of his family, for sharing her memories of his earlier years.

Thanks to my cousin, Sue Brown Crain, for providing the spark that ignited this project.

Thanks to Hobert Winebrenner and Mike McCoy whose "Bootprints" book gave me inspiration and opened up a new world of personal information about Uncle Bob.

Thanks to Howard Pemberton and Emmett Boyd for the many times they patiently shared their time and very personal memories of their service with Uncle Bob in World War II.

Thanks to those many others who contributed their time and provided valuable information and support in a variety of ways: Robert S. Wiley, Vaughn Skaggs, John B. Gordon, Sondra Gordon, Kathryn Robb Hall, June Robb Pritchard, Eddie Brown, Charlie Bowyer, Gene Anderson, Harold Conrad, Wayne Ivie, Byron Wolf, Cecil Clark, Duane Clark, Sherry Bailey, Bill Crabb, Carnell Cutbirth, Vena Custer Berglund, Gary Haas, Frances Wilshire Shahan, Tyler Alberts, Mildred Conrad, Dr. Robert Hackley, Sandy Clark, Donna Judd, Margaret Eaton Dillabough, Mabel Alice Thomas Redwing, Vance Shipman, Sam Weathers, and Bob Hayes.

Thanks to those many other unnamed individuals who constantly offered their encouragement and support.

Table of Contents

Prologue

Except for my superb parents, Maurice and Roxabel Wiley, the person who has most affected my life is someone I hardly knew—my Uncle Bob, Captain Robert Brown McHolland. This work is a tribute to him and is also intended to provide a lasting record of his short and remarkable life for family, friends, and their generations to follow.

Uncle Bob, Captain Mac as he was known to his men and fellow soldiers, was not only a bona fide war hero, but has been my hero from the time of my earliest memory. This story represents the culmination of my lifelong search to learn more about him. I hope that you will not be deterred by the some of the meticulous minutia contained in this effort to tell his story.

As you read this biographic portrayal of Uncle Bob's life, you will sense my unabashed admiration for him. With this work I have diligently endeavored to depict the impact this man has had on my life. However, I realize no matter how much I have tried to accomplish this, it remains that one must have walked in my shoes, dwelt in my soul, and known the deepest inner workings of my mind to grasp the depth and power of his impact.

Before I proceed with this tribute, my sincere hope is that the reader will understand it is not my intent in any way to glorify the death, devastation and destruction of war. I know first hand of the horror, misery, and dreadfulness of armed conflict and there is nothing glamorous or exalting about it. You will learn that Uncle Bob was a peace loving man who prayed for peace in the world and wanted it as much as anyone. It happens that a significant portion of his story involves the part he played in our nation's greatest struggle to protect our liberty and freedom.

In covering his war service I have relied on accounts from military history publications, national news media, personal recollections of Uncle Bob's combat comrades, and information from his official military personnel record to document the situation into which he was thrust in the service of his country. Some of the descriptions are graphic. However, they are necessary to better understand the disparaging, virtually hopeless situation Uncle Bob experienced merely doing his job as the ground war raged from Normandy across France and into Germany in 1944.

Through this story of his life, I hope the reader will come to know how, in the face of these constant unspeakable occurrences, the true character of the man never wavered. Until the end of his short, but fruitful life, it continued to show through his personality, integrity, moral uprightness, mental toughness, unshakeable belief in Almighty God, and the abiding consideration he had for the men he led into battle.

The Beginning--
A Heart-Rending Message

The date was December 11, 1944. How ironic was it that this was just one day after Uncle Bob's 26th birthday! I was very young, about two weeks from my fourth birthday, but even in a child's world I knew that something terrible had happened. With a telegram from the War Department, my mom, Roxabel McHolland Wiley (who was Uncle Bob's sister), was at the old crank wall telephone in the dining room of our home in Hurley, Missouri. My mother's personality was stoic in the most classic sense of the word. She was extremely reserved in the display of her emotions. But at this moment she was weeping profusely and through her sobs she was trying to deliver the gut wrenching message to her sister, Anna McHolland Hill' in Burleson, Texas, that their brother was missing in action. I do not remember the exact conversation my mother had with her sister, but I do recall (intermingled with her sobs) my mother saying something like "But it says he is missing, so there is still hope."

Somehow I knew the conversation was about Uncle Bob. He had already made a most favorable impression on me and clearly established himself as a good guy in my eyes. I remembered him as the fellow who only a few months earlier on his last visit home had taken my brother and me somewhere and bought us ice cream and candy. That clearly made him special to me as a three year old child. One could be certain that his name had been mentioned often in our family's daily routine, given the fact that he was serving with an army infantry unit in the thick of the battle in Europe. Even this small child was sensing there must be something unique about his Uncle Bob.

Since my mother was Uncle Bob's next-of-kin, she had received the dreaded telegram from the War Department with the information that he was missing in action somewhere in Germany. I cannot recall many more specific details about the days and weeks that followed, but I can imagine the terribly tough times that my mother and other family members and friends experienced. The anguish and uncertainty that a "missing in action" telegram brought must have been nearly unbearable.

I believe that my quest to know more about my Uncle Bob sprang from the situation involving the uncharacteristic reactions of my mother to the telegram along with the tumultuous days, weeks, and months that followed. Whatever its root, my life has been an endless mission yearning to learn more about this man.

MANY QUESTIONS BEGIN TO FORM

My relentless pursuit for information about Uncle Bob
was relatively unproductive for many years. I always had
so many questions, especially about his military service.
I knew he was an Infantry Company Commander in the
90th Infantry Division. I knew he was killed in action
November 24, 1944, in Butzdorf, Germany and, I knew
he received many combat decorations for heroism. Time
after time I heard good things said about him as I was
growing up.

So many things about Uncle Bob kept haunting me.
What was he really like? What was it about him that so
many people admired? Who were his friends? What did
they think of him? What did he do before he went into
the army? How did he obtain his commission? What
happened with his dream of flying? What did his men
think of him? Exactly where was his unit in the war?
How was he killed? Where is Butzdorf, Germany? What
were the circumstances involved in his awards? These
were but a few of the many more unanswered questions
I had.

Lacking the necessary knowledge or expertise in psycho-
logical terms to explain this insatiable need to know more
about a man I hardly remember in real life, I can only
deduce the real reason or reasons for my need to know. I
suppose the primary reason must be related to my memory of the situation on December 11, 1944, involving my
mother's reaction to the news contained in the telegram
from the War Department. Because this happened a few
days short of my fourth birthday one can probably un-

derstand why it was not possible for me to comprehend the gravity of the event, much less foresee the lasting impact it would have on my life. But, even at that age, I recognized that something was terribly wrong to cause the reactions that I observed from my mother. As seen through the prism of life experiences, I now believe that Uncle Bob became an integral part of my life from that moment on.

EARLY MEMORIES

I always had some vague memories of Uncle Bob. They must have occurred in early 1944 (while on his last leave before embarking with his unit to participate in the Allied invasion of Europe.) I have a clear recollection of an awards presentation at O'Reilly Army Hospital, Springfield, Missouri, in November, 1945. At that time, the hospital commander presented Uncle Bob's military decorations to my brother Bob, my cousin Tom Hill and me. I recall (prob-

ably in 1945 or 1946) the time that a box containing his personal effects was received at the Missouri Pacific Railroad depot in Hurley, Missouri, where my mother was the agent. There were the special services at the Hurley Methodist Church every Easter in

Easter Lily dedication to the memory of those which an Easter lily was
killed during World War II from Hurley. dedicated in memory
Hurley Methodist Church early 1950s— of those from the com-
courtesy Wiley family. munity who died serving

Uncle Bob's grave marker at the American Military Cemetery,
St. Avold, France. Inscription reads: Capt Robt B McHolland,
358th Inf 90th Div, Missouri, 24 Nov 1944. Courtesy—
Colonel Homer Bowman family.

their country in World War II. There was the hymnal in the church dedicated in Uncle Bob's memory and marked with a small gold star to denote that he was killed in action. There were the pictures of the white cross that marked his grave at the US Military Cemetery in France—pictures taken by dear friends, the Colonel Homer Bowman family, while stationed in Europe. These are only a few of the examples of how Uncle Bob seemed to always be near when I was growing up.

During my childhood years there were countless instances when Uncle Bob's name was brought up by friends and relatives. In every case the event or circumstance mentioned involved something favorable or complimentary about him. With all the nice things continuously being said about him, I began thinking very early in my life that there was something really special about this man. I started thinking that I wanted to be like my Uncle Bob. And, I wanted to know more about him.

My Mother's Reluctance to Talk About Uncle Bob

One would think that my mother would be an obvious source of information about Uncle Bob. But as far back as I can remember, she never wanted to talk about him. With the privilege of hindsight I have come to think it must have been her own personal way of dealing with the devastating loss of her beloved brother. I recall in those early years that the tears readily came when anything was said about Uncle Bob. Even in those younger years it was obvious to me that she got upset at the mention of his name. Because I did not want to take the chance of upsetting her, I looked for other ways to try to find out more about him.

The Scrapbook

During Uncle Bob's period of service my mother and her sister, Mary Lea McHolland Brown, kept a scrapbook about him. Among the items included in the scrapbook were letters he had written home to my mother, my aunt, and even some he had written to other relatives and friends while he was in the service. Included were many pictures of Uncle Bob. There were clippings from local newspapers about him as well as about other local men who were serving in the war. The most poignant part of the scrapbook was the section containing the cards and letters of condolence my mother and aunt received after he was killed in action.

I must have been only eleven or twelve years old when I first started going through the scrapbook reading everything posted. I was especially drawn to the letters that my uncle had written. I would go back to the scrapbook countless times over the years. I guess it was my way of trying to find out more about Uncle Bob.

NOTE: The scrapbook has been in possession of my Aunt Mary Lea for several years. She has always graciously shared it with me. Her unselfishness in sharing the scrapbook along with her memories of Uncle Bob has been invaluable to me in accomplishing this project.

REMINDERS OF UNCLE BOB FROM MY SCHOOL YEARS

There were other reminders of Uncle Bob as I went through elementary and high school at Hurley, Missouri—the same small community where he was born and raised. In my seventh/eighth grade classroom at Hurley Elementary School there was a plaque hanging on the wall in front of the classroom that read:

"For when that one Great Scorer comes to write against your name,
   He writes not that you won or lost but how you played the game."

These words, penned by the renowned sports writer Grantland Rice, were very meaningful to me even as a pre-teen. But the thing that meant the most to me was the fact that Uncle Bob was the person responsible for sending the plaque to the school sometime early in his Army service. There was the time when, as a high school student, I was in the high school library and noticed a copy of "Mein Kampf" by Adolph Hitler. It was written in German and had been sent to the library by Uncle

Bob. I can only guess that he had retrieved it from a battlefield as his unit moved across France.

COLLEGE, ROTC, COMMISSIONING, MILITARY SERVICE: LINGERING MEMORIES OF UNCLE BOB

I entered Southwest Missouri State College, Springfield, Missouri, in September 1958. As was the case at that time with all entering freshmen who had not completed their military obligation and had no physical disability, I was required to enroll in the Army Reserve Officer Training Corps program. I sensed the shadow of Uncle Bob as I began attending the ROTC classes. The first time I was designated as the leader of close order drill I was very unhappy with my performance. I even had the feeling that I had let Uncle Bob down. I imagined that Uncle Bob would have done things perfectly and wondered what he thought of my perceived ineptness in my first effort at directing troops.

With the encouragement of my father, I completed the ROTC program and was commissioned as a Second Lieutenant in the United States Army in May, 1962. My first assignment to the Army Infantry branch, coincidentally, was the same branch in which Uncle Bob served. I had some of his uniform insignia that had been returned with his personal effects and had somehow been kept over the years. I proudly wore his Infantry "crossed rifles" in my first Army assignment. During the Infantry Officer Basic Course, Ranger School, Airborne School and into my first assignment as platoon leader of an infantry rifle platoon, I thought of him constantly and strived to do a professional job like I thought Uncle Bob would do.

In October, 1965, I returned from a year in Vietnam. Upon reporting to my new assignment at the United States Army Administration Center (also called the Army Records Center) in St. Louis, Missouri, I learned that I had been promoted to Captain. I had a set of Captain's bars that had been returned with Uncle Bob's personal effects and I proudly wore those until I was discharged from the Army in August, 1967.

My assignment at the US Army Administration Center provided me another opportunity to find out more about Uncle Bob's military service. The center was the repository for all US Army personnel records. While I was there I was able to review his military service record. The record was somewhat disorganized and contained usual routine data that the military required. I actually did not gain much factual data from the record that I did not already know, but this kept alive my desire to know more about him.

CONTINUED HUNT FOR INFORMATION ABOUT UNCLE BOB

At this point there would appear to be quite a gap in my personal quest to gain more information about Uncle Bob. Although I have few specific examples to cite (from the time I was discharged from the Army in August, 1967, until November, 1994) my search for more information about him never ceased. When I picked up a copy of the American Legion magazine I always checked the section that showed unit reunion information hoping to see his unit mentioned. I never once saw information about a reunion of any of his units. I would go to libraries to check atlases and maps to try to locate the town of Butz-dorf, Germany, where he was killed. Never once did I find it. I would also return to the scrapbook periodically to read again the letters he wrote home. That would always leave me longing to know more about this man.

Through all these years Uncle Bob was never far from my mind. After I was discharged from active duty with the Army, I went back to work with the Army as a U. S. government civilian employee. Much of my civilian service was performed at Fort Leonard Wood, Missouri. In the late 1980s, a memorialization program was instituted at the installation. The purpose of the program was to honor former soldiers by naming buildings, training areas, streets, etc., in recognition of their service to our country. I submitted Uncle Bob's name through the bureaucratic channels hoping that his name might be used. His name was not used with the explanation given that the program at Fort Leonard Wood, the US Army Engineer Training Center at the time, was designed primarily for those soldiers who served with the Army Corps of Engineers. I was disappointed, but having worked for the Army for so long I could understand the basis for their decision.

A BREAKTHROUGH–
ENLIGHTENING INFORMATION FROM A COUSIN

The years continued to roll by and it seemed that I was at a standstill in obtaining any more new information about Uncle Bob. A call on November 24, 1994, from my cousin, Tom Hill, in Fort Worth, Texas was a turning point in my endless search for information about Uncle Bob. That date, November 24, 1994, just happened to be the fiftieth anniversary of Uncle Bob's death. Tom had called to honor the memory of Uncle Bob.

Tom and I had always shared a deep interest in knowing more about Uncle Bob. Being almost seven years older than me he had clearer memories of Uncle Bob. His mother, my Aunt Anna McHolland Hill, was an older half-sister of Uncle Bob. As mentioned in a previous paragraph, Aunt Anna was the person to whom my mother was speaking with on the phone about the telegram informing her of Uncle Bob being missing in action. Along with his father, my Uncle Earl Hill, Aunt Anna and Tom lived in Burleson, Texas, now a suburb of Fort Worth. Uncle Bob spent much time on weekends, in 1943, with Tom and his parents while on pass from Camp Wolters and later, Camp Barkley, Texas, where his unit, the 90th Infantry Division, was intensively training for its role in the upcoming invasion of Europe.

Tom and I had talked many times over the years and Uncle Bob was always a part of our conversations. This time Tom passed along some information he had learned about the action in Butzdorf, Germany, in which Uncle Bob was killed. As a result of our conversation he made copies of his finding and sent them to me. A part of what he sent happened to be an excerpt from the book *The Lorraine Campaign* by H. M. Cole. This was part of a nine volume series detailing the European Theater of Operations in World War II. It was compiled under the direction of the Historical Division of the United States Army and was published in 1950. I was intrigued and amazed at the intimate, detailed description contained of the battle at Butzdorf. It included actions preparatory to the battle, an aerial photograph of Butzdorf and the entire battle area. After almost forty years of near futile searching I finally had something that provided more detail about how and where Uncle Bob died.

I Found It on the Map--
Butzdorf, Germany!

But, I was still wondering just where Butzdorf, Germany, was located since I had never seen the town on a map of Germany. As luck would have it, I had a very good friend, Vaughn Skaggs, who had spent five years (1985–1990) working as a Department of the Army civilian in Germany. While there he and his family used vacation time to travel extensively throughout Europe. Much of their travel was by private vehicle which required the need for good road maps. After his return to the states it dawned on me to ask Vaughn if he might have any road maps of Germany. It turned out that he had a very detailed road map which appeared to show every little burg in the country. And, yes, in 1991, I finally found Butzdorf on a map!

Found--
A Valuable Source of Information

In the meantime, I kept my eyes and ears open for any information that concerned Uncle Bob and his unit. One day in the spring of 2000 a friend with whom I worked in the U.S. Army Engineer School at Fort Leonard Wood, Missouri, Sergeant First Class Sam Weathers, stopped by my desk on his way back from the post library. He was aware of my interest in World War II and informed me about some books he found on the "give-away" table at the library. He had picked up several copies of the book

*Road map of southeastern Germany. Butzordf located in
circled area--courtesy Vaughn Skaggs.*

and asked if I wanted one. Soon I discovered that the
book Sam gave me was the same one I mentioned in
a recent previous paragraph, *The Lorraine Campaign*, by
H. M. Cole. I immediately began scanning through the
pages and soon realized the book was the same one from
which my cousin, Tom Hill, had extracted the information about the actions of the 90th Division and Uncle
Bob's K Company at Butzdorf on November 24, 1944.
With my own copy of this extremely well-written and
well-documented book about the campaign, I was able
to meticulously study all aspects of the campaign and to
understand much more about the overall planning and
strategy involved which ultimately resulted in the unfortunate state of affairs that occurred at Butzdorf.

While I now had a few more answers to some of my long
searched for questions, a huge void remained. After all

of these years I still had never been able to locate anyone who actually knew or served with Uncle Bob while he was in service. Considering the passage of time I was beginning to accept the very real probability that most of those who had known him and made it through the war alive might no longer be around. I had virtually given up hope that I would ever be able to find any one who served with him.

Found, At Last, Someone Who Served with Uncle Bob!

It was the fall of 2003 and I never could have imagined the doors that were about to open. It started with a note from my brother, Bob, informing me that someone was writing a book that dealt with the 90th Infantry Division and was asking about Uncle Bob. Knowing of my particular interest in anything that might involve our uncle, my brother provided me with the name and telephone number of the person who was inquiring about Captain Robert McHolland.

I wasted little time in placing a call to Mike McCoy, the person who had contacted my brother. Mike lived in the small community of Albion, located in northern Indiana. In our first telephone conversation I learned that Mike was writing a book for a friend of his who had served with the 90th Infantry Division in Europe in World War II. The friend's name was Hobert Winebrenner. Hobert wanted to document his experiences in World War II and Mike, a writer and friend, had volunteered to assist him in this endeavor. In telling his story, one of Hobert's primary goals was to pay tribute to many of those with whom he served. As a part of his efforts to write the book, Mike had undertaken an extensive search to locate many of Hobert's old army buddies as well as relatives of those who did not make it back. Uncle Bob's name had come up during this search, and, knowing he had been killed in action, Mike was trying to find his relatives. Mike combined the skills of an accomplished detective along with the latest in computer search methods to locate a McHolland cousin in southwest Missouri who referred him to my brother, Bob. This search had ultimately resulted in my telephone conversation with him.

Mike explained that Uncle Bob, Captian Mac, was among those with whom Hobert had served in M Company, 3rd Battalion, 358th Infantry Regiment, 90th Infantry Division. Mike related that Uncle Bob numbered among those whom Hobert wanted to mention in his book. Surprisingly, I was about to learn an even more dramatic bit of information: Hobert was a part of the action at Butzdorf when Uncle Bob was killed. After all these years I finally had found out about someone who actually knew my Uncle Bob. This turned out to be just the beginning of new and exciting revelations about Uncle Bob. Through Mike and Hobert, I was introduced to Howard Pemberton, who was actually with Uncle Bob in the house at Butzdorf when he was killed.

OTHER CLOSE COMRADES DISCOVERED

So much more has happened in the three or four years since that telephone conversation with Mike McCoy. I have met and visited with him and Hobert Winebrenner at their homes in Indiana. My wife, Sheila, and I have visited numerous times with Howard and Ardys Pemberton. Responding to Howard's thoughtful invitations we

have attended the Pemberton family reunion at Osage
Beach, Missouri for the past four years. They have made
us feel as if we are part of the family. I became an associ-
ate member of the 90th Infantry Division Association and
began attending the annual reunions in 2007. Through
this organization I have met and formed a close friendship with Emmett Boyd who was Uncle Bob's Weapons
Platoon Sergeant in K Company. Each of these distinguished individuals has thoughtfully and patiently shared
with me so much information about the guy they knew as
Captain Mac—information about the man, his character, his leadership ability, and his genuine consideration
for his men.

Combined with the information about Uncle Bob that
I had been gathering for a lifetime, the opportunity to
meet face-to-face and talk about my uncle with close
friends who served with him and who were there when
he was killed seemed to provide some sort of closure to
my long search. I did not realize that even more was yet
to come.

A BOOK? ABOUT UNCLE BOB?

The idea to write this book did not come quickly. The
seed was actually planted by a dear first cousin, Sue
Brown Crain, who is a daughter of my Aunt Mary Lea
McHolland Brown. It came during a telephone conversation with Sue in which I was informing her of some
more information I had discovered about Uncle Bob.
On several occasions I had shared with Sue the latest I
had learned about him. It was during one of those conversations that Sue offered the comment that with all the
information I had about Uncle Bob I should write a book

about him. I dismissed the notion initially because I did not think I was capable of tackling such an overwhelming project. However, I suppose the seed began taking root as I found myself thinking more and more about it. A few weeks later in August, 2007, I attended the 90th Infantry Division Association reunion in Pittsburgh, Pennsylvania. The patriotism and dedication shown by the World War II veterans further inspired me to make the decision to attempt this project.

I continued to add to the mounds of information I already had. I included more from conversations and interviews from family and friends. Some of the additional information came from friends who attended elementary and high school with Uncle Bob, some were in the Boy Scouts with him, and some served under him as scoutmaster of the local troop. Other friends who provided valuable data include those who roomed with him in college and those who knew him when he taught in the small rural schools of Missouri. Two of his former students provided valuable insight about his teaching abilities. Much information was gleaned from friends and comrades who served with him at various points during his preparation for military service and during his time on active duty. Personal anecdotes and remembrances provided by these friends offered amusing and interesting insight into Uncle Bob's personality and were priceless in supporting the efforts of this project.

Along with the personal interviews and conversations I obtained Uncle Bob's college transcript, a record of his Masonic service, data about his Boy Scout Service, his official Army Personnel Record, and his Individual Personnel Deceased Personnel File. I scoured several books documenting the history of World War II. Among those most valuable to the completion of this project were *Battle History of the Third Battalion 358th Infantry*, Peragimus, 'We Accomplish," *War from the Ground Up*, and *Bootprints: An Infantryman's Walk through World War II*.

The personal rewards I have experienced in the undertaking of this project are incalculable. My only regret is that I did not begin earlier in this effort to detail the story of Uncle Bob's life. With the passage of time so many opportunities have been lost to speak with many friends and relatives who knew him and could have added much to his story.

In the chapters to follow I have tried my best to tell the story of a great man and a true American hero. It is my earnest hope and prayer that I have done justice to the memory of my Uncle Bob—Captain Mac.

Chapter 1
The Early Years -- Hurley and the
Spring Creek Valley

From an exhaustive search of weather information about the mid-western United States in 1918, it appears likely that December 10th of that year was a very cold day along the Spring Creek Valley of Missouri where the small town of Hurley is located. Notwithstanding the unseasonably cold temperatures of that late fall, I am certain it was a joyous time in the household of Orange Stanley and Nancy Jane Brown McHolland. On that date my Uncle Bob, Robert Brown McHolland, came into this world. He arrived inside a small two-story, stucco-sided frame structure termed the "Section House" in Hurley, Stone County, Missouri. "Section House" identified it among the local population as the house built by the Missouri Pacific Railroad for the purpose of housing local railroad employees. In this case it housed the family of the local depot agent.

The reason for giving this son the name of Robert has

been lost in the pages of time, but we know his middle name, Brown, came from the maiden name of his mother. Robert Brown McHolland would live a few days shy of twenty-six years on this earth. His life, along with almost four hundred thousand other Americans most appropriately identified by Tom Brokaw as the "Greatest Generation," would be shortened as a result of the actions of a ruthless, maniacal dictator thousands of miles away from the peaceful Spring Creek Valley. My Uncle Bob would never know of the relentless, lifelong quest of a proud nephew to learn more about him nor could he have envisioned the legacy he left during his limited time among us.

Uncle Bob was the fifth born of six natural children of Orange Stanley McHolland (who was known by his middle name, Stanley.) Before any of their natural children were born, Stanley and his first wife, Ettie Mary DuBois, *(NOTE: Some records reflect her name as Mary Ettie, but McHolland family genealogical researcher, Don Bearden, chose to identify her as Ettie Mary because that is how the earliest available census data identified her.)* had taken an infant, Jesse Fleetwood, into their home to raise.[1] Ettie Mary, died in July, 1913, leaving Stanley with Jesse and their three natural children: Eva (born 1903), Anna (1907) and Everette (1910) in his care. By March, 1915, Stanley met and married Nancy Jane Brown. Roxabel (my mother), had been born to this union in January, 1917, next came Uncle Bob, and then, his youngest sister, Mary Lea, arrived in January, 1921. As of this writing all of his siblings have departed this life except Mary Lea, whose assistance has been invaluable to me in completing this tribute to Uncle Bob. You will readily recognize her contributions as this story unfolds.

His Father--Stanley McHolland

In 1903 Stanley moved with his first wife Ettie Mary, step-son Jesse, and daughter Eva from Ava, Douglas County, Missouri to a small cabin a few miles east of Hurley near the James River. Soon afterward Stanley obtained his teaching certificate. He taught at the near-by Inmon School, a rural school with grades one through eight, from 1903 through 1905, after which he moved his family to Hurley. He then taught at another rural school, Union City, walking the four miles each day back and forth from Hurley to perform his teaching duties.

Inmon School, circa 1903-05, Stanley McHolland, teacher, kneeling at far right in second row. This is the same rural school where Captain Mac taught in 1941-1942—courtesy Wiley-McHolland family.

In addition to serving as Justice of the Peace for the village of Hurley, Stanley McHolland's primary job was depot agent for the Missouri Pacific Railroad station in Hurley. The railroad had been built through Hurley in

1907 and it is not clear whether Stanley was the first depot agent at Hurley. However, if he was not the first agent it is relatively certain that he was at least the second such agent. According to records of the 1910 census, he was shown as a depot agent as of May, 1910.

HIS MOTHER--
NANCY JANE BROWN MCHOLLAND

After Stanley's first wife (Ettie Mary DuBois) died in July, 1915, he was dutifully caring for the four children of this marriage: Eva, Everette, and Anna, as well as his stepson, Jesse Fleetwood. The task of looking after these young children had to be a tremendous burden for him. One could be certain that Stanley probably would have

had a natural desire for female companionship and would welcome some maternal assistance in the rearing of his family. The story of his courtship with Nancy, as related by family members, is one that speaks to accepted practices and customs of the era.

McHolland Family (minus Everette)-1917-Front: Anna, Nancy holding baby Roxabel; Rear: Stanley, Eva— courtesy Wiley-McHolland family.

As the depot agent, many of Stanley's contacts were of personnel associated with the railroad. Most of those workers were aware of his plight and undoubtedly were genuinely interested in helping him to find a solution for his unfortunate predicament. It is told that one of those among his railroad acquaintances informed Stanley of the presence of a certain young woman who resided in the small community of Evansville in northwest Arkansas. That young woman happened to be Nancy Jane Brown. She was single and apparently would welcome the visit of a suitor with the reputable credentials possessed by Stanley. It was likely in February of 1915 that Stanley took a ride on the train to Evansville to meet this eligible daughter of John and Phoebe Brown. After spending a week or so becoming better acquainted, Nancy accepted his marriage proposal and returned to Missouri with him. They were married March 3, 1915, and Nancy inherited Stanley's ready made family. Soon she was lovingly referred to as "Mama Nan" by his children. This is the name that stayed with her through the years.

By all accounts Nancy was readily accepted by her new family as she assumed the responsibilities of mother and wife. She was a strong woman who fit quite well into her new role and helped provide the foundation for a solid family structure. Every word written or spoken about her by family members reflects profound love and respect for her steadfastness and devotion to the entire family throughout her life.

HIS HOME TOWN--HURLEY, MISSOURI

The town in which Uncle Bob was born, Hurley, Missouri, was a quaint little village in southwest Missouri about 30 miles southwest of Springfield. It is located in northern Stone County about 50 miles north of the Arkansas border. Hurley is situated in a beautiful valley along the banks of a spring fed stream named Spring

Creek; aptly named because of its origin from a spring about five miles up the valley and north of Hurley. The creek is also fed by several other small springs.

When approaching the town from the north one readily notices a significant change in the topography of the area as it transitions from the flatter, more open area of the Ozark Plateau. Then begins a series of hills and valleys leading farther into steeper hills and deeper valleys in the region locally referred to as the Ozark Mountains. Most of the original settlers in the area of the Spring Creek Valley migrated from the rugged Appalachian areas of Tennessee, Kentucky, the Carolinas and Georgia. These folks had adapted nicely to the hill country of the Ozarks and were proud of their "hillbilly" heritage.

Not only is there a valley running north and south through which Spring Creek flows, but Hurley sits in the middle of a convergence of valleys from the east and west. It

Hurley in early 1900s view looking toward the northwest—

Courtesy Judge Robert S. Wiley.

was an ideal setting to grow up in during the 1920s and 1930s, not to mention the 1940s and 1950s when I was also fortunate enough to spend my childhood years in this idyllic setting.

Settlement in this area began in the late 1800s with the building of a dam and the establishment of a mill on the clear and briskly flowing waters of Spring Creek. The earliest settlers wanted to name their settlement Spring Creek, but when the application for a post office was made they learned that the name Spring Creek had already been assigned to another village and post office in

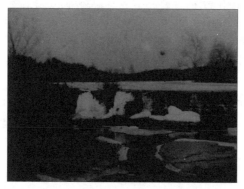

Dam and Mill Pond on Spring Creek in Hurley—
courtesy Judge Robert S. Wiley.

The Hurley Mill—courtesy Judge Robert S. Wiley.

the state. It is believed that some unknown government official ended up giving the new town its name of Hurley. The post office was established in 1898 and was located in a room of the mill. Not long after that a general store was added.[2]

Most of the people who settled in and along the valley made their living from the land. Except for the land in the low lying valleys the soil could not be described as fertile. However, the people in this area cleared hillsides to raise tomatoes and strawberries and to provide pasture for their livestock. Corn, wheat or oats were cultivated mainly in the more fertile valleys for livestock feed and also as cash crops. Almost everyone had a garden that provided fresh vegetables for the table as well as a sufficient amount to can or preserve for sustenance through the long winters. Most folks had at least one milk cow as well as some chickens for eggs. The cows and chickens were sources of food, too. Others also raised hogs for food. Whatever excess occurred over that, needed for one's own survival, would be sold to those fortunate enough to be able to afford to buy them.

The really BIG event that transformed Hurley from a one mill and one store village was the coming of the railroad. As the depot agent, Uncle Bob's father, Stanley, was an integral part of the significant event that occurred in the valley in the early 1900s. The Iron Mountain (later Missouri Pacific) Railway Company began surveying in 1904 for a rail line that would run from Springfield to Crane. The construction of the line was finished in 1907 and ended up as a spur running about 35 miles from Springfield to connect with the railroad's main line at nearby Crane.[3] Several of those miles of the spur ran along the Spring Creek valley and through the middle of the village of Hurley.

A celebration at the Hurley Depot in early 1900s—courtesy Judge Robert S. Wiley.

Within a year or so after the railroad line was completed three more general stores and dry goods businesses had sprung up in the community. By the early to middle 1920s there were at least seventeen businesses in Hurley along with a bank.[4] The railroad spurred growth by providing a better mode of transportation for agricultural goods being produced, as well as providing passenger service for travelers into and out of the valley. Even with this growth the population of the town itself never rose above 250. It is easy to understand that everyone knew everyone else in the community and were dependent upon one another for survival.

It was in this setting that Uncle Bob spent all his years until he completed high school in 1936. It would likely

seem to many of those spoiled by the affluence and con-
veniences we take for granted today that this must have
made for a dull, boring, mundane upbringing. But drawing from my own experience in being raised in the same
valley, before television and long before the electronic
and computer technology innovations, I believe Uncle
Bob would agree that he would not have traded his childhood experiences for those of any other person or any
other era.

Uncle Bob's Childhood Years

Throughout his childhood, Uncle Bob would be learning the means of survival in this rural setting by helping his father and mother with the various chores around
the home that were continuously required to make ends
meet. Those chores consisted of cutting wood for heat
and carrying it in for use in the cooking and heating
stoves, feeding chickens, gathering eggs, helping with killing and dressing chickens for food, butchering of hogs,
milking cows, cutting weeds, cutting sprouts to clear the
land for pasture, helping tend a large garden, helping
with the canning and preserving of fruits and vegetables,
and any other task that might be required for the family's
subsistence.

There was always something to do for Uncle Bob and
his young friends. They could be found traipsing along
Spring Creek swimming, fishing, or skipping flat rocks
on the surface of the creek. Then again, maybe it was
just exploring a cave or roaming the hills and hollows
hunting for small game. Kids played marbles and made
tops for spinning. They made hoops and tees. The hoop
was a steel ring that probably came from an old nail keg.

The tee was a flattened and bent Prince Albert tobacco can nailed to the bottom of a stick about three feet in length. By placing the hoop into the slot formed by the bent can the kids could guide and roll the hoop along the road or trail. They made slingshots and hurled rocks at birds; seldom ever coming close to their prey. They played cowboy and Indians, baseball, war games and oftentimes would make up their own games to entertain themselves. And, of course, every boy had a knife for whittling, carving, and just for show. Boring was not a part of the vocabulary or the life of a youngster growing up in the Spring Creek Valley.

THE "SECTION HOUSE"

Uncle Bob's earliest years were spent in the "section house" rented by Stanley from the Missouri Pacific Railroad. Although the rooms were small when compared to most houses of today, it contained a second story which provided ample space for the McHolland family. The house was situated between the tracks of the north-south railroad line and the large "Mill Pond." The Mill Pond was formed after the dam was built on Spring Creek in the 1890s to power the mill. The section house was about seventy-five yards north of the main east-west road that ran through town. It was sixty to seventy feet west of the railroad tracks and a bit farther east from the pond at its normal level. There are several photographs of family members taken during that period that show the railroad tracks in the background. You can also see portions of the house in the background of some photographs. It was a comfortable home and provided the family with essentials of warmth and shelter. However, the location of the house, between the railroad tracks on the east and the

Mill Pond on the west, was a constant source of concern for Stanley and Nancy because of the obvious hazards they posed for the safety of their children. Even though strict limits were set as to how far the children could go in each direction, there was a constant awareness of the ever-present dangers.

There are several photographs tucked away in family albums of Uncle Bob that were taken in the area of the section house during his first two or three years. Some of these included his first cousins Jerrel McHolland and Raymond McHolland. Jerrel and Raymond were sons of Stanley's brothers, James and Sam. Sister Mary Lea recalls happy times spent playing with these cousins along with another cousin, Nita, who was Raymond's sister. One of their favorite places to play was on the hill just across the railroad tracks. Mary Lea recalled other of Uncle Bob's playmates during those early years. Brent Conrad's older sons, Ray and Louis, were among his favorites as well as Dale "Rip" Dean with whom he remained close through the years until both gave their lives for their country and our freedom in World War II. There was another cousin who lived in Hurley and grew up spending a lot of time with Uncle Bob. Herbert McHolland, also a first cousin and the son of Stanley's brother John, was a few years older than him but many good times were shared with him and his family.[5] Herbert and Uncle Bob would remain close until Uncle Bob's death. More will be written about Herbert in later pages.

Mary Lea recalled a specific time during these early years when Uncle Bob caused some alarm within the family when he strayed away from home for a longer period

*Young McHolland Cousins, L-R, Raymond, Jerald, and
Uncle Bob 1920—courtesy Wiley-McHolland family.*

*Uncle Bob, about 4 years old, standing
in front of Section House in Hurley,
Note railroad tracks in background—
courtesy Wiley-McHolland family*

*The younger McHollands: Roxabel 4, Uncle
Bob 3, and Mary Lea, 6 months. In front
yard of Section House—courtesy Wiley-
McHolland family.*

than usual. Within an hour or so he returned home and was asked where he had been to which he replied he had been looking for his playmate and cousin, Raymond. He was only six or seven years old at the time and had not yet fully grasped the concept of distance. He did not realize that Raymond's home was about six miles away in the village of Crane. Mary Lea did not recall if there was punishment at the time, or if there was, what the punishment might have been. She did recall that Stanley was a strong disciplinarian and that Uncle Bob received the painful results of Stanley's spankings various times during his younger years.[6]

STANLEY AND RELIGION

Uncle Bob's father, Stanley, was known by his family as a very devout Christian who read and studied the Bible on a daily basis and endeavored to instill these beliefs in his children. He had the reputation in the community as a man of integrity and one who strived to practice the Christian principles he studied through the actions of his everyday life. Mary Lea recalls that Stanley always took his bible with him to work at the depot and hardly ever missed attending church on Sunday at the small Hurley Methodist/Baptist church. She remembered that the Baptists and Methodists used the church building on alternate Sundays and that Stanley, although he leaned more toward the Baptist teachings, attended services regardless of which denomination brought the message.[7]

During their early childhood years the younger siblings, Roxabel, Mary Lea, and Uncle Bob, would attend the church services along with Stanley. Mother Nancy usually stayed home busily preparing a delicious Sunday dinner. One of their favorite Sunday School teachers was a grand lady by the name of Lou Steele. This author can vouch for the wonderful nature of this angel on earth as he also had the good fortune of being a part of her Sunday School class in the 1950s when she was still teaching young folks the Christian way to live. As the years passed and Uncle Bob grew into his teenage years, Roxabel and Mary Lea continued to attend church regularly, but Uncle Bob, like most other boys of his age, was not as diligent in attending church every Sunday.[8]

A BIG FAMILY MOVE

While the McHolland family scratched out a living like most others in the community, Stanley's job as depot agent offered more of a sense of security than that of many others in the valley. He was fortunate to be receiving a regular pay check from the Missouri Pacific Railroad. Even before Uncle Bob was born Stanley had begun using some of this money to buy small parcels of property on which to raise a few cattle, sheep, and a hog or two. He would also have at least one horse for transportation.

Sometime in the early 1920s, probably 1923, Stanley purchased some property with a house on it about a quarter mile up the dirt road leading east of Hurley. Mary Lea remembers moving from the section house when she was about four years old. That would make 1925 as the year in which the McHolland family moved from the section house to the "new" home east of Hurley. Mary Lea recalls that Stanley had some work done before they moved and a part of the work was adding a room onto the house. The house was far from being described as a large mansion, but now they had their own home and it would provide room to comfortably house the family members who were still at home.[9]

By 1925 the size of Stanley's family at home had shrunk. Jesse had been gone from home for some time. From available genealogical information gathered by cousin Don Bearden, step-brother Jesse had left the area by 1919. Sisters Eva and Anna had left home in the early 1920s to attend the School of the Ozarks in Point Lookout, Missouri, and further their education.[10] Brother Everette was fifteen years old by this time and was also beginning to think about leaving home and making a living.

The move from the section house to the new home must have been a relief in many ways for Stanley and Nancy. It would have been a matter of pride to have their own home. More importantly, it must have eased their minds to get away from the section house and the persistent potential dangers posed to their young family from the nearby railroad tracks and the Mill Pond behind the section house.

Uncle Bob was seven years old when the big move occurred. The house was new, but the area where the house was located was not new to him. In increments over the years Stanley had accumulated over seventy acres of land to the south and east of the property the house sat on. He had raised cattle, sheep, hogs, chickens and a horse on the property for several years before they moved and Uncle Bob had undoubtedly been called upon to help with the feeding, milking, and caring for the animals. For several years he would help with the butchering of the hog which took place regularly on Thanksgiving for many years. Uncle Bob would have been called upon to help in maintaining the outbuildings and with keeping fences around the property in good repair.

HEALTH CONCERNS FOR STANLEY

By the time of the move, Stanley's health was becoming a great concern for the entire family. Mary Lea recalls that at some point in the early to mid 1920s Stanley had been diagnosed with tuberculosis by doctors in St. Louis. She also related that a local respected physician, Doctor Doggett, doubted the tuberculosis diagnosis. The specific root of Stanley's health problems will never be known, but Mary Lea indicated that it probably involved the lungs. One of her earliest memories occurred when she was four years old (1925). She remembers riding the train from Hurley with her mother and sister, Anna, to visit her father in the Missouri Pacific Employee's Hospital in St. Louis. She remembered that Stanley had a collapsed lung around the time of this visit. She believed that there must have been permanent damage to one of the lungs as she remembered through her early years when he was riding a horse or walking that he was always leaning to one side, possibly favoring the area because of pain. Poignantly, Mary Lea recalls that her father's condition was a constant factor that affected all aspects of family life from the time of her earliest memories.[11]

With Uncle Bob barely two years older than Mary Lea, he would also be aware of and experiencing the things that his sister recalled about Stanley's illness. According to Mary Lea, Uncle Bob also traveled to St. Louis to visit his father while he was in the hospital. Mother Nancy, benefiting from a family pass issued by the Missouri Pacific Railroad, traveled to St. Louis more than once to visit Stanley during his hospital stays. Mary Lea recalled that her mother would take one or two of the children at a time when she went. She specifically remembered her mother taking Uncle Bob and Roxabel one of those times.[12] Although brother Everette, 15 years old by this time, would be around home for a few more years to help pick up tasks left in the void of Stanley's disability, Uncle Bob would also be required to gradually perform more and more of the chores and to pick up more responsibility for doing all the essential things that needed to be done around the house and the farm.

EARLY EDUCATION

Education was a very important part of Stanley's philosophy of life and was something he imparted to his children. It is evidenced by the fact that he had worked to meet the necessary prerequisites to qualify for a teaching certificate which he earned in 1903. He immediately put these qualifications to use by teaching for two years at the rural school at Inmon and for another year at Union City.[13] He was very interested in seeing that all of his family received a good education.

Having been in existence since 1909, Hurley's school had been in full operation for several years by the time Uncle Bob began his education. The first Hurley school building was located on the south slope of a hillside on the west side of Spring Creek. As was the usual custom in the small communities of that time the school had begun with grades one through eight housed in the same building. At some point in the late 1910s the high school grades began to be added. Initially, the higher grades continued to be housed in the building with the elementary grades. This resulted in taxing the capacity of the small building on the hill. As conditions became more crowded and it became apparent that more room was needed, the building for a new Hurley High School was constructed and opened its doors in 1927.[14]

The first Hurley School—courtesy Wiley-McHolland family.

For a while in the mid to late 1920s, during the most crowded years for the Hurley school, another place was found to provide space for some of the lower grades. The recently constructed Primitive Baptist Church in Hurley turned out to be the place chosen to house the first, and possibly, the second grades. Mary Lea recalls spending at least her first grade attending school in the church building.[15]   It is also likely that Uncle Bob spent his first grade or two attending school in the same church building. After the new high school building was completed all of the elementary grades were again housed in the original school building.

Gathering further information from the memories of

Mary Lea, it appears that Uncle Bob was a good student, at least in his early years. Both he and Mary Lea were advanced two grades in one year early on in their schooling. She remembers an incident involving Uncle Bob a few years later when he would probably have been in either the fifth or sixth grade. At the end of the year when the report cards were passed out, he brought his card home but would not look at the portion that indicated whether the student was promoted to the next grade. Mary Lea recalled that he was afraid he was not going to be promoted. When he finally opened the card and read that he was promoted to the next grade, he was so happy he jumped for joy up and down on the bed yelling "I passed! I passed!"[16]

A dear friend of the family, Inez Inmon Bowman, whose father and mother, Howard and Winnie Inmon, owned and operated one of Hurley's general stores for many years, attended the school on the hill during Uncle Bob's early elementary years. She was one year older than him and in the same class as sister Roxabel. She has a photograph of all the students, which included Uncle Bob, Roxabel, and herself, which was probably taken in the late 1920s. Considering their ages and the normal lack of interest in the opposite sex during this period of development, it is understandable that Inez could not remember many details of that time about Uncle Bob. The one thing she did recall was that he had a scar on his chin; very likely the result of a childhood accident. Also, she recalled that Uncle Bob seemed pretty much like the rest of the boys of his age.[17]

With regard to Inez's memory of the scar on Uncle Bob's chin, additional information about the scar was discov-

Hurley Elementary School, 1928-29, grades 5-8. H. M. Thralls, teacher.
Roxabel, Uncle Bob (hands in pockets of overalls), and Inez Bowman are
the last three to the left on the front row—courtesy Inez Inmon Bowman.

ered. It is interesting to note that the report from the physical examination conducted upon Uncle Bob's entry on active duty in May of 1942, at O'Reilly General Hospital in Springfield, Missouri, had an entry describing a "two inch scar" on his right cheek.[18] His sister, Mary Lea, provided more information about the origin of the scar. She recalled that he had been playing on the outside basketball court down the hill from the school. The hill area between the basketball court and school had been pretty well covered with small tree sprouts which had recently been cut. While running up the hill to school Uncle Bob slipped and fell, cutting his chin on the sharp edge of what was left of one of the recently cut sprouts. Mary Lea remembered it as a nasty gash and thinks that it required stitches. In any event he would carry a permanent identifying mark on his chin from the injury.[19]

There was another entry under the medical history portion of Uncle Bob's entrance physical examination report that indicated he had suffered a fracture of his right wrist in 1930. No other details were stated regarding this injury. Mary Lea remembers him breaking his wrist but could not recall any details regarding the injury. A likely possibility of its origin could have been from a playground accident at school. It is also interesting to point out that the medical history portion of the report revealed that he had contracted the usual childhood diseases of measles, mumps, whooping cough, and chicken pox as well as scarlet fever. There was no indication of any severe effects from the scarlet fever.[20]

EARLY POLITICAL INFLUENCES

While Stanley's health remained a constant cause for concern he managed to hold down the job as depot agent and had the stamina and determination to run in the primary election on the Republican ticket for the office of state representative from Stone County in 1930. He must have had a true sense of purpose, not to mention a lot of pure grit, for him to take on the added challenge considering he had been back in the hospital in St. Louis at least two more times. It could be that Stanley's venture into local politics might have been the thing that sparked Uncle Bob's later interest in such matters. Mary Lea recalled that Uncle Bob accompanied Stanley as he took the train to make campaign stops in the Stone County towns of Crane, Galena, and Reeds Spring.[21] By the way, Stanley was soundly defeated in his bid for state representative. He finished third in a field of three candidates. Although he was defeated in his only run for political office, it is certain that his Stanley's stature was not diminished in the sight of his son.

YOUR SUPPORT WILL BE APPRECIATED

O. S. McHOLLAND
REPUBLICAN CANDIDATE FOR
REPRESENTATIVE OF STONE COUNTY

SUBJECT TO WILL OF VOTERS AT PRIMARY. AUG. 5, 1930

Stanley's Political Card—courtesy Judge Robert S. Wiley.

One of thee normal transitions of life approached as Uncle Bob finished the eighth grade at the elementary school on the hill in the spring of 1932. I can imagine that he experienced the usual variety of mixed emotions that most persons at that age deal with as they face a new unknown--the life of a high school student. However, awaiting him in the years to come were not only the challenges of high school, but other trying circumstances that would serve to test the mettle of Uncle Bob and his family.

Chapter 1 Endnotes:
1. Don and Sandy Bearden, Descendants of Hugh McHolland/Monholland (Self-published, Feb 13, 2007), 49.
2. Wayne Glenn, A Snapshot History: Clever, Hurley, Boaz, Brown's Spring, Oto, Possum Trot, Union City, Union Ridge (Self-published, 2006) 33, 34.
3. Mary Scott Hair, "Hurley," History of Stone County Missouri (Stone County Historical Society, 1989), 59.
4. Hair, 61.

5.   Personal interviews with Mary Lea McHolland Brown, 2007-8.
6.   Personal interviews, M. Brown.
7.   Personal Interviews, M. Brown.
8.   Personal interviews, M. Brown.
9.   Personal interviews, M. Brown.
10. Beardens, 48, 50.
11.   Personal interviews, M. Brown.
12. Personal Interviews, M. Brown.
13. Mary Lea Brown, "Orange Stanley McHolland," History of Stone County Missouri, Volume II (Stone County Historical Society, 1994), 210.
14. Green Thumb), "Hurley School," History of Stone County Missouri (Stone Country Historical Society, 1989), 133.
15. Personal interviews, M. Brown.
16. Personal Interviews, M. Brown.
17. Personal interview, Inez Inmon Bowman, 2008.
18.   Record of Physical Examination, May 1942, Official Personnel File, Robert B. McHolland
19. Personal interviews, M. Brown.
20. Physical Examination Record, May 1942, Official Personnel File, Robert B. McHolland.
21. Personal interviews, M. Brown.

Chapter 2
The High School Years, Tragedy,
Friends and Interests

For Uncle Bob, one could be certain the high school years would begin in the fall of 1932 with the normal anticipation of a teenager looking forward to new experiences. New friendships would be formed and he would be developing a variety of new interests. One of the interests that emerged during this period would be an important factor in his life few years later. That was his interest in the military service. Uncle Bob's youthful expectations during this time would be tempered by an element of uncertainty within his family. There was much concern about Stanley's worsening health situation, but Uncle Bob could not envision how much his world was about to change.

TRAGEDY IN THE FAMILY--
STANLEY'S PASSING

Mary Lea relates that the family had lived with the knowledge of their father's deteriorating health for some time.

As revealed earlier, one of her earliest memories of her
father was of the railroad trip to St. Louis to visit him in
the hospital. She recalls that he was back and forth to the
hospital a few more times over the next eight years when
his condition would worsen.[1] With the family painfully aware of Stanley's condition it was not a complete
shock when they learned that he had died on February 5, 1933 in the Missouri Pacific hospital in St. Louis
at the age of 57. He was brought back to Hurley by
train and funeral services were held February 8, 1933,
at the Hurley Primitive Baptist Church with burial in
the Crane Masonic Cemetery.

Even though Stanley had been ill for some time and
the family was well aware of the tenuous nature of
his health situation, the death of one's father is a life-
changing event for anyone. Stanley possessed a strong
personality and was dearly loved by all members of his
family. He was a man of faith, honesty and integrity
and he had the total respect of his family. Uncle Bob
had just turned fourteen and I can only imagine the
depth of the impact his father's death must have had
on him as well as the entire family. Uncle Bob's feeling
for and admiration of his father were clearly apparent
to one of his closest friends, John Brown. The closeness
of Uncle Bob and John will be revealed in the coming
pages. John has a vivid recollection of conversations
between them about Stanley. He recalled Uncle Bob's
reverence and respect for his father and related that he
was very proud of him always speaking of him with
high regard.[2]

Without Stanley's regular income from his railroad pay-
check things must have become tougher on the fam-

ily. Mary Lea recalls their mother, Nancy, was a good manager of what resources they had. Owing to their mother's prudent judgment and good sense in money matters it seemed to her that the family always had what they needed. She relates that while times were lean the family was able to earn a living by selling milk and eggs and maybe a cow or a hog as circumstances required. She pointed out that it did not take nearly as much to survive as it does today. After all, they did not have to worry about an electric bill, gasoline prices, a telephone bill, and various other things to "keep up with the Jones" because almost everyone shared the same living circumstances.[3]

Not long after Stanley died, the family and many others of the community, were dealt a tough blow when the Bank of Hurley failed. While the country was in the midst of the Great Depression, folks in the hills of southwest Missouri were known to recall they did not directly feel its effects. This is because, they would say, they were so poor they never noticed a difference in their own economic situation. However, those who had invested in the Bank of Hurley would not agree with this line of thought. The bank became a casualty of the times. With its failure most of the McHolland family's savings were lost. Although no amounts could be recalled, Mary Lea remembers that the family had some money from a small life insurance policy Stanley had bought as well as some other small savings. Whatever the amount, it was a significant loss to the family. [4]

Mary Lea remembers Uncle Bob pitching in even more after Stanley's passing to help the family make a living. He had always been expected to help with most of the work required to keep the farming operation running, but the types and extent of his assistance had constantly increased over the years as Stanley's illness left him unable to do much of the work. The work required to keep things going at home probably limited Uncle Bob's participation in school activities. As an example, Mary Lea does not remember him being involved in high school sports during these years when almost every school in the area had basketball and baseball or softball teams.[5] Although a few years later as a teacher, he became very much involved with his school softball team.[6] As a college student he organized and played on an intramural college basketball team.[7] On a questionnaire he completed a few years later as a part of his officer commissioning process in the army, he included "baseball player" and "volleyball player" as athletic skills he possessed.[8] There are also indications that sometime later he became a St. Louis Cardinal baseball fan.[9]

A Friendship Begins

One of Uncle Bob's closest friendships began developing while he was in high school. This friendship would endure throughout the remainder of his short life. Edwin Dean was two years behind him in school and recalls becoming more closely acquainted with him when he was a freshman and Uncle Bob was a junior. It seemed most everybody knew and liked Uncle Bob because of the good natured kidding and teasing he constantly dished out to those around him. The teasing and kidding of others was beginning to be a trademark of his personality. It was during this time of their acquaintance that both were involved in the local Boy Scout troop. With a local young man, Byron Young, as

Scoutmaster, Edwin remembered them attending scout meetings and participating in various scouting activities. The scout meetings were held at school and Edwin recalls playing basketball with him and other members of the troop after the meetings concluded. Another memorable time that Edwin remembered was when the

Best friends: Uncle Bob and Edwin Dean—courtesy Edwin Dean

scout troop was camping on Spring Creek about two miles north of town. They cooked out and slept under the stars, swam in the cold, clear waters of Spring Creek, and had a generally good time. One can be sure that there were other such outings. The friendship between Uncle Bob and Edwin would continue to grow in the coming years. The depth of their friendship will become apparent in the pages to come.[10]

As noted, Uncle Bob's personality was the primary factor that drew him and Edwin together. In the process of gathering information about Uncle Bob a dominant theme constantly emerged regarding his personality. He was always described in positive terms. Virtually everyone remembered him as being "good natured" and a really swell person who genuinely cared about people. He was not afraid to be in charge and readily accepted the role of being a leader. He seemed to be able to get along with everyone and his well meaning teasing and kidding was taken in the manner it was offered. More notably, his leadership qualities were also beginning to emerge during this period.

His Boxing "Career"

Mary Lea remembers that during his high school years Uncle Bob somehow developed an interest in boxing. The family has a picture of him taken outside the Hurley home that shows him without a shirt and posed in a boxer's stance appearing "ready for all takers." On the officer commissioning questionnaire previously mentioned he also noted "novice boxer" as one of the athletic skills he possessed. During his boxing phase Mary Lea remembers him coming home one day with a black eye. Her memory was vague about this incident, but she thought the injury might have occurred accidentally. She was unsure but seemed to recall that a high school friend, Leaford Gold might have had something to do with it.[11]

The boxing aspect of Uncle Bob's life appeared to be something of a mystery until I discovered that indeed there was more to his venture into the boxing arena. Through conversations with Charlie Bowyer, a younger friend of Uncle Bob about whom more will be written later, much more was learned about his boxing venture. Charlie clearly recalled details of the Bob McHolland-Leaford Gold boxing match. He remembered that the bout was "widely publicized around town" and that many of the local folks attended the big event. Charlie related that the fight took place south of the main part of town and just east of the railroad depot in an area called the "strawberry patch shed." Even with the reported black eye that he suffered, it was Charlie's recollection that although an official winner was not declared Uncle Bob seemed to get the best of the fight. It is interesting that Charlie also noted that he did not remember

Uncle Bob ever being involved in any kind of fight other than this one.[12] Taking it further, with all the stories that have been told by friends and relatives about Uncle Bob not one has mentioned anything about him ever being involved in another physical confrontation at any other time.

Uncle Bob, the boxer with a "Charles Atlas" physique—courtesy Wiley-McHolland family.

In recalling Uncle Bob's interest in boxing, Charlie Bowyer also noted Uncle Bob's close friendship with his brother, Delmar. Uncle Bob and Delmar were about the same age and were involved in many activities together and known to "run around together" during their high school years. Charlie, who was about ten years younger than his brother and Uncle Bob, hung around them as much as they would let him.[13]

A further connection to the boxing aspect surfaced during Charlie's recollections of Uncle Bob. He remembered Delmar's and Uncle Bob's interest in boxing led to them sending in their money for the Charles Atlas body building course. This was the course widely advertised in the boxing magazines and comic books during the 1930s and 1940s. Charlie remembers that they regularly bought and read boxing magazines.[14] The Charles Atlas advertisement used the catch phrase, "I was a 97 pound weakling," and promised to turn any one who bought the course into a perfect physical specimen just like him. The previously noted photograph of Uncle Bob without a shirt in his boxing stance might have been taken to show off the results of his progress with the Charles Atlas course.

A BUDDING INTEREST IN THE MILITARY

Mary Lea recalls another area of interest to Uncle Bob that began to develop during this period of his life involved the military. Ernest and Mary Scott Hair were well known citizens of the Hurley community. While

Ernest and Mary Scott Hair at their home in Hurley—courtesy Margaret Eaton Dillabough.

Mary came to be known for her exceptional writing ability and her devotion to teaching Sunday School classes and playing piano at the Hurley Methodist Church, Ernest was widely known as an avid fox hunter and a generally interesting fellow. Uncle Bob was drawn to develop a friendship with Ernest because of his service in the army in World War I. Mary Lea recalls Uncle Bob visiting with him many times to listen and to talk with him about his adventures in the "Great War." Years later, in his correspondence from

Europe during World War II, Uncle Bob would include messages to Ernest about seeing some of the same places Ernest had been in World War I and that they had talked about during their many conversations.[15]

OTHER ACTIVITIES

In addition to the continuing need to attend to the family farm there were other opportunities to work. Given the agricultural setting of the area, one can be certain that Uncle Bob was kept busy during the summers of this period with work such as helping to put up hay, combining or threshing the field crops, plowing fields for seeding and planting, picking strawberries and tomatoes. There was also the possibility of working at the local tomato canning factory during the active season. These and various other activities provided another way to earn some money.

Another certainty for Uncle Bob and his friends of these times would be the regular gatherings at the local swimming hole during the normally hot, dry and dusty months of June, July and August. An important "rite of passage" for any young boy growing up in the community was learning to swim. It is very likely Uncle Bob would have learned to swim by the time he was ten or eleven years of age. Swimming is another of the "athletic skills" he indicated that he possessed when completing the officer commissioning questionnaire.[16]

The favorite area swimming hole was known as the "Iron Bridge." It got the name from a railroad bridge with iron sidings along the top of the trestle that crossed Spring Creek about a quarter mile south of the Missouri Pacific depot in Hurley. The manner in which the creek curved in the area of the bridge made for a large hole of water deep enough in which to swim; not to mention that it was deep enough for some of the brave souls to jump into from the ten to twelve feet height of the bridge. No one needed a bathing suit as the usual practice was to swim in the nude. Neither the sometimes biting cold temperature of the spring-fed waters nor the occasional company of a water moccasin deterred the determination of the young swimmers.

Mary Lea recalls times when her high school friends would come to their place to visit in the evening. As Mary Lea was only two years his junior it would be natural that Uncle Bob might show an interest in entertaining her female friends. Some of those friends mentioned were Joan Young, Mildred Barnett, and Lynna Box. She revealed her amusement as she related that Uncle Bob's way of impressing them seemed to be that of telling scary stories that would leave her friends afraid to walk home in the dark. This would serve to provide Uncle Bob with the excuse to walk them home. While he showed the normal amount of interest in the opposite sex as that of the average teenage boy, Mary Lea does not recall him ever having one special "girl friend" during this period.[17]

Mary Lea recalls that after their father died they had purchased a car to provide them with transportation. Based on an assemblage of recollections of friends it is believed the car was an early 1930s Ford Model A coupe with a rumble seat. She remembers her brother Everette and Uncle Bob driving the car. It is believed this is the car that Uncle Bob continued to drive for the next several years. She remembers, too, that Uncle Bob would occasionally drive their Uncle John, Stanley's brother, to visit with McHolland relatives living in the Ava area of Douglas County. She recalls Uncle Bob being amused about Uncle John intently holding onto the passenger car door with apparent wariness of Uncle Bob's driving ability.[18]

A LOVE OF MUSIC AND SINGING

Another developing interest of Uncle Bob's during this period of life was music and particularly that of singing. This is an interest that continued to blossom throughout his life. This could have been the reason that he became more active in church activities. Among memories recalled by Inez Inmon Bowman was that of him singing Christmas carols. She remembered how he loved to sing and was part of a mixed group that went caroling in the community during the Christmas season. This was likely an activity of the Hurley Methodist Church. Another of Inez's memories of this period involved his interest in music. She recalled trading sheet music with him. A specific instance recalled was when he traded his copy of the words and music of a beautiful Christmas song entitled "Star of the East" to Inez for her copy of the words and music of a popular song of the day, "In the Valley of the Moon."[19]

Another story told about Uncle Bob by Inez Inmon Bowman was also related to music and singing. Uncle Bob and Inez had been chosen by Mary Scott Hair to sing a duet at a regular quarterly gathering of some of the churches in the area. It was the usual practice of the church groups to meet and to jointly review bible lessons. The activities always included some special singing. Inez cannot recall the name of the song they performed, but she did recall that the performance was held during a warm time of the year and that they had "dinner on the ground" at the gathering. Inez's mother had prepared a basket lunch that included fried chicken, pie, and other delectable morsels. After they had finished the delicious meal, and knowing that Inez's mother had prepared all of it, Uncle Bob seized upon the moment to start teasing her about her noninvolvement in preparation of the food. He continued to tease her about this and sometime later he presented Inez a rolling pin so she could learn to make pies. Inez still has the rolling pin as a treasured possession with this memory of Uncle Bob. His teasing had become a trademark as Inez also remembered him forever teasing her about the guys she dated.[20]

MOVIES: ANOTHER SPECIAL INTEREST

A favorite pastime of Uncle Bob was watching movies. According to Inez Inmon Bowman he enjoyed all types of movies. She remembers going with him to a movie at Hurley sometime during the summer months in the late 1930s.[21] A long since past practice that began during the 1930s and continued until the late 1940s was that of a traveling movie operation. Few of the smaller communities had a movie theater and some enterprising people came up with the idea of setting up a business of going from town to town on a regular basis and showing a movie. Flyers announcing the date, time, and title of the movie would be posted around town. The operation itself consisted of a covered truck that carried the projection and audio equipment, screen, chairs, and tent or canvas-type enclosure. Because this was an "outside" activity the movies were shown only during the warmer months. A tent was erected with a small projection screen placed at one end of the tent. The chairs were placed neatly in rows and the projector was set up on a table at the other end of the tent. Most people did not have an automobile to transport them to the nearest town with a movie theater and this offered a novel and convenient type of entertainment for the community. This was a good opportunity for people to gather and visit as well as watch a movie. Inez recalled that these events drew a lot of folks from the area..

Crane was the closest town with a real indoor theater. Aurora was a few miles further and also had an indoor theatre. As much as Uncle Bob liked to go to the movies it is likely that he would have used the Ford Model A coupe to take friends the six miles to Crane, or the longer fifteen mile trip to Aurora, as often as possible to take in a good western or maybe even a Garbo or Harlow movie.

OTHER HIGH SCHOOL FRIENDS

Undoubtedly there were many others in school and the community that were numbered among Uncle Bob's friends. Among those whose names I have heard associated with him over the years are: Delmar Bowyer, Lee Robb, Howard Irvin Dale "Rip" Dean, Leaford Gold, Billy Slentz, Arvene Conrad, boyhood friends Ray and Louis Conrad, and, of course, Edwin Dean. It can be assumed that there were many others who were counted among his circle of friends, but, in my tardiness to begin this documentation of Uncle Bob's life, I am guilty of letting Old Father Time rob myself of the opportunity to talk with many others who could have provided more stories and insight about Uncle Bob.

Classmate Lee Robb and Uncle Bob at Hurley High School, probably 1934— courtesy Kathryn Robb Hall.

HIGH SCHOOL GRADUATION

Uncle Bob graduated from Hurley High School in May 1936 in the upper twenty percent of his class. The ranking in his class is according to a statement made by the school principal at the time, John Vilhauer. The statement was a part of the character reference Mr. Vilhauer provided to accompany Uncle Bob's application for appointment as an army officer.[22] Since there were only twelve in his graduating class, the statement probably meant that he graduated third in his class. This would appear to be quite an accomplishment for someone who was never described as the studious type.

When I was attending the same high school in the 1950s I often wondered why there was no class picture of the 1936 class hanging with the other class pictures along the upstairs wall of the school. Except for the class of 1936, pictures of all the other classes from the 1920s through the 1950s were hanging in their rightful place. The most logical reason that Mary Lea, who graduated from Hurley High in 1938, could propose was that the cost of the usual formal pictures was too great and maybe the class had decided not to have them taken.[23] After all, the Great Depression was still taking its toll throughout the decade of the 1930s.

The story about a class picture for the Hurley High School class of 1936 has an interesting positive twist. The good news is that a picture of that class is now hanging in its proper place on the wall of the main hallway of the school where all of the other class pictures are displayed. The school has been greatly expanded and modernized over the years. The picture that hangs is a group picture of the class and it appears that it was probably taken with someone's old Kodak box camera. Those shown in the picture are identified as: Mr. Leroy Edison who was the Superintendent of Schools, Lee Robb, Howard Irvin, Gorden Merritt, Jack Spears, Kenneth Johnson, Loretta Robb, Marie Louise Jones, Rollie Scott, Jane Rickman, Kathryn Robb, Christine Tennis, and Robert McHolland.

Hurley High School—Class of 1936. Uncle Bob is last one
on right of back row—courtesy Sheila Wiley.

Included among some of Uncle Bob's personal belongings, a separate informal snapshot of Mr. Edison was found. This picture was apparently taken on the same day the group picture was taken as students, dressed in their graduation caps and gowns, can be seen in the background of the picture. Efforts to learn more about Mr. Edison were unfruitful, but since he had kept this single photo of him it is reasonably certain that he was admired and respected by Uncle Bob.

Uncle Bob, the graduate, 1936—courtesy Wiley-McHolland family.

During a period when finishing high school was quite an accomplishment, Uncle Bob had completed a huge step toward preparing himself for the future by successfully earning his high school diploma. Having completed this hurdle in the educational process it was now time for him to begin

Mr. Leroy Edison, Hurley Superintendent of Schools, 1936— courtesy Wiley-McHolland family.

looking ahead to decide the course for his future. While he was thinking about taking the next step in his education, another area of interest was also beginning to take shape. For some time he had shown more than a passing interest in the military. That interest would continue to grow. The next few years he would be alternating his efforts between furthering his education, teaching, and completing the requirements for commissioning as an officer in the United States Army. Although these activities would take him away from Hurley for short periods of time, Hurley remained his home. Because he still had livestock to tend, he did not venture far from home and would continue to keep his ties with the community through his involvement with various local activities.

Chapter 2 Endnotes:
1. Personal interviews, M. Brown.
2. Personal interviews, John Brown, 2008.
3. Personal interviews, M. Brown.
4. Personal interviews. M. Brown.
5. Personal interviews, M. Brown.
6. Personal interview, Wayne Ivie, 2008
7. Personal interviews, J. Brown.
8. Application for Appointment, May 1941, Official Personal File, Robert B. McHolland.
9. Letter of Robert B. McHolland, October 27, 1944.
10. Personal interviews, Edwin Dean, 2007-8.
11. Personal interviews, M. Brown.
12. Telephone interviews, Charles Bowyer, 2007-8
13. Telephone interview, Bowyer
14. Telephone interview, Bowyer
15. Personal interviews, M. Brown.
16. Commissioning Questionnaire, May 1942, McHolland
17. Personal interviews, M. Brown.
18. Personal interviews, M. Brown.

19. Personal interview, Bowman.
20. Personal interview, Bowman.
21. Personal interview, Bowman.
22. Letter of character reference, John Vilhauer,
23. Personal interviews, M. Brown.

Chapter 3
Hurley--Continued Ties and Activities

Throughout the years after his graduation from high
school in 1936 until his entrance on active duty in
the U. S. Army in 1942, Uncle Bob was occupied with
either attending or teaching school during the fall, winter and spring months. During the summer months
from 1936 through 1938 and in 1940 he was spending
a month participating in military training in the Citizens
Military Training Camp (CMTC) program.

With much of his time during these years dedicated to
preparing for a career by attending college, teaching, and
working toward a commission in the U. S. Army it would
seem that there would be little time left for other things.
However, he continued to maintain his close relationship to the Hurley community through church activities,
involvement in the Boy Scouts, tending to farm operations, joining the Masonic Lodge, and maintaining ties
with friends. After starting college in 1937, he returned

to Hurley almost every weekend during the two years he attended college. While teaching at the High Point rural school in Webster County from 1939 through 1941, he traveled back to Hurley on a regular basis to check in with friends and relatives and to work or check on things at the farm. Although one month out of four different summers was spent performing military training, much of the remainder of the time would find him at Hurley. It is noted that he spent his last year, (from May 1941 until May 1942) at Hurley before entering military service. He had moved back home after the 1940-41 school year at High Point to take a teaching position at the Inmon rural school near Hurley.

BOY SCOUTS AND YOUNG FRIENDS

His involvement with the local Boy Scout troop was mentioned previously at the beginning of Uncle Bob's friendship with Edwin Dean. Even as he grew older, past the usual age of scouting (ages11-13 for Boy Scouts, ages 14-18 for the older Explorer Scouts), he maintained an interest in helping with the local troop.

Two of the boys who were members of the scout troop were Eddie Brown and Charlie Bowyer. Both of these boys were born in 1929 making them eleven or twelve years old when Uncle Bob became a leader of the local troop. Charlie remembered that at some point he became the Scoutmaster of the Hurley troop.[1] This most likely occurred in 1941. This coincides with the time of his return to Hurley after his two years of teaching at High Point school.

(NOTE: The local Boy Scout council located in Springfield, Mis-

souri was contacted in an effort to verify the exact dates of Uncle Bob's service as scoutmaster. They were unable to confirm the dates of his service because their records only went back as far as the early 1970s.)

Several sources indicated that Uncle Bob was very interested in helping in the overall development of the younger boys in the community. This desire kept him very active in the troop's activities. He seemed to be drawn to boys that might benefit from special attention and the presence of a strong male figure. The extra effort directed toward these kids was a defining characteristic of his personality.

EDDIE BROWN

Born in 1929 Eddie Brown was about eleven years younger than Uncle Bob. He grew up in Hurley and was raised by his grandmother, Mary Hood. In the community Mary was affectionately referred to as "Aunt Mary" and was known for the beautiful flower garden she kept. Eddie, along with a couple of other boys around town lacked the influence of a strong father figure at home. Without this type of consistent, firm guidance from home, they were more prone to mischievous behavior and the possibility of getting into trouble. Echoing some of the things Uncle Bob's friend, John Brown, remembered about him during his teaching days at High Point, it was this type of kid that Uncle Bob seemed to be drawn to take under his wings.[2] It appears that something from deep inside the core of his being drove him to be a "self-appointed" guardian of any kid that he thought could use compassionate, morally based direction from a strong male figure.

Since the age for entry into the Boy Scouts was eleven and Eddie reached that age in 1940, most of the events he recalled must have occurred in 1940, 1941 or 1942. They could also have happened during the summers or possibly on the weekends before the summer of 1941. Most likely these events occurred when Uncle Bob was staying in Hurley from the summer of 1941 until the spring of 1942 when he entered on active duty with the U. S. Army.

Eddie Brown (left) with friend, Cecil Gardner, 1941—courtesy Eddie Brown

Eddie described Uncle Bob as "one of the good guys, somebody you'd look up to ….. one of the best." Many of his memories are centered on the activities of the Boy Scout troop and he recalled Uncle Bob and one of his friends, Arvene Conrad, as the leaders of the troop. Eddie related that Uncle Bob was always "keeping an eye on the kids." It is understood that Eddie meant that Uncle Bob was forever watching out for the ones that might need an extra bit of guidance or encouragement. Eddie recalled some of the others that were involved with the scouting activities during this period. Among those mentioned by Eddie as possibly involved were Cecil Gardner, Charlie Bowyer, Milford Jenkins and Donald Dean.[3]

It is evident that Uncle Bob made a strong, positive impression on Eddie Brown. For several years he carried a wallet-sized photograph of Uncle Bob clad in his army uniform. Uncle Bob had most likely given him the photo to sometime in 1942 when he was home on leave after he entered service. A larger version of the photo was found in a family album. It appeared to be one of those taken by the army for inclusion in his official personnel file. Over sixty years after Uncle Bob gave him the photograph and Eddie, in a very thoughtful gesture, had several touched-up prints made of the photograph and presented them to members of Uncle Bob's family.

Eddie Brown's photo of Uncle Bob— courtesy Eddie Brown.

An incident recalled by Cecil Clark, cousin Herbert McHolland's stepson, would appear to be a part of a scout troop outing. Cecil related what he recalled as one of his earliest memories. He was four or five years old at the time when he remembers Uncle Bob driving an old farm wagon with a team of horses up the dirt road near the McHolland home place east of Hurley. There were several boys on the wagon laughing, talking and obviously having a good time. Cecil specifically remembers one of the boys on the wagon since he shared the same rare first name with him. That boy was Cecil Gardner who was also one of the boys Eddie Brown mentioned as being a part of the Boy Scout troop.[4] Because the time period (sometime in 1940, 1941 or 1942) of Cecil's recollection is consistent with Uncle Bob's active involvement with the scouting activities, it can reasonably be deduced that this was likely a scouting event and Eddie Brown was possibly a part of it.

One other incident recalled by another Hurley resident, Mildred Leath Conrad, who grew up on a farm near the McHolland place also lends credence to Uncle Bob's Boy Scout connections. It was during this time frame that she remembered seeing him with a team of horses pulling a wagon on the road that ran by the McHolland home. The wagon was loaded with members of the Boy Scout troop headed somewhere for an outdoors experience.[5]

Apart from the scouting activities, Eddie recalled another memory about Uncle Bob. Eddie and Charlie Bowyer, who was his age (and about whom more will follow) climbed into the back of Uncle Bob's car, the Model A Ford, and hid out while he took a trip about fifteen miles to Aurora. He remembered Uncle Bob had a car with a rumble seat. From the conversation they had overheard, they knew that Uncle Bob was going to drive to Aurora taking Arvene Conrad along with him. Eddie said he and Charlie never had a dime and were always looking for something to do; and this was something to do at the time. They believed they were really pulling a good trick on Uncle Bob by "hiding in the rumble seat." Uncle Bob "discovered" them when they got to Aurora exclaiming "What have we got here?" all the while pretending to be surprised at his young passengers. He got a good laugh out of it and then treated them by taking them to a movie.[6]

CHARLIE BOWYER

The young man mentioned in the previous paragraph was a subject of tremendous concern for Uncle Bob. Charlie Bowyer would probably be described in present-day terms as a "troubled kid." My journey in gathering information for this story turned up a large amount of interesting information about Charlie from various sources including much from Charlie himself. Edwin Dean remembered that Uncle Bob was always concerned about Charlie and trying to look out for his best interests.[7] Uncle Bob's sister Mary Lea and John Brown echoed these sentiments.[8,9] The distance from Hurley to John's home in Niangua was around sixty miles, but John knew a lot about Charlie and Uncle Bob's interest in helping to keep him out of trouble. I was struck by the many details that came out about Uncle Bob's relationship with Charlie and was led to the conclusion that Charlie Bowyer probably fell into the category of a "special project" for him.

Like his Hurley cohort, Eddie Brown, Charlie was born in 1929. He had come to Hurley from Potwin, Kansas, with his parents in 1934 when he was five years of age. Charlie had a brother, Delmar, who was about ten year's his senior. Delmar was one year younger than Uncle Bob. When the Bowyer family moved into the house up the road just east of the McHolland home, Delmar and Uncle Bob became close friends. This was another friendship that endured through school and later years. Delmar also attended one or two of the Citizen's Military Training Camps (CMTC) along with Uncle Bob. Their parents were older than most parents of Charlie's peers. Possibly because he was the "baby" boy of the family he grew up doing pretty much what he wanted to do. His younger years were devoid of discipline and he came to be known in the community as a kid that was always in trouble. During his pre-teen and teenage years it seems that if something happened involving mischievous, or sometimes destructive, behavior around the town Charlie would be the first one to whom the fingers were pointed.

Charlie's memories of Uncle Bob are of a "very good natured" fellow whom he admired and respected. Charlie remembered following him around "like a little puppy while he was milking, plowing, or whatever he was doing." He recalled that among the animals Uncle Bob cared for on the farm was a flock of sheep. A part of caring for sheep is the spring ritual of lopping of the lambs' tails. Charlie remembers helping Uncle Bob with this task by holding the lambs as Uncle Bob lopped the tails. Charlie recalls that Uncle Bob surprised him (probably on purpose) during the process of lopping the lambs' tails by quickly castrating one of the young male lambs. Charlie, thinking that Uncle Bob was making a bad mistake, yelled something like, "Hey, that's not his tail!" Charlie remembers Uncle Bob having a good laugh about Charlie's reaction and told all who would listen about Charlie's pained reaction to his "awful deed."[10]

Snapshots of Charlie with Uncle Bob make up a part of the family scrapbook. A couple of those pictures show Uncle Bob, Charlie, and another friend, Garland Honeycutt, proudly displaying a young mule that Uncle Bob

At left: Uncle Bob, Charlie Bowyer with Sarie the mule—courtesy Wiley-McHolland family. At right: Garland Honeycutt, Uncle Bob, and Charlie Bowyer with Sarie—courtesy Charlie Bowyer.

had bought. Charlie remembers the mule was named Sarie and that he also had a stock dog named Elmer.[11] Charlie has other memories of "tagging along" with Uncle Bob on various trips. One of those trips he recalled was to the Civilian Conservation Corps camp at Shell Knob, Missouri. The camp was located about forty miles south of Hurley. The purpose of the trip was to visit Billy Slentz, another of Uncle Bob's friends. There was another vague memory of a time that he went with Uncle Bob to Niangua when he was teaching at High Point school. Uncle Bob took him to school with him and he remembers watching a softball game while he was there.[12]

Charlie remembers participating in a Boy Scout paper collection drive under the direction of Uncle Bob while he was Scoutmaster. Along with providing them something meaningful to do and to keep the boys busy, the primary purpose of the drive was to raise money for a worthwhile charity. Charlie does not remember the amount of money they collected from the sale of the paper, but the drive was successful. He remembers Uncle Bob calling a meeting of the scout troop to decide the organization that would be the recipient of their proceeds. The American Red Cross turned out to be the benefactor of the Hurley Boy Scouts' paper drive.[12] This was yet another example of the positive influence he had on the young men of the community.

Another memory recalled by Charlie has some similarities with one of those related earlier by his friend, Eddie Brown. Charlie recalled Uncle Bob's car, the Model A Ford, was a coupe with a rumble seat and that he and a friend (usually Eddie) often rode in the rumble seat on various trips with him. Charlie recalled an event that he believed included a young lady from Crane by the name of Vena Custer. (When interviewed, Vena Custer Berglund did not remember this event.) It is known that Uncle Bob tried to woo this young lady after he was on active duty in the Army. Charlie believes the trip took them to Aurora where Uncle Bob dropped off Eddie and himself to see a movie while Uncle Bob took his date elsewhere. The boys were picked up after the movie and all of them returned to Hurley.[14]

There will be more to report in the pages to follow about Charlie. Uncle Bob's continued interest in Charlie's welfare was evident from his references to Charlie in letters he later wrote from overseas.

GENE ANDERSON

Although not connected with Boy Scout activities, Gene Anderson was another of the young Hurley boys who admired Uncle Bob. Like Eddie Brown and Charlie Bowyer, Gene was born in 1929, but his home and family situation was quite different than that of either Eddie or Charlie. Gene was an only child and was blessed with a comfortable family life. His father and mother, Onus and Osa, operated one of the local general stores in Hurley in the late 1930s through the late 1940s. You might say it was a forerunner of the local convenience store as there was a lunch bar in a section of the store where Osa served sandwiches and a daily luncheon special. There was an area in the rear of the store where the family lived.

Gene proudly stated that, "Bob was my boyhood hero." It was probably sometime in 1939 or 1940 that Gene recalls the beginning of his relationship with him. There was something about Uncle Bob that drew Gene away from the store to follow him around and to help him with his work on the farm. Gene recalls often walking the short distance up the valley to the farm. It was not unusual for him to take the walk to the farm every day for several days at a time. Many times he would stay at the farm all day and would have lunch and supper with Uncle Bob and others of the family. He fondly recalls Uncle Bob allowing him to do a lot of the work and treating him almost as an adult. He also recalled going to the farm at times, maybe with Charlie Bowyer or another friend, catching Uncle Bob's horses and riding them over the pasture. He sensed that even at his young age he was fully accepted by Uncle Bob and he always felt at ease while he was around him.[15]

Gene recalled a particular incident in which he was help-ing Uncle Bob put up hay. Gene's job was to handle the team of horses pulling the hay wagon. He remem-bers the horses were named Duke and Minnie and that Uncle Bob would often add the term "Few Brains" to Minnie's name for obvious reasons. In addition to guid-ing the team Gene also had the job of spreading the hay evenly on the wagon as Uncle Bob and his friend, Delmar Bowyer, used pitchforks to load the loose hay on the wagon. Gene remembers Uncle Bob and Delmar working together much of the time he was at the farm. They worked well as a team, but he recalls Uncle Bob was clearly the leader of the team.

The standard practice was to load the wagon with as much hay as possible in order to reduce the number of trips to the barn. One of the loads happened to be piled higher than usual. It should be noted that Gene was only eleven or twelve years old at the time and was prob-ably only about five feet in height. As he was driving the horses with this large load to the barn he had trouble seeing over the sides of the load. The trail to the barn passed through a narrow gate. Because of limited vis-ibility caused by the large load the wagon caught one of the gate posts as he was guiding the wagon through the gate. This caused him to lose a part of the load. Gene feared he might be in big trouble, but it turned out to be a minor disaster. Uncle Bob was unfazed as he coolly backed up the wagon and they reloaded the lost portion of the hay. Uncle Bob then guided the load through the gate and to the barn. Gene was impressed with Uncle Bob's demeanor and how he calmly handled the misfortune without getting upset. They continued to gather and put up hay as if nothing had happened.

One of the most indelible memories Gene has about Uncle Bob concerns the assistance he provided to Uncle Bob in completing an army extension course. The course encompassed the basic knowledge required of an army infantry officer and consisted of several sub-courses covering subject areas such as unit organization and function, chemical warfare, map reading, aerial photography, etc. As a prerequisite for appointment as an officer Uncle Bob was working on these courses during the period of January 1941 through September 1941.

Gene recalls sitting at the kitchen table of the McHolland home with a large army topographical map spread across the table and aiding Uncle Bob with the map reading sub-course. Uncle Bob would read the problem giving Gene the azimuth (direction) and distance from a starting point on the map. The solution to the problem required that a compass be used to plot the azimuth. By using the legend one would then calculate the distance to the required destination point. The coordinates of that point would be the correct answer to the map problem. Gene assisted Uncle Bob with these problems by plotting the azimuth, determining the distance to the destination, and providing him with the coordinates of the destination. Uncle Bob would then record the coordinates Gene gave him as the answer. Gene marveled at the confidence Uncle Bob had in his abilities as he took the information Gene gave him and wrote it in as the answer without a question.[17]   Uncle Bob's confidence in the ability of young Gene Anderson was rewarded as the actual course records show that Uncle Bob satisfactorily completed the

A young Gene Anderson—courtesy Colonel Gene Anderson, Ret USAF.

map reading sub-course on August 4, 1941. [18]

Gene is another person that recalled Uncle Bob's inclination of teasing. He said he "loved to tease" but it was never in a malicious manner. Gene admired and respected him because, even as a naïve, young fellow he was always treated with dignity and respect by Uncle Bob. He was yet another of the youth of Hurley whose life was affected in a most positive manner. He movingly added that hearing the news of Uncle Bob's death really hit him hard.[19]

LATER SUCCESSES FOR THE YOUNG FRIENDS

Eddie Brown, Charlie Bowyer, and Gene Anderson accounted for but three young boys of Hurley whose lives were touched, and possibly influenced, in some way by Uncle Bob's charismatic manner and caring personality. Undoubtedly there were others who would have been available and gladly would have shared their memories of Uncle Bob had I begun this project sooner. All of these three individuals gained a measure of success in their lives beyond their Hurley experience.

After Eddie Brown completed high school he worked several years for the local farmers' exchanges in Hurley and Crane before securing a position with a large manufacturing company in Springfield. He retired from the company in 1991 after a career of almost thirty years in their production and inspection functions.[20] Charlie Boyer entered the military service shortly after World War II and had a successful career in the United States Army retiring in 1968 as a Sergeant First Class with over twenty-two years of service to our country.[21] Gene Anderson obtained his Bachelor of Science degree in Education from Southwest Missouri State College (now Missouri State University) with the original intent of a coaching and teaching career. By this time the Korean Conflict was raging and shortly after be began teaching at his alma mater, Hurley High School, he received his draft notice. He enlisted in the United States Air Force before he was drafted and later attended Officer Candidate School and received his commission as

Lt. Col Gene Anderson (retired as full Colonel), United States Air Force—courtesy Colonel Gene Anderson, Ret USAF.

an officer. He later received a degree in Electrical Engineering from the Air Force Institute of Technology and was involved in the earliest stages of the computer technology revolution in the air force. He retired as a full Colonel with twenty-two years and six months of service to our country.[22]

FARMING OPERATIONS

It can readily be recognized from previous references that farm work had been an integral part of Uncle Bob's life from his earliest years and continued to be important as he was attending college and started teaching. He was usually home on the weekends and through the summer months, except for his CMTC military training. He would be attending to the usual chores associated with caring for the animals and upkeep of the buildings and fencing. After he got his first teaching job at High Point School, he began investing some of his income in buying more livestock. The family still had the seventy five plus acres that Stanley had accumulated over the years and had continued to keep a cow or two, some sheep, some chickens and a team of horses. As mentioned before, at some point he also bought a mule. The acreage provided ample pasture for several head of livestock. Later, when he went on active duty in the army, he enlisted the services of his cousin Herbert to help care for his investments.

Harold Conrad lived with his family in the house just up the road east from the McHolland home. Harold related an amusing incident about Uncle Bob that must have occurred sometime in 1940 or 1941. Harold was only seven or eight years old when he recalled a time that Uncle Bob was bargaining with his father, Marion, for a young calf he wanted to buy. They had been talking for a while when Uncle Bob ended up offering Marion twenty-five dollars for the calf. Marion told Uncle Bob that he needed thirty dollars for the calf. Uncle Bob replied that he could not go that much and it appeared the bargaining was about over. It was at this time that the young and naïve Harold told his father he thought that twenty-five dollars sounded like a good deal to him and that his father ought to make the deal. After Harold made his opinion known, Marion relented and made the deal with Uncle Bob taking twenty-five dollars for the calf. That was not the end of the story for Harold. He said that once Uncle Bob took the calf and left, his dad informed him that he was going to be working hard to make up for the money Harold had cost him.[23]

Cecil Clark's brother, Duane, another of cousin Herbert McHolland's step-sons, remembers little about Uncle Bob as a person. But he does recall Herbert taking care of Uncle Bob's livestock on the farm after he went on active duty. Duane remembers making the short trip with Herbert up the valley to the farm east of Hurley and helping to feed cattle, sheep and a mule. He also remembers the time that his uncle (mother's brother), who was serving in Europe in World War II, sent home a copy of the Stars and Stripes (Warweek) edition that highlighted Uncle Bob's infantry company.[24]

Another incident recalled by Edwin Dean portrays Uncle Bob's involvement in another aspect of farming. When Charlie Bowyer recalled that he followed Uncle Bob around everywhere, one of the things he mentioned was he followed him as he was plowing. This would tend to agree with a memory of Edwin's which through a process of deductive reasoning must have occurred sometime in the spring or summer of 1941. Edwin had tried to enlist in the Marines, but the Marines had refused his enlistment. He received word that the results of his physical examination revealed that he had a perforated eardrum. (Edwin said this was the result of a childhood injury that occurred when a firecracker exploded near his ear.) He received this information in Springfield and as soon as he returned to Hurley he wanted to tell Uncle Bob about it. He remembers delivering his disappointing news to Uncle Bob as Uncle Bob was plowing corn in a field. The field was about a quarter mile south of Hurley on a small strip of land the family owned and was located between the railroad tracks and Spring Creek.[25] It might be noted that Edwin was not deterred by this rejection as he joined the army a short time later and bravely served as an original member of the celebrated Darby's Rangers in North Africa, Sicily and Italy in the Second World War.

MASONIC ORDER

One of Uncle Bob's most treasured accomplishments was that of becoming a member of the Masonic brotherhood. In becoming a Mason he followed in the footsteps of his father, Stanley, and was no doubt also positively influenced by his uncle, John McHolland, both of whom were Masons.

Uncle Bob was a member of Crane, Missouri Lodge Number 519. That lodge has since been merged with Galena, Missouri Lodge Number 515 which maintains the record of his membership. The lodge records show that he passed the proficiencies of Entered Apprentice degree on June 24, 1941, Fellowcraft degree on July 22, 1941, and Master Mason degree on August 19, 1941.

The Grand Lodge of Missouri records show the officers of the Crane lodge at the time of his degrees were: Worshipful Master, Wade Garroutte; Senior Warden, Lee

Dewitt; Junior Warden, Martin Crumpley; Treasurer, Harold Crumpley; Secretary, Harry D. Wilson; Senior Deacon, Louie D. Wilson; Junior Steward, Curtis Hayes; and Tiler, Ross Farmer.[26] Considering his Boy Scout activities, farming operations, preparations for teaching and the time involved in reaching the Master Mason level, the summer of 1941 was clearly a very busy time for Uncle Bob.

Masonic Certification—courtesy Wiley-McHolland family.

A prized possession of Uncle Bob's was his Masonic ring. On his last leave before he went overseas he left his ring in the care of his Uncle John McHolland. He told Uncle John that in the event that he did not make it back home alive, the ring was to be his. After Uncle John died in 1961, his family presented the ring to one of Uncle Bob's namesakes, my brother, Robert S. Wiley, who also is a Mason. The ring is presently in the possession of Robert's granddaughter, Mary Claire Wiley, in whom he has entrusted the care and safekeeping of the ring. [27]

OTHER ACTIVITIES

There were two other job activities worthy of mention that occurred between the period of Uncle Bob's high school graduation and his entry on active duty with the army. Along with his full time teaching jobs at High Point and Inmon, these two jobs were listed on the Classification Questionnaire of Reserve Officers he completed in January of 1942 after he had received his temporary appointment as a second lieutenant in the Army of the United States. He showed that he had worked at the Hurley Canning Factory as a time checker in August and September of 1936. This would have been a seasonal job as the sole purpose of the factory was to can tomatoes during the relatively short period the tomatoes were

L-R, Brother-in-law, Maurice Wiley, sisters Roxabel and Mary Lea, and Uncle Bob, 1940—courtesy Wiley-McHolland family.

ripe and ready for canning. He also listed that he had
worked as telephone operator for the Hurley Telephone
Company from 1935 until 1939. This work was indicated as being a part time situation.[28] His sister, Mary
Lea, related that his other sister, Roxabel, was the principal operator of the telephone company switchboard for
a few years in the mid to late 1930s. She confirmed that
it was not unusual for any one of the three siblings to be
performing duty as the local switchboard operator during this period. Uncle Bob was regularly called upon
to sit in and handle the telephone calls in and out of
Hurley.[29]

ANOTHER TRAGEDY IN THE FAMILY

Uncle Bob was over halfway through his first year of
teaching at High Point when tragedy again struck the
McHolland family. His mother Nancy had begun to suffer
a decline in her health sometime in 1938 or 1939. Even
with her declining health, Mary Lea remembers that their
mother never seemed to slow down and continued about
her daily tasks. She recalls that mother Nancy had been
diagnosed with high blood pressure and was under treatment for the condition when she suffered a severe stroke
in February of 1940.[30] Uncle Bob was immediately contacted at the Brown household in Niangua where he was
staying when his mother had the stroke. John Brown remembers being with him as he drove to Hurley as quickly
as possible to be at his mother's bedside.[31] Because of the
severity of the stroke his mother never regained conscious-
ness and died shortly after Uncle Bob arrived on February
10. Funeral services were held two days later at the Hurley High School and she was laid to rest beside Stanley in
the Crane Masonic Cemetery. Although the family was

aware of her high blood pressure problem, it was another tough loss especially when considering she was only 52 years of age. Uncle Bob returned to High Point school with a heavy heart and surely immersed himself in his job to help in dealing with the grief process.

In this chapter I have endeavored to cover the various home and community activities in which Uncle Bob continued to be involved around Hurley from his high school graduation in 1936 until he entered military service in May 1942. Throughout those same years he was wrestling with questions and decisions about his future. It was during this journey to discover solutions, that his time and attention were focused in three areas: college, teaching, and preparation for military service. In the next three chapters each of these aspects will be separately addressed for these years.

Chapter 3 Endnotes:
1.　 Telephone interviews, Bowyer.
2.　 Personal interviews, J. Brown.
3.　 Telephone interviews, Eddie Brown, 2008.
4.　 Telepjpme omterview, Cecil Clark, 2008.
5.　 Personal interview, Mildred Conrad, 2008.
6.　 Telephone interviews, E. Brown.
7.　 Personal interviews, Dean.
8.　 Personal interviews, M. Brown.
9.　 Personal interviews, J. Brown.
10.　 Telephone interviews, Bowyer.
11.　 Telephone interviews, Bowyer.

12. Telephone interviews, Bowyer.
13. Telephone interviews, Bowyer.
14. Telephone interviews, Bowyer.
15. Personal interview, Gene Anderson, 2008.
16. Personal interview, Anderson.
17. Personal interview, Anderson.
18. Extension Course Records, August 1941, Official Personnel File, Robert B. McHolland.
19. Personal interview, Anderson.
20. Telephone interviews, E. Brown.
21. Telephone interviews, Bowyer.
22. Personal interview, Anderson.
23. Telephone interview, Harold Conrad, 2008.
24. Telephone interview, Duane Clark, 2008.
25. Personal interviews, Dean.
26. Letter, Grand Lodge of Missouri, March 18, 2008.
27. Personal Conversation, Robert Wiley, 2008.
28. Classification Questionnaire, January 1942, Official Personnel File, Robert B. McHolland.
29. Personal interviews, M. Brown.
30. Personal interviews, M. Brown.
31. Personal interviews, J. Brown.

Chapter 4
Uncle Bob's College Experience

As Uncle Bob embarked upon the next phase of his life after his graduation from high school, the ominous early clouds of war were forming in other parts of the world. Hitler's designs for world domination were becoming more evident with similar warnings emerging from the other side of the globe in the Pacific. Uncle Bob was taking the first steps toward preparing himself for the future. Throughout the next few years he would attend college with the idea of a possible career in teaching. He would continue to pursue his interest in the military, as well as continuing to be active in local church and Boy Scout activities.

TOUGH ECONOMIC TIMES
THROUGHOUT THE COUNTRY

During the middle 1930s as our country was still in the process of recovering from the economic depression, efforts to make a living remained a struggle for most families. Things were not much different in the Spring Creek Valley. While the amounts of money involved were meager for most people, virtually everyone in the community was affected by the failure of the local bank. As was mentioned, the McHolland family was among those who lost money when it closed. The sum they had in the bank could not have been a huge amount, nonetheless it was a significant loss at that time. Combined with Stanley's death in 1933, the challenges of the family to manage with fewer resources made for an even more austere standard of living and increased their need to be prudent in the use of what money they had.

Roxabel Goes to Work

Uncle Bob's older sister, Roxabel, had graduated from Hurley High School one year ahead of him in 1935. Owing to her father Stanley's emphasis on education and along with her strong personal desire to become a registered nurse, she enrolled in the Springfield Baptist Hospital School of Nursing. She successfully completed her first year of training at about the same time Uncle Bob graduated from high school. As noted before, mother

Hurley Missouri Pacific Depot—courtesy Wiley-McHolland family.

Nancy was a good manager of the household, but it would seem likely that financial pressures might be beginning to stretch the budget of the family. It is possible it was becoming more apparent that additional income would be required if all family members were to be afforded the opportunity to continue their education beyond high school. It was at this point that some changes occurred

Roxabel Wiley, Hurley Depot Agent 1936-1962—courtesy Wiley-McHolland family

which would aid in bringing in some additional income to meet the expenses associated with educating the family.

From the time that Stanley died in 1933, the filling of his position of depot agent could be described with the "musical chairs" analogy. Numerous individuals had served as depot agent during this time. It seemed that no one wanted the job because of the location.[1] It was at this point in 1936, after Roxabel had completed her first year of nurses training, that officials of the Missouri Pacific Railroad offered the depot agent position to her. It was a very tough decision for her because of her passion for nursing, but the practical considerations of a solid, permanent job and a good steady income were the deciding factors in accepting the position.

(NOTE: Roxabel's passion for nursing and patient care never wa-

vered. After the Hurley depot closed in 1962, she obtained certification as a Licensed Practical Nurse and performed those duties for almost 25 years. She also continued her work with the railroad at other locations retiring with 45 years of service.)

Although Uncle Bob had graduated in the spring of 1936 it was a year later that he began his college studies. It is likely that financial considerations were the primary reason for this delay. It is assumed that Uncle Bob probably benefited from Roxabel's decision to take the depot agent job. With her additional income for the family, she likely helped him to fulfill a desire to continue his education. He enrolled at State Teachers College (now Missouri State University) in Springfield, Missouri in the fall of 1937. The tuition cost was one dollar per course hour. The full course load for a term (quarter) was ten dollars. Thus, taking a full load through the fall, winter and spring terms would cost a grand total of thirty dollars.[2] His initial plans were to become a teacher.

COLLEGE--THE FIRST YEAR

The title of the college, "Southwest Missouri State Teachers College," defined the primary purpose of the institution—one of training elementary and secondary school teachers. There were no dormitories at the school so the students whose home was from outside of Springfield traditionally stayed in one of the many rooming houses that had sprung up around the campus area. Uncle Bob ended up renting a room at the same place where a student from the small farming community of Niangua, John Brown, rented a room.

MA FORSYTHE'S ROOMING HOUSE

The rooming house was located only a half-block from the campus. It was run by a matronly lady known by all her tenants as "Ma" Forsythe. Ma was a widower with a young son who made the most of space in the house to assure that she could accommodate as many roomers as possible. Ma watched over the boys in her home with a mother's interest and was aware of their comings and goings.

John Brown recalled that there were always young men that she seemed to favor over others. He believed

that Uncle Bob and he numbered among those she liked very much. Ma had rented out rooms for some time and was especially proud of former roomers who had gone on to successful careers. Two of those former roomers she liked to tell about were Hubert Wheeler, the long-time Commissioner of Education for the state of Missouri, and Willard Graff. a long-time Springfield Superintendent of Schools.[3]

*John Brown, college buddy and good friend—
courtesy John and Florence Brown.*

You could say that Ma Forsythe's house was fairly typi-

cal of many houses located near the college campus, being used to accommodate students. Many of the rooming
houses were two story structures with a basement. Their
owners made maximum use of the space in order to house
as many roomers as possible. John recalls there must have
been twelve to fifteen other students staying at Ma's house.
There was not much space for the individual roomer. A
small desk or table, with chair for studying, along with a
bed was furnished. It was understood that cooking and
bathroom facilities would be shared. John believes that the
spaces in the basement area were rented for a dollar or a
dollar-and-a- half a week, while the better upstairs spaces
were rented for two or two-and-a- half dollars a week.[4]

A Close Friendship Begins--John Brown

Because many roomers came from small towns and shared
many common interests and common goals, friendships
would often develop with others in the house. This is
where Uncle Bob's friendship with John Brown began and
continued to develop in the coming years. John graduated from Niangua High School in 1936 and had moved
to Springfield that summer to take a job running a paper route. He enrolled in college that summer and had
been at Ma Forsythe's for a year when Uncle Bob arrived.
Their common background and interests would serve to
open the door to an enduring friendship.

John Brown recalls that he and Uncle Bob connected from
the first time they met. According to John, making friends
was not a difficult task for Uncle Bob. "People just seemed
to like Bob. He was a very caring person. He really got
to know everyone and always made time for everyone,"
John recalled.[5]

SCHOOLWORK AND STUDIES

Drawing again from John Brown's memory of Uncle Bob, it was clear that he possessed a great amount of intelligence and common sense with an active mind. But he was not inclined to spend a lot of his time reading and studying. He did study enough to make passing grades in his classes. One subject that interested him the most was history. John recalls him being in a history class under Dr. Shannon.

(NOTE: Dr. Shannon's reputation as a tough professor was still well known over twenty years later when I attended the same institution.)

Because of his interest in history Uncle Bob applied himself enough in the course to earn a passing grade. He fared better in Dr. Shannon's taxing introductory history course than many of his peers. [6]

OTHER INTERESTS--
POLITICS AND THE MILITARY

John Brown noted that Uncle Bob was interested in almost anything to do with history, current events, or politics. Following the example of his father Stanley, he would proudly voice his Republican preference when a political subject arose during conversations with friends. A favorite political figure of his was Dewey J. Short, the congressman from his district.[7] Uncle Bob was personally acquainted with Dewey and others of the Short family. Dewey also hailed from Stone County and a few years later would honor Uncle Bob's service and memory in the halls of the United States Congress.

John Brown also recalled Uncle Bob's interest and involvement in the military during this time. From conversations with Uncle Bob, John was aware that he was working toward getting his commission. Uncle Bob often spoke of his participation in the Citizens' Military Training Camp program and that he was determined to complete the requirements for commissioning.

An "Organizer"

A personal quality of Uncle Bob that began to emerge during his first couple of years at Ma Forsythe's place was his organizational ability. John recalls an example from his years at Ma's house when he organized an intramural basketball team made up of other roomers at the house. John was a member of the team. The team participated in games on campus, but John remembered them loading up in a car or two and driving to Hurley to play a game at the Hurley school gymnasium. Uncle Bob made arrangements for a game with a town team made up of local players. John said that Uncle Bob was not the fastest or quickest person on the court, but was a pretty good player. One of the things that really stood out about Uncle Bob was his penchant and ability to be an organizer.[9]

Uncle Bob's friendship with John Brown continued to grow during the year they stayed at Ma Forsythe's rooming house. It was after this year that John accepted an offer to teach in a rural school, High Point, near his home in Webster County. John would later be instrumental in an important career decision involving Uncle Bob.

COLLEGE--THE SECOND YEAR

In the fall of the 1938-39 school year Uncle Bob returned to Springfield and resumed his college studies, but he had a new roommate and a new residence. His roommate was his friend, Edwin Dean, who had graduated from Hurley High School in the spring of 1938 and enrolled at State Teachers College. They rented a one-room apartment near the campus at the corner of National and Cherry Streets. Edwin recalled that they had a coal oil stove to cook on, but he does not remember doing much cooking (He does remember going out often to a place near the St. Agnes School, where they could get three hamburgers for twenty-five cents.) There was a bed and a cot in their room. Edwin slept on the cot because Uncle Bob "outranked" him. They got along well and enjoyed one another's company. However, school and studies did not agree well with Edwin and he left school after the first term.[10]

Because of the expense in renting the room it is very likely that Uncle Bob found another roommate to pick up Edwin's share of the rent. Whether he actually found another roommate is not known. The specific facts of the situation have been lost with the passage of time, but it is known that Uncle Bob continued his studies throughout the remainder of the school year.

It was during this second year in college that he joined the Springfield YMCA. With his inclination to be involved with the activities and direction of younger people it is understood how he could quickly become involved as an instructor's helper with the YMCA. His organizational ability along with his desire to be a positive influence un-doubtedly were welcome assets to the program. [11]

A New Challenge Ahead

A new challenge would present itself to Uncle Bob as he completed his second full year of college. Although the change occurring in his life at this point would pre-clude his return to college in the fall of 1939, he would return again to Springfield to enroll for the summer term in 1940. This would be his final college experience. His college transcript shows that he successfully completed a total of 69.4 semester hours while at Southwest Mis-souri State Teachers College. As his friend John Brown had indicated, he was not an outstanding student, but he managed to compile a respectable 2.2 grade point aver-age during his time in college.[12]

Chapter 4 Endnotes:
1. Personal interviews, M. Brown.
2. Personal interviews, J. Brown.
3. Personal interviews, J. Brown.
4. Personal interviews, J. Brown.
5. Personal interviews, J. Brown.
6. Personal interviews, J. Brown.
7. Personal interviews, J. Brown.
8. Personal interviews, J. Brown.
9. Personal interviews, J. Brown.
10. Personal interviews, Dean.
11. Classification Questionnaire, May 1942, Official Personnel File, Rob-ert B. McHolland.
12. College Transcript.

Chapter 5
His Teaching Years

Uncle Bob's friend from the year at Ma Forsythe's rooming house, John Brown, would play a principal role in the change that occurred in Uncle Bob's life beginning in the fall of 1939. Uncle Bob had attended college for a little over two years and perhaps by this time a shortage of finances could have been a contributing factor that caused him to begin pursuing job possibilities. After all this time he had amassed just over sixty credit hours so it is also possible that he could have become tired of the grind of attending classes and was ready to try something else that would earn some money. Whatever the case, a welcome opportunity for change presented itself.

HIGH POINT SCHOOL--THE FIRST YEAR

It was noted that after two years of attending college John Brown had accepted a teaching position at the High

Point rural school near his home of Niangua in Webster County. After John had completed his first year of teaching at High Point he was offered and accepted a teaching job at Strafford which included an attractive raise in pay. Because of his attachment with the good people at High Point, John was interested in helping them in finding a suitable replacement. He got to know Uncle Bob very well from their year together at Ma Forsythe's and thought he would be a good choice to fill his old job. John asked Uncle Bob if he would be interested in teaching and Uncle Bob was more than willing to try something different for a while. John talked with the High Point school board and recommended Uncle Bob for the position. John recalled that Uncle Bob's name was the only name submitted for consideration. Upon John's strong recommendation the board hired him for his first teaching position provided he could meet the state's certification requirements to teach.[1]

The next step for Uncle Bob was to get in touch with the county superintendent of schools to assist him in obtaining the necessary credentials for teacher certification. Of course, John was very well acquainted with the Webster County Superintendent of Schools, Mr. Oscar Carter, who had established a fine reputation as the county superintendent. John introduced Uncle Bob to Mr. Carter who assisted him with the required paperwork for his certification.[2] Mr. Carter's assistance and recommendation enabled Uncle Bob to be duly certified to teach at the High Point School. Uncle Bob's relationship with Mr. Carter turned into a friendship that endured through the remainder of his years.

High Point was a typical southwest Missouri rural school

of the period. The name High Point was derived from the fact that it was located on the high ground in the area. It was not really at the top of an obvious hill, but actually sat on the highest point of some gently rolling hills. The school building consisted of one large room, heated by a wood stove. The building housed grades one through eight and one teacher taught all eight grades.

A rural school was called such because it was located in a rural area, a few miles from the nearest town. There were several other rural schools in the county as well as in most counties of the state during that period. All who attended walked to school. Some of the students had quite a distance to walk everyday. Those who finished the eighth grade and wanted to move onto high school would have to find their own way to get back and forth to the nearest high school. It was not until a few years later that buses would be made available to transport those who wanted to attend high school. Typically, the community was tight knit and drawn together through its common interests in making sure their children were afforded the opportunity for schooling.

Through John Brown's connections Uncle Bob quickly found a place to stay. That place was with John's father and mother, Percy and Edith Brown. Known for their hard work and integrity, the Brown family was highly respected in the community. Along with John, there was another brother, Travis, and three sisters: Laura Mildred (Bug), Pauline (Polly), and Faye. Polly who is now deceased would be one of Uncle Bob's students at High Point. With his ability to get along with people and his willingness to pitch in and help with things around the farm, Uncle Bob was soon accepted as one of their own and enduring friendships were established. It was this early association with the Brown family that fostered a permanent tie between them and the McHolland families. Within a few years, Travis Brown would marry Uncle Bob's sister, Mary Lea McHolland.

The transition from that of a student to being a teacher would undoubtedly have some rough spots for Uncle Bob. However, it took little time to establish himself as an integral part of the school and the community. His likeable, magnetic personality along with his organizational talents served him well in his new endeavor as he made new friends and began to earn the respect of the members of the community.

Uncle Bob had a full house when the school year began at High Point in August of 1939. He was going to earn his salary of ninety dollars a month. There were thirty-

High Point School, August 25 1939. Uncle Bob is at far right—
courtesy Wiley-McHolland family

four students counted in a picture taken on August 25, 1939 -- the first students he taught at High Point. Several families had more than one member attending. Among the students were five Crawfords, four Ivies, three Weavers, three Wardens, three Lawrences, two Addymans, two Jones, and two Cantrells.[3]

John Brown kept in close touch with the school board and community through these times. John remembers that "People liked Bob. He was a very caring person especially with those that were underprivileged. He made a special effort to give attention to the kids that needed the extra time. He was never in a hurry and took time with those that needed it whether it was for the school work or for something like self-esteem or moral direction." [4]

Once again, Uncle Bob's organizational abilities came to the forefront. John Brown recalled he had several boys at High Point that liked to play baseball. From all accounts, with some practice and guidance they were able to field a pretty good team. John believes that sometime during this first year Uncle Bob began arranging baseball games with neighboring rural schools. Over a period of time the baseball games began drawing a crowd from the local community. Clarence "Boss" Cantrell, the first baseman for High Point was a special attraction with his ability to hit the long ball. Along with Boss' exceptional slugging talent he is also remembered for always playing in his overalls. During the warm months the baseball competition with other schools became a regular Friday afternoon event that drew rooters from the rival school as well as many of the loyal High Point supporters. This became a popular event and continued throughout his teaching tenure at High Point. [5]

Wayne Ivie was one of the four Ivie family members that were students of Uncle Bob's at High Point during both years he taught there. Wayne described Uncle Bob as "a good teacher who was well liked by all." Of his teaching approach he said Uncle Bob "was not harsh or unfair and he kept order not by fear but through respect for him." Wayne remembered that Uncle Bob had confidence in himself and instilled that confidence in others and that "he enjoyed his job and the kids." [6]

High Point School Softball Team 1939. Wayne Ivie is in second row, second from the left. Clarence "Boss" Cantrell is fourth from left in second row. Uncle Bob is kneeling at far right—courtesy Wiley-McHolland family.

HIGH POINT--THE SECOND YEAR

After attending his last Citizens' Military Training Camp session during the summer, Uncle Bob returned for his second year at High Point in August of 1940. The school

High Point School, August 28, 1940, Uncle Bob at far left—courtesy
Wiley-McHolland family,

picture for this year included seven fewer students leaving a total of twenty-seven in the group. While there were not as many students as the year before, many of the family names remained the same. Wayne Ivie looked forward to playing baseball again. A photograph was taken of the baseball team and Wayne was listed as the shortstop. Other team members and their positions were: Hugh Ivie, leftfield; Bud Lawrence, third base; Verg Warden, pitcher; "Boss" Cantrell, first base; Otis Wolf, catcher; Robert Weaver, second base; Don Weaver, centerfield; Dean Lawrence rightfield; Bobbie Warden, reserve; and Jack Addyman, reserve. Coach McHolland sported a baseball cap and was wearing striped pants with suspenders for the team picture. [7]

Wayne Ivie recalls that Uncle Bob "enjoyed playing baseball and enjoyed winning, but you won fair….and, win or lose, you walk off the field with your head up." [8] Along with the photograph of the High Point baseball team of 1940 was a handwritten record of the scores of

High Point School softball team, 1940. Clarence "Boss" Cantrell in middle of back row, Wayne Ivie last one on right in back row, Uncle Bob kneeling at far right—courtesy Wiley-McHolland family.

the games played. Their record was a respectable six wins and five losses for the season.

Everyone in the community remembered Uncle Bob for his interest in his softball team. However, he had a broader impact on the students and the community through his genuine interest in helping each student develop the most of their potential. As a member of the community, Mrs. Joe Layman, simply put it, "He taught the children (of High Point) to live upright lives... and surely his teaching will go with them through all the trials they meet."

John Brown recalls that during his teaching stint at High Point, and even after he left, he never heard a complaint or harsh word about Uncle Bob from a child or parent. There was universal admiration for him throughout the community, as a person, because of the open and evenhanded manner in which he dealt with people as well as respect for him in the way he lived his life. [7]

Lasting friendships were formed during Uncle Bob's years at High Point. This will become evident later from letters he wrote and received while serving in the army. After Uncle Bob left High Point he remained interested in the people with whom he had become acquainted and was always asking about friends and former students. When inquiring about someone he often used a nickname he had given the individual. Identifying people by nicknames had become a distinctive characteristic of his.

High Point School building as it is today, converted into a home--
courtesy Jerry and Sheila Wiley

THE BROWN FAMILY AND TRAVIS--
ANOTHER CLOSE FRIENDSHIP

More must be written about Uncle Bob and the time he spent with the Brown family during his tenure at High Point. Much has been covered about his relationship with John, the oldest of the family. Since John had taken the teaching position in Strafford he had rented a place there to stay. Strafford was located over twenty five miles away, a far distance at the time, so John was home only on weekends. Travis, John's younger brother by about three years, was still at home. With John living in Strafford most of the time, the obvious opportunity presented itself for Uncle Bob to become better acquainted with Travis. As with his brother John, Travis' personality meshed well with Uncle Bob's and they became close friends. During Uncle Bob's second year with the Brown's he and Travis had another thing in common. Travis also became a teacher and started his first job at Washington, one of the rural schools in the area.

Travis recalled many happy times during the two years Uncle Bob stayed with the Brown family. He remembered that Uncle Bob and his hard working father, Percy, got along well. Together they enjoyed listening to the popular radio shows of the time. One of the radio shows that came to mind was the Bob Hope Show. Travis remembered they especially liked this show and recalls them having many good laughs together while they listened to Bob Hope crack his corny jokes. [10]

As Uncle Bob and Travis became more closely acquainted they often traveled about ten miles away to the larger town of Marshfield on the weekends. Uncle Bob had his Model A Ford coupe with the rumble seat that served as their transportation. Going to the movies, roller skating and bowling were some of the activities which they enjoyed together. Travis remembers Uncle Bob as a good bowler and, true to his knack for organizing, assembled a team for the local bowling league in Marshfield. The team was good enough to win first place in the local league. [11]

Recalling "there were a lot of pretty girls around Marsh-field," Travis chuckles when he recalls their efforts at attracting those of the opposite sex. It seems that both young men were rather shy and hesitant to ask a girl for a date. Travis remembers after a period of time with neither able to muster up the nerve to ask a girl out, something of a ritual became established with them. In an effort to bolster their courage, before they went out they began to ask each other "Are we going to be mice or men?" Travis said that no matter how much they tried to

Good friend, Travis Brown, teacher, Washington rural school, 1940— courtesy Travis and Mary Lea McHolland Brown.

build up their courage, more often than not they turned out to be "mice."[12]

Uncle Bob must have overcome his shy propensities with the women at times. John Brown recalls going with him in his coupe as they double-dated a couple of the local ladies. They went to the movies in Marshfield at the Ritz. John remembered it was crowded in Uncle Bob's coupe as all four of them were jammed into the front seat. What made for an even cozier situation was that the girls, who were sisters, were a bit on the hefty side. Nonetheless, their size and a crowded car did not deter all from enjoying themselves--that night and as well as on other occasions. [13]

In another story with regard to Uncle Bob's female interests, Travis Brown recalls that he seemed to take a liking to Travis' oldest sister, Laura Mildred. She was in high school during the time Uncle Bob stayed with the Brown family. Another local fellow, Carl "Cowboy" Layman had set his sights on Laura Mildred before Uncle Bob came into the picture. Travis relates that Carl had dropped out of school before Uncle Bob arrived on the scene, but when Uncle Bob started showing an interest in Laura Mildred, Carl began attending high school again to "better protect his interest" and make clear his romantic designs with Laura Mildred. Carl's efforts in continuing his academic progress apparently paid off as he and Laura Mildred ultimately were married.

Although Uncle Bob left High Point after his second year, he continued to keep in touch with the Brown family. There were visits, phone calls, and letters after he moved back to Hurley and later when he was in the army. Uncle Bob and John continued to exchange letters while both were in the army. Efforts were made to get together while both were stationed in Texas, but John cannot recall them ever being able to get off duty at the same time long enough to link up. As already noted, Travis' connection with the McHolland family was later turned into a lifelong commitment with his marriage to Mary Lea.

INMON SCHOOL

After the two years at High Point, Uncle Bob moved back to Hurley to take a similar position at a local rural school. He was hired to teach at the Inmon School which was located about eight miles east of Hurley. This is the same school where his father began teaching just after he moved to the area in the early 1900s. The school was close enough to home that he could drive back and forth everyday. Being back in Hurley afforded him the opportunity to spend more time tending to his farm activities, It was during this time that he was serving as Scoutmaster of the local troop, becoming involved in the Masons, and taking various actions to secure his army commission. He had many irons in the fire as the school year began for him in the fall of 1941.

When compared to the relative ease of obtaining information about Uncle Bob's tenure at the High Point School, I was considerably less fortunate in my quest for information about his time spent teaching at Inmon. John and Travis Brown along with Wayne Ivie were able to provide valuable first-hand experiences of his time at High Point. Because of the consolidation of most of the Stone County rural schools into larger districts by the early 1950s many records of these schools cannot be located. It can be established that Inmon school was one of forty-one rural schools operating in Stone County in the early 1940s.

All of these Stone County rural schools had been consolidated into larger schools by the middle 1950s. [14] A principal purpose of the position of County Superintendent of Schools was to serve as primary administrator of the county rural schools. With the rural schools no longer in operation the position of county superintendent was abolished. Many of the records associated with that office cannot be found. None of the records kept by the school itself could be found.

BYRON WOLF--
AN ADMIRING STUDENT

Although no official records of the school are available, one of the students who attended Inmon School during the 1941-42 school year, Byron Wolf, was located. He provided a good deal of interesting information about his teacher of that year. That teacher, of course, was Uncle Bob. Byron was one of his sixth grade students at Inmon that year. Byron stated that Uncle Bob "was a wonderful guy" whom he really liked. He said that Uncle Bob seemed to "take a shine to him" and that he was "the type of guy who seemed more like the kids than a teacher." But he also made it clear that he was a good teacher. Byron warmly recalled that Uncle Bob loved to sing and would often lead the students in singing old hymns that everyone knew. He remembered that Uncle Bob left a few weeks before the end of the school year to enter the army.[15]

Byron Wolf, student at Inmon School in early 1940s—courtesy Byron and Jessie Wolf

Byron corresponded with Uncle Bob while he was in the army. He thought it was a special thing for him, just a young boy, to get letters from Uncle Bob, his teacher and now an officer in the army. Uncle Bob also sent a picture of himself in his uniform. Byron said he kept the letters and picture, along with some group pictures of Inmon school for many years, He sadly related that a few years ago a mouse found its way into the box containing the letters and pictures and completely destroyed them. [16]

Early Release from Teaching Duties

It is certain that actions connected to his application for appointment in the Army would have caused him to be away from his teaching duties several times during this school year. It was during this time that he would be required to appear before a board of officers in Kansas City, go through another physical examination, and execute his oath for appointment.

Although Uncle Bob spent most of the school year of 1941-2 at Inmon, the exact date he had to give up his teaching duties to report for duty with the United States Army cannot be determined. As noted above, Byron Wolf recalled that he left before the end of the school year and his sister, Mary Lea, also remembers that he did not finish the school year.[17] A considerable amount of specific information about this period is available about the activities Uncle Bob had been involved in to obtain his army commission. This information sheds light as to the approximate time of his departure from his teaching duties at Inmon.

Uncle Bob's military records show that a letter dated January 16, 1942, was sent to him from the War Department informing him of his temporary appointment as a Second Lieutenant in the Army of the United States. The effective date of this appointment was the same date as that of the letter. The letter included an Oath of Office form that Uncle Bob signed on January 24, 1942, and notarized by Oda H. Plowman. He also received correspondence within the next few days from Headquarters, Third Military Area, St. Louis, Missouri, with a suspense date of February 18, 1942. The letter requested information about his availability for active duty. Uncle Bob responded that he desired extended active duty and would like to be ordered to duty on or about May 15, 1942[18]. In his response he further stated, "I will require fourteen days to arrange my business affairs after I am notified that I am to be ordered to extended active duty." Then he added, "I will be needed (at Inmon) until this school term is over." Despite his obvious efforts to inform the War Department of his desire to complete the school year, he was ordered to report for active duty to O'Reilly General Hospital in Springfield, Missouri, on May 8, 1942. Based on the assumption that at least two weeks were required to take care of personal business, it is likely Uncle Bob relinquished his duties at Inmon sometime in mid to late April of 1942. School records found in the Stone County, Missouri, County Clerk's files contain Uncle Bob's signature on graduating eighth grade students' report cards dated April 17, 1942. That date was on a Friday in 1942 and was likely his last day of teaching at Inmon.

Although he had to leave Inmon before the school term was over, most assuredly those in the school district understood the reason for his action. Almost everyone who knew Uncle Bob knew of his interest in the military. They were aware of his years of participation in the CMTC program and satisfactory completion of all the training stages. Even before Japan's earth-shattering attack on Pearl Harbor in December of 1941 those around

Uncle Bob knew he had been working for several months toward completion of the necessary prerequisites for obtaining his commission as an officer in the United States Army.

Chapter 5 Endnotes:
1.   Personal interviews, J. Brown.
2.   Personal interviews, J. Brown.
3.   High Point school picture, August 25, 1939.
4.   Personal interviews, J. Brown.
5.   Personal interviews, J. Brown.
6.   Personal interview, Ivie.
7.   Picture, High Point Softball Team, 1939-40.
8.   Personal interview, Ivie.
9.   Personal interviews, J. Brown.
10. Personal interviews, Travis Brown, 2008.
11. Personal interviews, T. Brown.
12. Personal interviews, T. Brown.
13. Personal interviews, J. Brown.
14. Robert S. Wiley, "Rural Schools in Stone Country," History of Stone County Missouri, Volume II (Stone County Historical Society, 1989), 90.
15. Telephone interviews, Byron Wolf, 2008.
16. Telephone interviews, Wolf.
17. Personal interviews, M. Brown.
18. Various documents and correspondence from Official Personnel File, Robert B. McHolland.

17. Personal interviews, M. Brown.
18. Various documents and correspondence from Official Personnel File, Robert B. McHolland.

Chapter 6
Early Military Experience and Preparation for the Service

As noted, Uncle Bob began to show an early curiosity with the military. At this point I will digress from the chronological timeline of his story in order to provide a clearer picture of his evolving interest in this area. In addition, further information will be included about the steps he began taking to prepare himself for military service. These actions ultimately led to his commissioning as an officer in the U. S. Army.

Uncle Bob had shown an affinity toward the military for some time. His enthusiastic involvement as a Boy Scout and later as a scout leader, were indications of his inclination toward this type of activity. Recalling the times in Hurley of his frequent visits with Ernest Hair, to hear about World War I exploits is another indication that he had more than a passing interest in the military. The progressively deteriorating world situation and the beginning signs of our nation's preparation for action were other likely influencing factors kindling his interest in military service. The opportunity to pursue this interest occurred after his first year of college. His first exposure to actual military training began during the summer of 1937.

THE CITIZENS' MILITARY TRAINING CAMP (CMTC) PROGRAM

The opportunity for Uncle Bob to become involved in the military opened in the form of a United States Government program entitled the Citizen's Military Training Camp (CMTC). Shortly after World War I, Congress passed the National Defense Act of 1920 which authorized the establishment of the CMTC program. Based on lessons learned from World War I regarding our nation's defense posture, this program was instituted with the intent to provide another source of commissioning officers for the U.S. Army Officer Reserve Corps.[1]

Uncle Bob must have been made aware of the CMTC program sometime shortly after he graduated from high school in 1936 through the publicity efforts of the program. It was advertised throughout the country as "A Free Summer Camp" that provided transportation, food, uniforms, and medical care for 30 days for young men interested in serving their country in the military. The stated purpose of the program was shown in a flyer advertising the camps held in the Midwest area:

> *"The object of these camps is to bring together young men of high type from all sections of the country on a common basis of equality and under the most favorable conditions of outdoor life; to stimulate and promote citizenship, pa-*

*triotism, and Americanism; and through expert physical
direction, athletic coaching, and military training, to benefit the young men individually and bring them to realize
their obligations to their country."* [2]

CMTC PROGRAM LEVELS

Completion of the CMTC program required attendance
and satisfactory performance of training requirements
at four of the thirty-day summer camps. The program
consisted of four courses that progressively increased in
difficulty over the four year span of training. The four
courses were titled and described as follows:

> *"The Basic Red Course. Age limits, 17 to 24. Ap-
> plicants must possess average general intelligence, be able
> to read and write English, and be of good moral charac-
> ter. This provides preliminary military training, including
> physical development, athletics, school of the soldier, squad
> and company drill, rifle marksmanship, camp sanitation,
> personal hygiene, military courtesy, meaning of discipline,
> and studies in citizenship. Those taking this course will
> be given the opportunity to qualify for the next higher, or
> Advanced Red Course.*

> *"The Advanced Red Course. Age limits, 17 to 24. Phys-
> ical requirements same as for Basic Red Course, and must
> be a graduate of a Basic Red Course, or have had military
> training equivalent thereto. This course provides training
> in Infantry, Field Artillery and Cavalry, with demonstra-
> tions in Air Service and Tank Corps, advanced instruction
> in the subjects covered in the Basic Red Course included.
> Those who take this course will be given the opportunity to
> qualify themselves to perform the duties of a private in the*

National Guard or Enlisted Reserve Corps and to qualify for the next higher or White Course.

"The White Course. Age limits, 18 to 24. Physical requirements slightly higher than those of the Red Courses. Applicants must have a grammar school education, possess qualities of leadership, and be of good moral character. This course provides training in Infantry, Field Artillery and Cavalry with demonstrations in Air Service and Tank Corps, for the purpose of qualifying selected enlisted men in the Regular Army, National Guard, and Enlisted Reserve Corps, and selected citizens who indicated their willingness to serve, at some future time, an enlistment in the Army of the United States, and who have had military training equivalent to the Advanced Red Course, for service as noncommissioned officers capable of training recruits and leading them in active service, and also to qualify themselves as specialists. Those who attend will be given the further opportunity to qualify for the next higher or Blue Course.

"The Blue Course. Age limits, 19 to 24. Physical requirements and qualities of leadership not lower than for the White Course. Educational requirements will be those prescribed for appointment as second lieutenants in the Officers' Reserve Corps; the minimum is a high school education or its equivalent. This course provides training with the object of qualifying selected warrant officers and enlisted men of the Regular Army, National Guard and Enlisted Reserve Corps, who have completed the White Course or who have had military training recognized by regulations as equivalent thereto, for service as second lieutenants." [3]

Although there was no guarantee of a commission, satisfactory completion of all four courses of the CMTC program could provide an important first step toward appointment as an officer in the U. S. Army.

CMTC-THE FIRST SUMMER

Information taken from his application for appointment as a reserve officer reflects that Uncle Bob began his

CMTC training at Fort Leavenworth, Kansas on July 30, 1936 in the Red Course. His rank for that session was shown as Private, his organization was "Infantry" and his commanding officer was Lt. Col. W.G. Jones. While specific information is sparse about his performance at the camp, his marksmanship ability was recognized as he became qualified with a rifle during this session. He must have done well in acclimating himself to the overall military environment as he satisfactorily completed all requirements of this course on August 28, 1936.[4]

Uncle Bob at Fort Leavenworth, Kansas, CMTC,
1936—courtesy Wiley-McHolland family.

CMTC-THE SECOND SUMMER

It is quite probable that Uncle Bob was pleased with his initial experience in military training. The next summer he returned to the CMTC at Fort Leavenworth, Kansas to tackle the Advanced Red Course. The course began on July 6, 1937. Information gained from friends indicates that he had some company from Hurley as this time his friend, Delmar Bowyer, likely accompanied him on his trip back and forth to the camp. Uncle Bob's rank for this session was Corporal, his organization remained "Infantry" and his commanding officer was Lt. Col. D. F. McDonald. He met all the requirements for satisfactory completion of the Advanced Red Course on August 4, 1937. [5]

Fort Leavenworth, Kansas CMTC, 1937. L-R, Dale (Rip) Dean, unidentified, Uncle Bob with Corporal stripes—courtesy Wiley-McHolland family.

From all appearances, Uncle Bob found continued interesting and rewarding challenges in the military environment. All of those around him remembered his enthusiasm for his military training. Perhaps he was beginning to feel he might have found his niche in life.

CMTC-THE THIRD SUMMER

As the summer of 1938 arrived he had completed his first full year of college and was probably more than ready to get back to Fort Leavenworth for the third level of the CMTC program. His close friend, Edwin Dean, accompanied him this time on his trip back and forth to camp. He began his training in the White Course on July 26, 1938. His rank was now Sergeant, an achievement

Edwin Dean second from left and Uncle Bob last on the right at CMTC, Fort Leavenworth, Kansas, 1938—courtesy Edwin Dean.

of which he was very proud. Edwin still has a photo of him with his shirt off and proudly showing off the recently earned sergeant's strips on his bare arm.

Uncle Bob remained in the Infantry portion of the course and Lt. Col. Thomas Taylor was his commanding officer. He satisfactorily completed the White Course on August 24, 1938. This gave him just enough time to return to Springfield and prepare for enrollment in his second year of college.[6]

Edwin Dean in the center and Uncle Bob at right holding his Sergeant stripes on his left arm, CMTC, Fort Leavenworth, Kansas, 1938—courtesy Edwin Dean.

A BREAK FROM CMTC

According to the information Uncle Bob entered on his application for appointment as an officer he did not participate in the CMTC program during the summer of 1939. The probable reason for not attending the camp this summer is likely linked to his decision to apply for the teaching position at High Point school for the 1939-40 school year. Even with the strong recommendation he had received from his friend, John Brown, for the position there were various administrative processes that would have required a lot of Uncle Bob's time and attention during this period. He would need to obtain teaching certification and his new job would require organization and preparation for class activities. With the challenges and anticipation of a new job awaiting him, completion of the fourth CMTC program course was put on hold until the next summer.

Having completed his first year of teaching at High Point in the spring of 1940, Uncle Bob was probably more than ready to resume his military training, particularly when an important goal was close at hand. Having successfully completed the first three levels of the program, it was imperative that he finish the final level if he was to attain his ultimate objective of becoming a commissioned officer.

COMPLETION OF CMTC-THE FOURTH SUMMER

In the summer of 1940, location of the CMTC program training was moved to Jefferson Barracks, Missouri. The installation was situated on the Mississippi River just a few miles south of St. Louis, Missouri. Edwin Dean also attended and accompanied Uncle Bob on the trips to and from camp. Uncle Bob began his training in the Blue Course as a "Cadet" on July 3, 1940. It was during this training that he became qualified to fire the .45 caliber pistol. With Lt. Col. E. L. Pell as his Commanding Officer, he satisfactorily completed the course requirements on July 31, 1940.[7] Although completion of the CMTC program did not guarantee that he would be commissioned, it was a giant step toward that end.

MORE CMTC MEMORIES

As noted, one of Uncle Bob's closest friends, Edwin Dean, became involved with the CMTC program during the summer of 1938. He recalls traveling back and forth to the camps with Uncle Bob and that each person earned $30 for the 30 days of training. Edwin remembers Uncle Bob's intensive interest in and enthusiasm for the training. As always, during this time, Uncle Bob was exhibiting his sense of humor and keeping everyone on their toes.[8] Another friend, John Brown, confirms Uncle Bob's passion for and interest in his military training experiences. From the beginning of the training he had expressed his determination to finish all of the four phases and to obtain his officer's commission.[9]

There are several photographs of Uncle Bob taken during the camps he attended. Some of the photographs are of Uncle Bob by himself and there are other shots with men who were also in training. One photo provided by Edwin Dean was taken in a photo booth at the train station in Kansas City either on the way to or back from one of the camps at Fort Leavenworth. It shows him with a particularly comical expression. There were others from the community in some of the photos who also attended camp. Along with Edwin, his cousin and good friend Dale "Rip" Dean, and good friend Delmar Bowyer were present at some of the camps he attended.[10]

Uncle Bob acting up at the train station in Kansas City, 1938—courtesy Edwin Dean.

Attending the four CMTC camps and completing all the requirements were to become very important for Uncle Bob in the not too distant future. The satisfactory completion of all four levels of training, along with his teaching experience and college records, were to later provide the basis for his commissioning as a second lieutenant in the U. S. Army Officer Reserve Corps.

A TRIP TO LOUISIANA--CHECKING OUT THE ARMY AIR CORPS

Two of Uncle Bob's closest friends, Edwin Dean and John Brown, were part of another military-related experience. This was an excursion planned, organized, and carried out by Uncle Bob that occurred in August of 1940 shortly after he completed the CMTC White Course at Jefferson Barracks. Having just finished the CMTC program, it is believed that he was seriously thinking about gaining entry on active duty as soon as possible.

With amusement Edwin and John recall a trip to Shreveport, Louisiana with Uncle Bob. Edwin remembered that Uncle Bob had voiced his interest in becoming a pilot for some time.[11] The purpose of the trip was for him to take an Army flight physical examination at Barksdale Army Air Base. Neither Edwin nor John could remember whether Uncle Bob had made prior arrangements for the exam or that he intended to report and request an examination. John recalled that Uncle Bob borrowed his brother-in-law's car. Maurice Wiley (my father) owned the car. The reason Uncle Bob borrowed it was because his Model A coupe was too small for the long trip. The borrowed car was a late 30s Ford. It was a sedan and provided more room for the three travelers.[12] Edwin also remembers it was a Ford sedan and that they drove all night to get to Shreveport. He recalls sleeping in the car which possibly could have been on the trip down. They must have arrived early in the morning while it was still dark because Edwin recalled them sleeping for a while in the car before entering the base.[13]

Another of Edwin's vivid memories about the trip was his recollection of the many black workers toiling away in the cotton fields throughout southern Arkansas and Louisiana.[14] John, who had seldom experienced eating out at restaurants or cafes, remembered having some fine southern cooking in the places where they stopped to eat on the trip.[15]

A DISAPPOINTING EXPERIENCE

The purpose of the trip resulted in disappointment for Uncle Bob. He failed to pass a portion of the very stringent eye examination required for entry into flight training. On the report of Physical Examination for Flying, dated August 7, 1940, the examining Flight Surgeon stated that Uncle Bob did not meet the physical requirements because of a "defective angle of convergence."[16] As explained in laymen terms by my former optometrist Dr. Robert Hackley this meant that a tendency toward double vision beyond normal limits was probably detected during the stringent eye examination that is required for pilots.[17] Although he was disheartened with the results, his failure to pass the physical at this time did not keep Uncle Bob from continuing to pursue his dream of being a pilot. There will be more about his desire to fly in the pages to come.

MORE WORK ON THE COMMISSION-- THE ARMY INFANTRY EXTENSION COURSE

It was not long after the trip to Louisiana that Uncle Bob returned to Niangua to begin his second year of teaching at the High Point school. As the winds of war were swirling in Europe and the Far East, he was experiencing a sense of urgency about his preparation for military service. Even while he was teaching his desire to obtain the officer commission kept him looking ahead toward that goal. From the early part of 1941 he began a series of actions that would lead to the attainment of his commission.

In January of 1941 he enrolled in the Army Infantry Extension Course. Satisfactory completion of this course was a basic commissioning requirement. The Army Infantry Extension Course consisted of ten sub-courses. Based on his CMTC program credentials Uncle Bob was given credit for three of the sub-courses leaving a total of seven sub-courses he was required to complete. He began the extension course program by enrolling in the Organization of the Army sub-course On January 28, 1941. As he completed a sub-course he enrolled in the next one on the requirements list. Uncle Bob completed the remaining six sub-courses (Organization of the Infantry, Defense Against Chemical Warfare, Military Law, Map Reading-- with a young Gene Anderson's capable assistance, Aerial Photograph Reading, and Infantry Drill) by September 5, 1941. [18]

APPLICATION FOR APPOINTMENT AS AN OFFICER

Information gained from his official Army personnel records shows that Uncle Bob completed his Application for Appointment and Statement of Preference for Reserve Officers on May 21, 1941. His sister, Mary Lea, remembers assisting him with the tedious process involved in the typing and assembling of the application.[19] Several other documents of supporting information were required to be submitted along with this application. The first among those documents was a Report of Physical Examination conducted by Dr. Kenneth L. Kelsey in Aurora, Missouri. Although Dr. Kelsey signed the report on May 29, 1941, his examination was obviously conducted a few days before that. This is evident as Dr Kelsey had attached to his report the results of an x-ray examination conducted at the Missouri State Sanatorium, Mount Vernon, Missouri, on May 26, 1941 and a Kahn (blood) Test conducted by the State Board of Health Laboratory in Springfield, Missouri, on May 27, 1941. Dr. Kelsey determined that Uncle Bob met the physical requirements for appointment as a reserve officer.

Other documentation accompanying his request for appointment included: a copy of his college transcript from Southwest Missouri State Teachers College, Springfield,

Missouri, certifying his 69.4 hours of college credits; a statement from the Army Extension School certifying satisfactory completion of the Army Infantry Extension Course; and a copy of the comprehensive final examination administered by the Army Extension School.[20]

Uncle Bob with sister Mary Lea at Hurley Depot, probably 1941—courtesy Wiley-McHolland family.

The specific date is not available, but Uncle Bob must have mailed his application for appointment to Headquarters

Third Military Area in St. Louis, Missouri, during the first week of June, 1941. Documentation is available showing that headquarters referring to his application and requesting, on June 10, 1941, the verification of Uncle Bob's CMTC service from the Seventh Corps Area in Omaha, Nebraska. On June 12, 1941 the Seventh Corps Area responded to the request with the following statement: "The records show that applicant satisfactorily completed the Blue Infantry CMTC Course at Jefferson Barracks in 1940 and was recommended for the extension course." [21]

From the time of Uncle Bob's submission of his application for appointment in June and of the actions described to verify his CMTC service, there is a gap in documentation until September. Keep in mind that during the summer of 1941 Uncle Bob was involved in other activities: tending to his farm, serving as Scoutmaster for the local troop, accomplishing the requirements to become a Master Mason, readying for teaching school at Inmon, and giving much attention to completing the Army Infantry Extension Course. It is obvious that he was a very busy person with a lot of things on his mind. Receiving the word on September 8, 1941, that he had satisfactorily completed the extension course was a key in the quest to attain his commission. Now all that was left in the documentation process was to obtain three character references.

CHARACTER REFERENCES

Uncle Bob wasted no time in getting the three letters of recommendation concerning the quality of his character. The three letters, all dated September 8, 1941, are quoted in their entirety: [22]

Typed Letter of Howard Inmon, owner of the H.A. Inmon Store, Hurley, Missouri:

Dear Sir:

I am a merchant in the grocery business here at Hurley and I have been asked to write a letter of recommendation by one, Robert McHolland.

I have known Robert McHolland for about fifteen years and have found him to be of good character. He has been honest in his business dealings with me and so far as I know he possesses a good moral standard.

He has never to my knowledge run afoul of law but always supports it as a good citizen should. He has shown himself as an ardent support of American ways and ideals.

Very truly yours,

H.A. Inmon

Handwritten Letter of J.L. Baker on letterhead of J. L. Baker, General Merchandise, Hurley, Missouri:

To the Commanding Officer, Third Corps Area, Omaha, Nebraska,

I wish to recommend Robert McHolland as a young man of sterling character who has led a life which is above reproach.

I have known him all of his life and am glad to say that he will conscientiously fill any position to which he is assigned.

Respectfully yours,

J.L. Baker

Typed letter of John Vilhauer, Superintendent, on letterhead of Hurley Public Schools, Consolidated District No. 1, Hurley, Missouri:

Dear Sir:

I have known Robert B. McHolland for seven years. Robert graduated from the Hurley High school in the spring of 1936 and was in the upper 20 percent of his class which was 12 in number. Immediately following his graduation from high school he enrolled in Southwest Missouri State Teachers College at Springfield, Missouri, where he has completed approximately 70 hours of college work.

Robert is a young man of excellent standing in his community. His character is unquestionable. He comes from a very highly respected family.

In my opinion Robert is 100% all American. He has always been an outstanding leader of good citizenship in his community.

Very truly yours,

John Vilhauer

BOARD OF OFFICERS CONVENED

With all required documentation completed, the next step for the Army was to convene a Board of Officers with the purpose of personally examining the applicant's "ability, leadership and personality for the appointment he seeks." The board was convened at ten o'clock A.M. on October 16, 1941. Although the location of the board was not specified, it is assumed the board was held in Kansas City, Missouri, as the record indicated that both officers on the board, Major Ross C. Henbest and Major

Harry A. Huncilman, were from Kansas City. [23]

Uncle Bob's appearance before the board lasted approximately two hours. The board determined that the moral qualifications were "established by the letters attached," (This referred to the letters of H.A. Inmon, J.L. Baker, and John Vilhauer regarding his character.) Further, the board determined that he possessed the necessary general qualifications for appointment "by reason of his general education, neatness, appearance, bearing and general adaptability for the military service." The board also administered a written examination which covered the basic subjects that were included in the Army Infantry Extension Course. [24]

The board adjourned at noon on October 16, 1941 with the finding that Uncle Bob was "physically, orally, generally, and professionally qualified for appointment as Second Lieutenant, Infantry-Reserve, and does recommend his appointment accordingly." [25] He had reason to be elated with the recommendation but was advised by the president of the board that this was only its recommendation and that final approval for appointment rested with the War Department.

DELAYS AND ANTICIPATION

Uncle Bob undoubtedly returned to his teaching duties at Inmon anticipating that it was now a matter of time before he should receive the news that his appointment as an officer was approved by the War Department. If he was not already aware of the snail's pace of the Army bureaucracy, he was about to sense a new meaning of the word patience. The recommendation for his appointment wound its way through two headquarters levels before it reached the War Department on November 8, 1941. Although the physical examination completed in May was included in the documentation, the War Department decided it needed a "final type report of physical examination." The War Department sent the application package back through the command levels requesting that another physical examination be completed. [26]

Although a copy of this Report of Physical Examination could not be found in the record, there is correspondence indicating that another physical examination on Uncle Bob was completed on December 3, 1941. For some unknown reason the report of the physical examination laid on desks in headquarters until the War Department on December 12, 1941, sent a memorandum through channels requesting status of the physical examination. Even with this higher level interest the report of physical examination did not reach the War Department until December 26, 1941. Notwithstanding that the United States had declared war on Germany and Japan barely two weeks earlier, it is possible the usual slower pace of the Christmas season could have had something to do with the delays.

FINALLY...A GOAL ATTAINED!

Uncle Bob would need to exercise even more patience as it was almost another month before he received the letter from the War Department informing him of his temporary appointment in the Army of the United States as a Second Lieutenant. The letter from the War Department was dated January 16, 1942, but it appears Uncle Bob received the letter on January 24, 1942.[27] He finally had the letter in his hands and now all he needed was to

Uncle Bob on the date of his commissioning January 24, 1942—courtesy Wiley-McHolland family

execute the oath of office using the enclosed form, have it notarized, and return it to the War Department. When the properly executed oath of office was received in the War Department Uncle Bob had finally accomplished the goal he had worked toward for almost six years.

With his appointment finally in hand Uncle Bob applied for extended active duty. He informed the War Department that he was teaching and would not be available for active duty until May 15, 1942, when the school term was finished. In addition, he requested two more weeks to get his personal affairs in order before reporting for active duty. As one might expect, little if any consideration was given to his desire to complete the school year at Inmon. In

Uncle Bob with his Aunt Elva Brown Milliken shortly after receiving his commission in January or February 1942—courtesy Wiley-McHolland family

late April he received orders from the War Department to report for active duty at O'Reilly General Hospital in Springfield, Missouri, on May 8, 1942.[28]

Chapter 6 Endnotes:
1. Donald M. Kington, Forgotten Summers: The Story of the Citizens Military Training Camps, 1921-1940 (San Francisco, CA: Two Decades Publishing, 1995), 1-7.
2. Informational Flyer, "A Free Summer Camp," 7th Corps Area, 1923.
3. Informational Flyer, 1923.
4. Training Record, Official Personnel File.
5. Training Record, Official Personnel File.
6. Training Record, Official Personnel File.
7. Training Record, Official Personnel File.
8. Personal Interviews, Dean.
9. Personal interviews, J. Brown.
10. Personal interviews, Dean.
11. Personal interview,s Dean.
12. Personal interviews, J. Brown.
13. Personal interviews, Dean.
14. Personal interviews, Dean.
15. Personal interviews, J. Brown.
16. Record of Physical Examination, August 1940, Official Personnel File.
17. Telephone Interview, Dr. Robert Hackley, 2008
18. Training Records, Official Personnel File.
19. Personal Interviews, M. Brown.
20. Documents, Official Personnel File.
21. Documents, Official Personnel File.
22. Official Personnel File.
23. Documents, Official Personnel File.
24. Documents, Official Personnel File.
25. Documents, Official Personnel File.
26. Documents, Official Personnel File.
27. Documents, Official Personnel File.
28. Documents, Official Personnel File

Captain Mac

Chapter 7
Introduction to Military Life and Flight School

With the bombing of Pearl Harbor by the Japanese on December 7, 1941, the United States was violently shaken from its long-standing isolationist position in world political affairs. Along with Japan, war was soon declared on the other Axis Powers of Germany and Italy and the nation began the initial steps toward a massive mobilization of military forces and the establishment of an enormous production structure to support the war effort. More than any other conflict in which our nation had been involved, this war would present a clear situation of "good versus evil." American citizens rushed to enlist and the nation was united as never before in an ultimate struggle for individual rights and freedom throughout the world. In accepting his appointment as an officer and entering on active duty in the United States Army, Uncle Bob joined the thousands upon thousands of young Americans who volunteered to fight the evil forces of Nazism, Fascism, and Japanese imperialism.

Author's Note: Uncle Bob was a relatively prolific letter writer. From the time he went on active duty in May 1942, until he was killed in November 1944 his sisters, Roxabel and Mary Lea, saved many of the letters he wrote home and kept them in a scrapbook. In addition, several friends and relatives graciously turned over to Roxabel and Mary Lea letters they had received from Uncle Bob for inclusion in the scrapbook. There are some rather lengthy gaps between letters at times. The reasons for the gaps could likely be related to more pressing issues in his life involving duty, training, or combat requirements. It is also likely that some of the letters he sent home were lost, misplaced, or destroyed. Contents of these letters will be used profusely throughout the coverage of Uncle Bob's period of military service. The contents of these letters are important aids in providing insights into the core of Uncle Bob's personality and character. His mischievous sense of humor and teasing nature are parts of many letters. In them he expresses his moral values, religious and political beliefs, and hopes and dreams for the future. Telltale signs of frustration are also conveyed especially during exhausting periods of combat. My goal is to weave the contents of these letters into this tribute in a way that will clearly portray the fundamental nature of this decent and honorable man.

ORDERED TO ACTIVE DUTY

April 25, 1942, was the date of the official document from Headquarters Seventh Corps Area, Omaha, Nebraska, ordering Uncle Bob to active duty.[1] Given two or three days for the mail to reach Hurley, Missouri, it is likely he received the orders sometime the last week in April. The orders informed him that his active duty date would be May 8, 1942. On that date he was to proceed "without delay" to O'Reilly General Hospital in Springfield, Missouri, for the purpose of undergoing a complete physical examination. If he was found to be physically qualified, he would then proceed to the Replacement Training Center at Camp Robinson, Arkansas.

Uncle Bob remained at the O'Reilly General Hospital for a few days. The records reflect that the probable reason for his extended stay at O'Reilly was to have some dental work completed.[2] Considering the massive number of enlistments and calls to active duty occurring in this period, he likely waited in several long lines during his physical examination as well as for the dental work to be done. He did not have to spend all of his time at the hospital during this period. He revealed in a later letter to his friend, John Brown, that he stopped by Ma Forsythe's rooming house at some point while he was there and visited with Paul Nichols, a mutual friend of theirs.[3] When the army was finished with the physical examination requirements, he was released from O'Reilly General Hospital on May 25, 1942, with orders to report to Headquarters, Replacement Training Center, Camp Robinson, Arkansas.[4]

CAMP ROBINSON, ARKANSAS-- A SHORT STAY

Uncle Bob reported for duty at Camp Robinson on May 26, 1942 and was assigned to Company D, 67th Training Battalion, 14th Infantry Training Regiment with duty as "Company Officer." He was at Camp Robinson for only about a week. But, as he reported in a letter dated June 5, 1942, it was long enough for him to meet "several boys from Texas" and one fellow who had stayed at Ma Forsythe's rooming house when he was there. From here he was soon assigned to his "permanent" unit, Company F,

3rd Infantry Regiment, Fort Snelling, Minnesota, as of June 5, 1942. [5]

FORT SNELLING, MINNESOTA--
FIRST PERMANENT ASSIGNMENT

Uncle Bob departed Camp Robinson on June 2 and reported for duty with Company F, 3rd Infantry Regiment, Fort Snelling, Minnesota, on June 5, 1942. It is likely the army provided transportation by train as that was the usual mode of official travel at the time. He reported the following in a letter addressed "Dear Folks" dated June 5, 1942: "Well I'm here at Ft. Snelling and it is a much better set up than down at Camp Robinson. It is an old post and is one of the oldest outfits in the army. I spent one day in Chicago. I went out to see the Great Lakes. I didn't get to see the Cubs or White Sox play though." It is noted that when he wrote to the "Folks" he was writing to sisters Roxabel and Mary Lea.

HIS FIRST UNIT--THE THIRD INFANTRY
REGIMENT (THE OLD GUARD)

The Third Infantry Regiment was indeed, as Uncle Bob wrote home in that first letter, one of the oldest outfits in the army. Knowing the importance the army attaches to unit tradition and history, I am certain he quickly learned that his outfit was the very first American army unit. The unit was organized in 1784 and became known as "The Old Guard." The Third Infantry Regiment is presently based at Fort Meyer, Virginia and is the unit that provides the soldiers for Presidential and White House special ceremonies and events. In addition, it provides soldiers who guard the tombs of the unknown soldiers at Arlington

Good friend John Brown, circa 1942-1943—courtesy John and Florence Brown.

National Cemetery.[6]

Within a week of his reporting for duty with the Third Infantry it was apparent that Uncle Bob had been thoroughly educated in the tradition of the Old Guard. In a letter dated June 11, 1942, to his friend John Brown, who was now in the army at Camp Leonard Wood, Missouri, he wrote proudly about his new unit; "The 3rd Inf is the oldest organization in the army and has more streamers and citations than any other outfit in the army. It fought at Lundy's Lane, Chapeau, Fredericksburg, Gettysburg, Appomattox and Antietam, Luzon in 1896-1900, and Vera Cruz and Monterey. It was on the Mexican border during last war but we are promised action for this one. I wish we would before I get to thinking serious. The morale is high and the spirit is good. Much better than in the R. T. Co at Robinson." In the last sentences of this passage one can sense hints of his apprehension and anxiety about the task ahead.

WELCOME TO THE ARMY, LIEUTENANT

While Uncle Bob had become somewhat familiar with requirements of the military way of life through his four summers of participation in the CMTC program, new

Official Army Photo-2d Lt. Robert McHolland, 1942—
courtesy Wiley-McHolland family.

lessons were to be learned about the life of an army officer. In the June 11 letter to John Brown he wrote about one of the social expectations of an army officer. Uncle Bob began by writing "Well I'm waiting for a fellow to come for me to go to a regimental party. Two days ago I went on a fourteen mile hike and are my feet sore and tonight (it is Col Brown's desires) for us to attend what is probably our last party." His statement about it being the unit's "last" party appears to imply that the furious pace of the training ahead would not allow time for many of these social events.

MORE FROM THE JUNE 11 LETTER

There are several passages in the June 11 letter Uncle Bob wrote to John Brown that warrant mentioning because they are illustrations of his sense of humor. Of what he was experiencing in the Minnesota summer he wrote, "The mosquitoes are my third worst enemy of course Hitler is No. 1, Hirohito No 2, mosquitoes 3 and Mussolini is 3rd. (sic)"

With an apparent reference to a rival Webster County rural school he joked about his logic as he added "I guess I studied Ed. (education) good over at Black Oak." He poked fun at his McHolland family in his next statement, "Well Uncle Green's widow divorced him this week and Herb married a widow so the McHolland's are keeping up. Eh?" He continued with more family news about being an expectant uncle proudly writing, "I am expecting a new nephew ? by name of Robert Stanley McHolland Wiley Jr. in the very near future."

His sister Roxabel was eight months pregnant at the time. The event occurred about three weeks later on June 29 and Uncle Bob would have his "Junior" as the new nephew was given the name of Robert Stanley Wiley. (He

Judge Robert S. Wiley—courtesy Dale Wiley.

Robert Maurice Wiley—courtesy Robert   *Robert Edward McHolland—courtesy*
Maurice Wiley   *Dr. Sharon McHolland.*

would never know that he would have two more namesakes; Robert Edward McHolland, son of his brother
Everette, and Robert Maurice Wiley, grandson of Roxabel's son, John Wiley.)

One more item from the June 11 letter to John Brown
tells of one of the typical numerous extra duties assigned
to junior officers in the army. He sounded proud of this
added assignment as he wrote "I am the athletic and recreation officer for the company. Our baseball team has
lost 4 and won 0 so you see McHolland will have to get
down to serious business. I have two ex-minor leaguers
on my team one is a pitcher and one is a first baseman
and he is in the hospital with claps." There is no way to
determine whether he got the team "shaped up" as no
more information is available about his efforts to pro-
duce a winning team.

Based on what is known of his inclination to write we
can be assured that Uncle Bob continued to keep in

touch with family and friends. However, from the time of the June 11 letter to John Brown there is a space of about four months in which none of his letters are available. As a company officer in a unit readying itself for combat he would have been busy directing his troops in training activities such as weapons familiarization, physical training, small unit tactics and other subjects vital to preparation for the enormous task ahead. The records show that he spent the period June 27 through July 10 on temporary duty to Camp Ripley, Minnesota which was another army training facility.[7] As one familiar with army infantry training I can reasonably presume that he was leading his unit in some special training conducted at Camp Ripley during this time.

THE NAGGING URGE TO FLY

It can be certain Uncle Bob had his hands full at Fort Snelling learning the many new requirements and nuances that went along with being an army officer as well as the day to day tasks associated with being the leader of a combat unit. But the burning desire to become a pilot had remained within him even after his disappointing experience in Louisiana described in the previous chapter. He had been at Fort Snelling less than two months when he decided to take another stab at flying. In a letter dated July 18, 1942, addressed to the Chief of Air Corps Uncle Bob requested an application for pilot training. [8]

Within a couple of weeks the Army Air Corps responded to Uncle Bob's request and forwarded the application. His Application for Pilot Training in Officer Grade was dated August 3, 1942. Of course, one of the requirements was another physical examination for flying. The paperwork was sent forward and moved with a usual slow pace through the army channels. It was during this period that his unit, the 3rd Infantry Regiment was re-designated as the 73rd Infantry Regiment for reasons known only to the army. The physical examination for flying was subsequently scheduled for September 14, 1942. Uncle Bob traveled from Fort Snelling to Sherman Field, Fort Leavenworth, Kansas, for the examination. [9]

With the nation now at war, the situation within the army air corps had changed significantly from that at the time Uncle Bob took the flight physical examination in Louisiana. There was now the need for an unlimited number of qualified pilots to wage the all important air war. It is not known whether the minimum physical requirements might have been eased to attract more potential pilots. Whatever the reason, unlike the results of his first flight physical, Uncle Bob passed the physical examination for pilot training. The records show that he took three days leave after he passed the examination.[10] It is only conjecture but with the additional time off duty it is possible he made a quick trip home to share his good news with family and friends.

PRE-FLIGHT TRAINING

Uncle Bob returned to Fort Snelling to learn that he had received orders to attend a two week pre-flight training course at Camp Curtis Guild, Boston, Massachusetts. He departed Fort Snelling, Minnesota, on September 22, 1942, and arrived at Camp Curtis Guild on September 25, 1942. The pre-flight course consisted of two weeks of classroom work on related subject matter. He satisfactorily completed this course on October 9, 1942.[11]

From Camp Curtis Guild Uncle Bob moved to San Antonio, Texas, to attend the Air Force Pre-Flight School (Pilot) beginning October 12, 1942. Training at the school concentrated on various academic subjects such as aircraft identification; maps, charts, and aerial photographs; mathematics; physics; and information about air, naval, and ground forces.[12] It must have been an intensive eight or nine weeks of primarily classroom work designed to prepare them for the actual flight training.

The next letter available from Uncle Bob was written during the first week of this pre-flight school and provides his initial impressions of the training. The letter was written to John Brown on October 17. He said his normal routine went like this:

> *"Up at 6 am for reveille*
> *630-700 breakfast*
> *700-800 Shave, make bunk, etc.*
> *School from 8 to 12*
> *From 1 to 2 a beauty rest*
> *From 2 to 4 physical training and athletics*
> *From 4 to 6 drill."*

He went on to say "I weigh 177 lbs now. I'm getting little a heavy but this work will take it off. I go to bed at 10:00 every night because we have bed check. This is all funny to me because no where else in the US Army does an officer have such a strenuous routine. I hope to make flier but don't be too disappointed if I don't because only about 40% of all who enter does. I have passed two of the toughest exams the army gives. My eyes are OK now." Note that he made specific mention of the condition of his eyes. You will recall that John Brown was with him in August 1940 on the Louisiana trip to Barksdale Army Air Base when he failed to pass the flight physical examination.

It was by design that the pre-flight school training was obviously very strenuous with students treated alike regardless of rank. Perseverance, strength of character, and other important intangible traits were also being tested as an integral part of the training. It was an element in the process to eliminate those with weaknesses and undesirable traits as early as possible before the actual flight training began. In a letter to his Aunt Zona and Uncle Arthur Singleton in Ava, Missouri, dated November 11, Uncle Bob proudly wrote "I am trying to learn to be a flight officer. If I make the grade I'll graduate in May." He also wrote about the training, "In this school it is necessary for us officers to step down a notch or two. We have to make our own bunks, mop our own floors, and clean our own bunks. We also have to march to mess and that is out of the ordinary for officers but I don't think it has hurt any of us. I was getting too fat and sassy anyway."

In that same letter to Aunt Zona and Uncle Arthur, Uncle Bob touched on politics, "Well, I see by the papers that we Republicans are back in power in Missouri as the only state office went to a Republican. Friend Dewey J. got back in as usual." He was referring to his friend Dewey Short, the U.S. Congressman from his district. His humor was exhibited as he wrote about his sister Mary Lea whom he nicknamed "Droopy", "I suppose Droopy is getting rich teaching like I did." He turned serious when he wrote of the observance of Armistice Day and the current war, "Today our only observance of Armistice was one minute of silent prayer at eleven o'clock for those who died in the last war. We hope this time we will have kept them from have dying in vain. My prayer was for those like Forrest and Raymond who is holding them until we can get there in larger numbers." Forrest McHolland was a cousin serving on a submarine in the U.S. Navy in the Pacific, and another cousin, Raymond McHolland, was serving in the U.S. Army in North Africa.

Uncle Bob satisfactorily completed the pre-flight course at San Antonio on December 12. His final grade report reflected scores in the 80s and 90s in all subject areas with the exception of a 76 in Physics.[13]   He probably spent more time and effort studying the physics subject than any of the others. Hurley High School did not offer a physics course and there is no record on his college transcript that he took a physics course. Considering this was his first exposure to the subject it was also probably a great accomplishment for him. From here his next assignment was to the 315th Army Air Forces Flying Training Detachment, Hatbox Field, Muskogee, Oklahoma, where the actual flight training was to be conducted.[14]

ON TO THE REAL THING--FLIGHT SCHOOL

Uncle Bob reported for flight training at Hatbox Field in Muskogee, Oklahoma on December 14, 1942. With an overall score of 89 achieved on the tough academic portion of the training he would have been feeling pretty good about his prospects to attain pilot status. But, as he wrote to John Brown in the October 17 letter, he was well aware of the fact that only about 40 percent of those who start flight training are successful in becoming a pilot.

By this time the nation's war efforts were approaching full throttle. With Christmas season approaching, Uncle Bob's flight training began on December 16. The Individual Flight Record shows that he participated in training flights, accompanied by an instructor, on that date as well as on the dates of December 17, 18, 22, 23, 24, 30, 31 and January 1, 2, and 3 of 1943. With exception of Christmas Day through the 29th of December, he was in the air everyday. On eighteen training flights he logged a total of almost nine hours of flight time with three different flight instructors. Because there were no training flights shown in his Individual Flight Record from Christmas Day, the 25th, through December 29, it appears the school observed the holiday season with a break from training.[15]   There is nothing in the record about Uncle Bob taking leave at this time and close relatives and friends could not recall memories of that particular 1942 holiday season. Although lacking any specific details, in noting the relative closeness of Muskogee, Oklahoma, to Hurley, Missouri, one would think that Uncle Bob probably made it home during that period.

PROBLEMS WITH LANDINGS

It is likely, during this period at home among close friends and relatives, that Uncle Bob would have been sharing thoughts and concerns about his flight training.   In my relentless search for the least bit of information I could gather about Uncle Bob, at some point I picked up a tidbit that concerned the troubles he encountered while learning to fly. I can no longer recall the exact source of that data, but whoever it was recalled Uncle Bob saying he experienced problems with landing the plane. At this time, he had been through about two weeks of training and would have known he was having some problems. This is another point in his story where I must depend upon conjecture, but I believe information about his flight training difficulties quite possibly originated during this period of time.

DISAPPOINTMENT--RECOMMENDATION FOR CESSATION OF FLIGHT TRAINING

Because there are no notes in the flight record about the individual flights until January 1, it is not possible to know how Uncle Bob felt about his progress, but it is very likely he had been made aware of deficiencies in his performance. The Progress Check which occurred on that date left little doubt that he was having problems with piloting a plane. The instructor who had accompanied him on all training flights to this point, H. L. Davidson, pulled no punches when he provided the following written assessment about Uncle Bob's potential to be a pilot: "He has been instructed in all pre-solo maneuvers, including take-offs and landings, and has a total of 7 hours and 47 minutes dual instruction. This student's basic faults are: failure to absorb or retain instruction; slow reaction time, judgment of speed and distance very poor. He has very little feel of the airplane and his coordination and torque correction are mechanical. I consider this student a source of danger to himself as well as to others and I therefore recommend that he be eliminated." [16]

When a student was recommended for elimination, apparently the next step was to change instructors for the

purpose of obtaining the assessment of another qualified person. On January 2 the records reflect that an
instructor by the name of Mr. A. L. Bastone accompanied Uncle Bob on another training flight. No remarks
about the flight could be found in the record. The next
day, January 3, another instructor, 2nd Lt. F. Wheeler,
was assigned to accompany Uncle Bob on what would be
his last flight. Again, no remarks could be found in the
record about this flight, but the records do contain a final
grade sheet on that date which recommended Uncle Bob
for elimination from the course. [17]

FACULTY BOARD ACTION

Once the recommendation for elimination had been made
regarding a flight student, the next step taken by the flight
school was to convene a Faculty Board to examine the
student and all records connected with his training. The
board was made up of flight school faculty members all of
whom possessed pilot qualifications. The board met on
January 4, 1943, to perform the examination and records
review in Uncle Bob's case. The board recommendations
were: "That this student officer: a. Be eliminated from
his present course of air crew training; b. Is not recommended for further air crew training." Further information included in the "Remarks" section of the board report
read: "Relieved from further flying training due to he fact
that he has exhibited traits while actually operating Army
Air Corps aircraft at this station, which are a source of
danger to his own life as well as the lives of others." This
report was forwarded on January 5, 1943, by radiogram
to the Commanding General of the Army Air Forces.
The radiogram read "Second Lieutenant Robert Brown
McHolland 0433315 Student Officer Class 43F eliminat-

ed January 4, 1943. Because of flying deficiency is not recommended for further air crew or glider pilot training. Officer desires to remain in Air Corps." [18]

OTHER FACTORS?

With regard to Uncle Bob's unceremonious dismissal from flight training, a couple of pertinent issues, apart from the findings of the board, warrant further discussion. Although he passed the flight physical examination required to enter flight school, one cannot completely ignore the findings of the flight surgeon who conducted his first flight physical examination in August 1940, at Barksdale Army Air Base in Louisiana. You might recall that Uncle Bob was disqualified at that time because the examination revealed a problem with his eyes termed by the examiner as a "defective angle of convergence." An obvious question would be "What physical changes occurred to correct this problem?" A plausible correct answer would be that nothing had really changed, but rather the urgent need for pilots was the overriding factor that either eased the physical requirements or led to an oversight in detecting the abnormality in his vision. The slightest physical defect could have been a significant factor in his inability to meet the exacting requirements of actual flight training.

The second issue concerns thoughts Uncle Bob shared with his sister Mary Lea about flight training. She recalls him telling her of the tremendous burden of responsibility he felt when flying a plane. The feeling was not only related to all the tasks involved with actual piloting of the plane, but especially for the personnel aboard. Mary Lea indicated that it seemed to be an overpowering burden for him.[19] Perhaps this was the key factor that adversely affected his judgment and performance and led to the final result.

In the meantime, Uncle Bob would await the decision of the army as to his next assignment. In the radiogram sent to Army Air Force Headquarters he had expressed his desire to stay with the Army Air Corps in some capacity. He did not have to wait long for his new orders. With the need for ground troops it is doubtful that his desire to remain with the air corps was given much consideration. Within the next few days he learned he would be returning to the infantry with assignment to the Infantry Replacement Training Center at Camp Wolters, Texas.

Chapter 7 Endnotes:
1. Document, Official Personnel File.
2. Document, Official Personnel File.
3. Letter to John Brown, June 11, 1942.
4. Document, Official Personnel File.
5. Document, Official Personnel File.
6. Website, www.oldguard.org.
7. Document, Official Personnel File.
8. Letter, Official Personnel File.
9. Documents, Official Personnel File.
10. Documents, Official Personnel File.
11. Documents, Official Personnel File.
12. Documents, Official Personnel File.
13. Documents, Official Personnel File.
14. Documents, Official Personnel File.
15. Documents, Official Personnel File.
16. Documents, Official Personnel File.
17. Documents, Official Personnel File.
18. Documents, Official Personnel File.
19. Personnel Interviews, M. Brown.

Chapter 8
The Infantry--
More Training and Some Personal Time

In November 1942 the United States had entered
World War II in earnest by committing large numbers
of ground troops in North Africa to assist the British in
their struggle to defeat the German and Italian armies.
While the U.S. Navy was battling to gain control of the
seas in the South Pacific, it was apparent that many more
ground troops, U.S. Army and U.S. Marines, would be
needed in the capture and occupation of the Japanese-
held islands in the Pacific. Beyond this, many long and
arduous battles lay ahead for the Allies in their war
against the forces of evil. Although the need for many
new pilots would continue, that number would be small
in comparison to the need for hundreds of thousands of
soldiers to staff many new divisions that would make up
the ground forces. Uncle Bob certainly would have been
painfully aware of the manpower situation in the army
so it is doubtful he would have been surprised to learn
of the decision of the War Department to return him to

the infantry.

Although the year of 1943 began with obvious disappointment for Uncle Bob, there would soon be much more to occupy his time and thoughts and to help him get past his tough flight school experience. He would return to an infantry training center (as an infantry rifle platoon leader for a time) to direct the intensive combat training. He would also receive more individual training that included attendance at the Infantry Officer's Basic Course at Fort Benning, Georgia. Upon completion of this course he would receive a permanent assignment to a unit readying for combat in the near future. While the next few months would be a very busy phase for him it was not "all work and no play." He would also squeeze in time to keep in touch with relatives and friends as well as to strike up new acquaintances with lady friends.

BACK WITH THE INFANTRY--
CAMP WOLTERS, TEXAS

Within a week or so after the decision of the flight school faculty board, Uncle Bob received orders to report to the Infantry Replacement Training Center, Camp Wolters, Texas. On January 22, 1943 he was assigned to the 63rd Infantry Training Battalion at Camp Wolters. Upon reporting to his new unit he was granted fifteen days leave which he took from January 23 through February 6.[1] It can be assumed with a great degree of certainty that he took advantage of this free time from the rigors of military life to return to his home town of Hurley. In these friendly surroundings he would have some time to reflect on his recent setback and to contemplate the new direction the army had in store for him. Because he always enjoyed visiting with friends and relatives it is certain much of his time was dedicated to calling on favorite aunts, uncles, cousins and old friends. It is also quite possible it was during this time that he made his first acquaintance with a young lady from the nearby town of Crane.

Upon expiration of his leave time, Uncle Bob returned to Camp Wolters and reported for duty on February 6. While his assignment here would be interrupted for three months to attend additional required officer training, Camp Wolters would be his permanent station for the next six months.[2]

Uncle Bob immediately began his platoon leader duties with Company A of the 63rd Infantry Training Battalion. Keeping up with the ever increasing requirements to staff the many new combat divisions being formed was a tremendous task for the army and much of Uncle Bob's time at Camp Wolters would be occupied with training soldiers in the effort to fulfill these needs. In a letter dated February 11, 1943 (only five days after returning from leave,) written to his friend John Brown, he expressed some of the pressure he was feeling:

> *"I guess I won't go to Ft. Worth this week either. They put me in a school down here that lasts for five weeks. It really takes lots of time. On Wednesday, Mondays and Fridays we put in about 18 hours a day and that is not exaggerating either because we do night problems on those nights and we have school the next day just the same. It's kindly rough for an Air Corps Officer just home from leave …. I like this place better than I did. Tho I'm not crazy about it yet. I haven't seen town all week. I just don't have time ….   I'd like to come over but I couldn't stay long*

> *enough to make connections. I don't get off Saturday until*
> *5:30 and then I'd have to do the four S's before I could*
> *leave. I wrote Anna and told her our presence would not*
> *be there Sunday."*

John Brown had recently completed Officer Candidate School and was assigned to the 86th Infantry Division located at Camp Howze, Texas, near Gainesville.[3] It was close enough to the Forth Worth area that they had made plans to meet at Uncle Bob's sister, Anna's, home in nearby Burleson for a visit over that weekend.

Amid the pressures of the new job, Uncle Bob's sense of humor also emerged in the letter to John as he wrote, "I'm sure proud Strafford beat the Bull Dogs, aren't you? Well I'd be in favor of a little pasture party. Wouldn't you?" In the first sentence he was referring to a softball game someone had heard about between two rival schools back home. In the second sentence it was clear that he was all for playing a softball game (pasture party) right now. Uncle Bob and John Brown apparently missed their last opportunity to see each other. John Brown cannot recall meeting up with Uncle Bob during his time in Texas. No doubt the pressure of the business of training for war kept these two young infantry second lieutenants from getting together for a visit.

There were other indications of the busy times Uncle Bob was experiencing while at Camp Wolters. In a letter dated March 3, 1943 Uncle Bob wrote, "Dear Folks, How is everybody? I am still OK but I am hard pressed for time but I sure don't get to spend much money. I've gone a whole month since returning and haven't spent $10 yet but I will have to pay about $50 for the usual things like Mess, Club Dues, Orderly Fee and etc." In the letter he was interested whether there were any new calves and asked of Roxabel, "Who is taking care of the kids?" He ended the letter with the following request "Why don't you send me some clippings of the Dr. Palmer case and the details in the next mail. I'd like to use that case in a talk at Officers Pool School this next week sometime. Please."

The request for information about "Dr. Palmer" is most intriguing. There was a person who went by the name of "Dr. Omar Palmer" who had operated a clinic in Hurley during the 1930s. He became known locally as the "Herb Doctor" for his profuse use of herbs gathered from the surrounding area in the treatment of his patients. His fame had spread beyond the community through articles printed in St. Louis, Kansas City, and Springfield newspapers about him and reports of the miraculous results of his unconventional treatment practices. In her book, *The Wizard of Oto*, written about Dr. Palmer, Carly Andrus noted that Dr. Palmer "remained a mystery to the reporters and the curious who tried to secret out his past. He would at times grant interviews but still refused to have photographs taken or discuss his past or his alleged medical education." The mystery deepened within the local community when Dr. Palmer suddenly decided to close the clinic in 1938. He moved for a short time to nearby Aurora, and then to an even more isolated area in extreme southwest Missouri. There were rumors, never confirmed, that maybe Dr. Palmer was even a Nazi spy.[4] Perhaps the subject of the Officer Pool School session concerned intelligence or counterintelligence and Uncle Bob was planning to use the information in his presentation.

Spending Time with Relatives

From the content of the February 11 letter to John Brown it is apparent they had made plans for the coming Sunday to visit with Uncle Bob's sister, Anna, and family in nearby Burleson, Texas.

His sister, Anna, had been a resident of Texas for some time. After completing high school at the School of the Ozarks in Point Lookout, Missouri, she moved to the Fort Worth area of Texas where she completed nurse's training and became a Registered Nurse. It was in Texas that she met her future husband, Thomas Earl Hill, Sr. They settled in the small community of Burleson, Texas, located a few miles south of Fort Worth, Texas. They had a son, Thomas Earl Jr., who was Uncle Bob's first

Earl and Anna Hill—courtesy Wiley-McHolland family.

nephew.

Camp Wolters was less than an hour's drive from Burleson. Conveniently, this offered Uncle Bob a home away from home when he was able to get away from the demanding requirements of infantry training. Uncle Bob's nephew has many cherished memories of those visits.

MAKING LASTING IMPRESSIONS ON A NEPHEW

Thomas Earl Hill Jr., whom I will refer to as Tom, has many cherished memories of Uncle Bob from the period of his assignment at Camp Wolters. I must note that Tom and I have shared for years the same fervent passion to learn more about our Uncle Bob. Tom was an admiring and impressionable boy who turned ten years of age during this period. He vividly recalls riding with his father and mother in their 1940 Ford as they made trips to Camp Wolters on weekends to pick up Uncle Bob to spend some time with them. He believes they must have usually picked him up on Friday evening as the soldiers were released for a short pass. He remembers the family waiting in an area outside the main gate and seeing the soldiers streaming out in droves to the lines of waiting buses and cabs to catch a ride into Fort Worth for some fun time away from the grueling routine of training. Pretty soon they would spot Uncle Bob, always sharply dressed in uniform, looking for their familiar vehicle. They would head back to Burleson where he would often spend a night or two with them relaxing, catching up on family news, and enjoying some good home cooking. [5]

Young Tom Hill especially enjoyed the attention he could

expect from Uncle Bob who always seemed to enjoy spending time with kids. These were exciting times for Tom and he always looked forward to having this special uncle around. He would bring Tom surprises and treat him like he was more than just a kid. One of Tom's treasures is a gas mask he still has that Uncle Bob gave him on one of the visits. Another prized possession of Tom's is a letter dated September 17, 1944, addressed specifically to him from Uncle Bob that he sent from overseas. The suggestion that in the midst of combat operations Uncle Bob would take the time to write him was yet another gesture that showed the genuine nature of this man. [6]

Tom recalls a time during one of the visits when he and Uncle Bob were in the living room while his mother, Anna, was in the kitchen preparing supper. Uncle Bob was playing with Tom's Daisy BB gun when he pulled

the trigger leaving a tiny BB embedded in the ceiling of the living room. Hearing the noise and commotion, Anna yelled from the kitchen, "What is going on in there?" Tom, fearing that he might be in trouble, recalls Uncle Bob quickly letting Anna know what had happened and explaining to her that it was all his fault, that Tom had nothing to do with it.[7]

A young Tom Hill—courtesy Wiley-McHolland family.

Another treasure of

Tom's is picture taken of Uncle Bob in the front yard of their home in Burleson. Tom recalls that as they were leaving the house one Sunday afternoon to take Uncle Bob back to Camp Wolters, his mom had Uncle Bob stop and pose for the picture she took with her handy Kodak box camera. Uncle Bob, as usual, was in uniform and dressed as sharply as ever. He posed while standing at attention beside a crepe myrtle bush near their driveway. The picture was enlarged with Uncle Bob's erect figure carefully cut out and pasted on particle board and placed in a stand. The resulting image was about a foot tall figure of Uncle Bob proudly and impressively standing at attention. Over sixty years later Tom Hill, with an admiring nephew's profound respect, displays that figure in a special place at his home along with Uncle Bob's combat decorations.[8]

Today, Tom Hill also honors his revered uncle with a restored 1944 Ford Jeep which he proudly displays in various activities that honor World War II veterans. The

Tom Hill and his "Uncle Bob" jeep—courtesy Arrowhead Chapter,
Military Vehicle Preservation Association

jeep is often included as a part of Tyler Alberts' Mobile 90th Infantry Division Exhibit. Painted clearly under the windshield of the jeep are the words "Uncle Bob". Uncle Bob's combat ribbons are shown on the left windshield. The numbers shown on the jeep, along with U.S. Army, are his birthdate—10121918.

INTEREST IN THE LADIES

In the interest of placing events in chronological context, this is the proper point to include certain pertinent events that occurred sometime during this period. Simultaneously, it is fitting to address a subject that has been scarcely mentioned so far in this account of Uncle Bob's life. It concerns his interest in and relationships with the fairer sex. References were made previously by John and Travis Brown citing instances of efforts to connect with young ladies and of some casual dating during the two years Uncle Bob spent teaching at High Point school. It is evident that he was a "normal, red-blooded American boy" when it came to interest in the ladies. But, according to his sister, Mary Lea, it seems that he was never seriously involved with one person. However, it was discovered during this period of time that there were at least two young ladies that deserve further mention. It seems that he might have had a particular interest in one of the young women.

A bit of intrigue and romanticism surround Uncle Bob's association with a young lady by the name of Vena Custer who hailed from the town of Crane, Missouri, which is located about six miles from Hurley. The story has it that Uncle Bob first saw Vena playing basketball at a girl's high school basketball game at Crane. The date of this occurrence is not known, but it could have been sometime in 1941 or 1942. This story has an interesting twist that was unknown to Vena at the time. She learned much later that Uncle Bob upon seeing her told someone he had seen the girl he was going to marry. Apparently some time had elapsed before Uncle Bob took further steps to make contact with the pretty young lady he had spotted on the basketball court. The reason for Uncle Bob's hesitancy to approach Vena might have been related to their age difference. After all, Uncle Bob was about six years older than Vena, who was still in high school.[9]

Vena Custer (Berglund)—courtesy Wiley-McHolland family.

Over sixty years later Vena Custer Berglund graciously provided her unique perspective of her acquaintance with Uncle Bob during this period. Vena was a senior at Crane High School in the 1942-43 school year. She was also editor of the school paper. She recalls her first contact with Uncle Bob was a telephone call he made to her in her capacity as editor of the paper. He had concocted a tale about a "mystery" involving some occurrence around Hurley that he believed Vena as editor of the paper should look into. The so-called "mystery" probably involved the infamous "Herb Doctor," Dr. Omar Palmer. This was likely Uncle Bob's clumsy way of arranging some way to meet her because it was

shortly afterward that he asked her for a date. Vena remembers dating him on two separate occasions. On one
of the dates they went to Springfield to have dinner at
the Kentwood Arms, one of the finer places to dine in
Springfield at that time. Vena recalled that both of Uncle Bob's sisters, Mary Lea and Roxabel, accompanied
them on that date. On the other date, she remembered
going with him to a war movie at the theater in Crane.
She recalled clearly that the movie seemed to upset Uncle Bob and they left before it was over.[10]   In assembling
the pieces of information and giving consideration to the
dates provided by Vena, it is believed their dates most
likely occurred during Uncle Bob's leave in January and
February of 1943.

Vena Custer Berglund offered a few more of her memories and observations concerning Uncle Bob. She could
not recall a time that she ever saw him when he was not
in uniform. She remembered that because of their age
difference her parents had reservations about her dating this older man who was already in the army. However, she said that her parents liked him and that he was
always a perfect gentleman. She recalled talking with
Uncle Bob by phone one more time after the two dates.
She believed he called from Kansas City as he was traveling between assignments. She remembers also that they
corresponded after these dates but never considered that
theirs was anything but a casual relationship. It was not
until a few years later that she discovered that Uncle Bob
might have had plans to carry their acquaintance into
something more serious. [11]

On at least one occasion, possibly more, of Uncle Bob's
visits to his sister's home in Burleson while stationed at

Camp Wolters, his nephew, Tom Hill, recalls him dating a lady whom he described as "the prettiest girl in Texas." The young lady's name was Frances Wilshire. Miss Wilshire was from Burleson and was a student at Texas Wesleyan College in Fort Worth, Texas. Tom remembers her later as being prettier than ever when she was his Burleson High School health and civics teacher in the late 40s and early 50s. Tom recalls Uncle Bob borrowing his dad's 1940 Ford and going out on a date with Miss Wilshire on a few occasions while he visited them.[12]

Mrs. Frances Wilshire Shahan confirmed Tom Hill's

The "prettiest girl in Texas," Frances Wilshire (Shahan)— courtesy Wiley-McHolland family.

memories of her dating Uncle Bob during the time he was stationed at Camp Wolters, Texas. Frances was a student at Texas Wesleyan College in Fort Worth majoring in Home Economics. She was born and raised on a dairy farm near Burleson and was acquainted with Tom's dad and mom, Earl and Anna Hill. Frances remembers she and Uncle Bob were good friends and he was "very much a gentleman … outgoing, honest … and someone who found a way to do things and got things done." She recalled that he loved to sing. Their dates often involved gathering with friends at a place called Bar-Walk Farms located between Burleson and Joshua where they would join their voices in popular songs of the day. Uncle Bob did not hesitate to lead the others in singing old country and gospel songs.

Frances recalled with a touch of melancholy that Uncle Bob conveyed to her he did not think he would come back from the war alive. She believed his training at the Infantry School in Fort Benning, Georgia (March-August 1943) particularly influenced his thinking as these thoughts occurred after his return from that training. Frances recalled that there was some exchange of correspondence after he departed Camp Wolters remembering particularly a profusely censored V-mail she received from him while his unit was in England.

A Home Economics major, Frances recalled participating in a patriotic project involving the baking and sending of fruitcakes to soldiers during the Christmas season of 1944. She sent her fruitcake to Uncle Bob, but, unfortunately, he never received it. She received a letter sometime early in 1945 from a sergeant in his unit thanking her for the delicious fruitcake and informing her that

Uncle Bob had been killed. Frances finished her degree work at Texas Wesleyan and taught for a few years. She later worked several years as a Home Demonstration Agent for the university extension service in Texas before she married a rancher, Art Shahan, and settled in the Pleasanton, Texas, area to raise their family.[13]

OFFICER DEVELOPMENT TRAINING

Uncle Bob had been on active duty as a second lieutenant for about ten months when he was scheduled to attend the Infantry Officer Basic Course at the "Home of the Infantry" at Fort Benning, Georgia. Completion of this course was an essential requirement of all infantry officers. At that time this was a three month course of instruction designed to cover every important subject of concern to an infantry small unit leader. The emphasis was on leadership, tactics, coordination of fire and air support, familiarization with weapons, and other areas critical to success in combat.

Uncle Bob was at Fort Benning when he received a consoling letter from his friend, Edwin Dean, who was with the famed "Darby's Rangers" in North Africa. Edwin, having received a letter from Uncle Bob that he had not made the grade as a pilot, wrote on March 10, 1943, "Was glad to receive your letter but sorry to hear you didn't get your wings. Anyway the man who wins this war will be none other than the old Infantry man himself." In his typically modest manner Edwin went on to write "I had quite an aeroplane ride recently myself. We were dumped out over the front lines where we've been raiding enemy outposts and strong points. You have, no doubt, read about some of the rangers' activities in the newspapers. I was presented with the Silver Star medal for my small part in the operation." With an award of a Silver Star, Edwin's part in the action would not be termed as "small." The Silver Star medal is the third highest medal for heroism in combat. Specifically, it is awarded "For distinguished gallantry in action against an enemy of the United States…"

Uncle Bob spent three months at Fort Benning attending the Officer Basic Course from March 22, 1943, to June 22, 1943. He made it through the course with flying colors finishing with an academic rating of "Excellent." He returned to Camp Wolters with assignment to the Infantry Officer Replacement Pool on June 23, 1943, with the duty of Rifle Platoon Officer.[14] From this point it was evident that he was awaiting War Department orders for permanent assignment to a combat division. The army keep him occupied with various platoon leader duties and he probably visited with the Hill family on some of the weekends. The records show he took advantage of this time to have some dental work done. It was also during this period that he heard again from Edwin Dean.

Edwin's letter was written on June 6, 1943, and was addressed to Uncle Bob's Fort Benning, Georgia, address. It had been forwarded to his Camp Wolters unit on June 28, so it would probably have been the first week in July when he actually received Edwin's letter. Edwin wrote:

> *Dear Bob,*
>
> *Sorry I haven't answered your last letter sooner but I've been busy.*

I've seen practically all of North Africa. Since I've been here I landed at Arzew on the invasion. 3 January I went to the front by air. On Feb 12 I seen my first real action at Sened Station where I was decorated. My remaining time on the front was spent in the vicinity of Gafsa and El Geutar. Jerrys are good soldiers but he can be beaten just the same as anyone else. I think the American soldier is better with a little combat experience under his belt.

I suppose your school days are about over and you will be assigned to an outfit soon. Maybe I will see you over here sometime in the near future. Will close now as I have more letters to write. Notice the changed address

Edwin

With his expected terseness, Edwin got directly to the point but left out many details. With the 1st Ranger Battalion he definitely had seen much of North Africa. More specifically, he was a part of very intense fighting at Sened Station, Gafsa, and El Guettar. The battalion was awarded the prestigious Presidential Unit Citation for its part in the battle at El Guettar. At the end of the letter Edwin advised Uncle Bob to "notice the changed address." Based on the impressive performance in North Africa of the 1st Ranger Battalion, the commander, Lieutenant Colonel William Darby, was authorized to form two additional battalions; the 3rd and 4th Ranger Battalions. Edwin was selected to be a part of the cadre that formed the 4th Ranger Battalion. There is no doubt that he had been busy, as he stated, At the time he wrote, his new unit was training for their next action; the invasion of Sicily which occurred on July 10, 1943.

The wait for news of his next assignment was not long in coming for Uncle Bob. Orders were issued on July 29, 1943, assigning him to the 90th Infantry Division, Camp Barkley, Texas with a reporting date of August 3, 1943.[15] He would become a part of a unit, with a storied tradition that had already been training intensively for over a year, for the most important and gravest challenge it would ever encounter.

1LT Edwin Dean, Darby's Rangers—courtesy Edwin Dean.

Chapter 8 Endnotes:
1. Documents, Official Personnel File.
2. Documents, Official Personnel File.
3. Personal interviews, J. Brown.
4. Carly Andrus, The Wizard of Oto (Self-published, 1985), 88, 101-116.
5. Telephone interviews, Thomas Earl Hill, Jr., 2008.
6. Telephone interviews, Hill.
7. Telephone interviews, Hill.
8. Telephone interviews, Hill.
9. Telephone interviews, Vena Custer Berglund, 2008.
10. Telephone interviews, Berglund.
11. Telephone interviews, Berglund.
12. Telephone interviews, Hill.
13. Telephone interview, Frances Wilshire Shahan, 2008
14. Documents, Official Personnel File.
15. Documents, Official Personnel File.

Chapter 9
A Proud Unit and Preparation
for the Real Thing

By August of 1943 the Allies had defeated the Axis
armies in North Africa and Sicily and were preparing to invade Italy. The American Navy had won major
battles in the Pacific and the Allied forces in that area
were beginning to make some progress. Although war
was being waged on two major fronts, more emphasis
was being directed toward the European Theater. While
large numbers of troops and material were being provided on both fronts, the American strategy was to give
priority to winning the war in Europe as soon as possible in order that all our energy and resources could be
directed toward winning in the Pacific.[1] Experiencing
meteoric growth, the American war production machine
had reached unbelievable levels. The rate and propor-
tion of mobilization of the armed forces paralleled the
remarkable progress of the production of material and
supplies. The activation, manning, and training of the

unit to which Uncle Bob was assigned was an integral part of this extraordinary achievement.

Authors note: At this point it is significant to note a conspicuous gap that exists in Uncle Bob's personnel records from the time he reported to Camp Granite, California in September, 1943, until he departed for overseas in March, 1944. His promotion is the only document in his file for this period of time. Punch cards showing changes in personnel status, duty assignment, location, etc. were available for virtually every change up to this time. Other reliable sources, particularly the Battle History of the Third Battalion 358th Infantry Regiment, *were used to document many of Uncle Bob's movements throughout the remainder of the text*

THE 90TH INFANTRY DIVISION

Uncle Bob's new unit, the 90th Infantry Division, had been reactivated in March of 1942 at Camp Barkley, Texas, a base located a few miles south of Abilene, Texas. The division was first activated in August 1917 at Camp Travis, Texas as a part of General John J. Pershing's American Expeditionary Force. The division became known as the "Texas-Oklahoma Division" because most members came from those two states. The division patch even denotes this heritage as it consists of a red "T" superimposed over a red "O" on a khaki background.

The division distinguished itself in World War I in the St. Mihiel and Meuse/Argonne operations. The unit was inactivated after the war in June 1919. The tradition of the 90th Division lived on with the forming of the 90th Division Association and was among the first of the inactive units to be reactivated after declaration of war against the Axis powers. This time members of the

The 90th Infantry Division "Tough Ombres" patch—courtesy John Colby

division came from all parts of the country and the "T-O" aptly came to represent the "Tough Ombres."[2]

The 90th was what was known in the army as a "standard triangular infantry division." It consisted of three infantry regiments, each with three battalions of three rifle companies (and one heavy weapons company.)[3] Uncle Bob was assigned to the Headquarters Company of the division. Initial assignment to this administrative and support company was the normal practice while the person was going through the usual in-processing routine. It also allowed time for the division personnel staff to determine the most appropriate assignment.

DUTY ASSIGNMENT

After in-processing was completed, Uncle Bob was assigned to Company M, 3rd Battalion, 358th Infantry Regiment. His specific duty assignment was that of Machine Gun Platoon Officer and, as such, he headed one of the M Company machine gun platoons. The parent unit of M Company, the 3rd Battalion, 358th Infantry Regiment, consisted of three line rifle companies; I Company, K Company and L Company, and a Heavy Weapons Company, M Company. The three "line" companies made up the riflemen or "foot soldiers" who were trained for the front line fighting. Heavy Weapons Company, M Company, was the battalion's "artillery" and provided 81mm mortar and .30 caliber machine gun (water-cooled) support to the line rifle companies.

Captain John Marsh, M Co., 3rd Battalion, 358th Infantry commander, killed in action in France on Hill 122, 10 July 1944--Ft. Dix, New Jersey, M Company photo by David Pond Willis.

M Company was commanded by Captain John Marsh, a very able and competent officer from Montana, with a Masters of Business Administration from prestigious Stanford University. Captain Marsh was a member of the original cadre that formed the 90th Division at Camp Barkley. First Lieutenant Donald Benedict, a graduate of the University of Idaho and a former high school vocational agriculture teacher was the M Company Executive Officer.[4] M Company would be Uncle Bob's home and these two capable men would be his immediate superior officers for several months.

1LT Donald Benedict, Executive Officer of M Co. 3rd Battalion, 358th Infantry--Ft. Dix, New Jersey, M Company photo by David Pond Willis.

As noted, the 90th Infantry Division was activated in March of 1942, and had been exhaustively training for combat from that point until Uncle Bob officially joined the unit in August, 1943. In addition to undergoing a seventeen week basic training course the division had continuously participated in a variety of combat training exercises under both the hot summer sun and in the cold winter weather of Texas. The division also participated in a two-month long maneuver in Louisiana against the 77th Division in early 1943.[5]

Uncle Bob officially reported for duty with his new unit on August 14, 1943, and would soon learn the division was preparing for another lengthy maneuver to be conducted several hundred miles from Texas. No doubt he would have immediately been thrust into a flurry of activity involved in readying his platoon for a major move to participate in desert training maneuvers in California. In fact, Uncle Bob would spend only a couple of weeks at Camp Barkley. By the first of September the division would be moving in its entirety to Camp Granite, California.

A NEW FRIENDSHIP BEGINS

Sergeant Howard Pemberton, Heavy Machine Gun Section Leader, M Co., 3rd Battalion, 358th Infantry—courtesy Howard and Ardys Pemberton.

Staff Sergeant Howard Pemberton was a section leader in the machine gun platoon to which Uncle Bob had been assigned and remembers well this new officer from his home state of Missouri. Sharing common backgrounds and interests, there was an immediate, positive connection between them. Howard, who would later receive a battlefield commission, was very familiar with the fraternization rules concerning officers and enlisted personnel and

spoke of those officers who carried it to extremes. However, with high regard for Uncle Bob as an officer and a
friend, he stated "He wasn't like that, he was more like
one of us."[6]   Howard would serve under Uncle Bob's
command for the remainder of his tenure with M Company. His close relationship with Uncle Bob would continue even after Uncle Bob took command of K Company several months later in the heat of battle in France.

A Few Months in the California Desert

Along with the entire battalion, M Company would move
by rail from Camp Barkley, Texas, to Yuma, Arizona, the
first week of September, 1943,[7]   Howard Pemberton recalls the unit unloading at Yuma and moving across the
Colorado River several miles into the vast desert area of
southeastern California. Howard remembers "there was
nothing there but sand everywhere." The area designated as Camp Granite was still under construction and
Howard recalled that for several weeks everyone had to
sleep in their pup tents. It was two or three months later
before they were able to move into small crude structures
consisting of a foundation with low walls and a canvas
covering. This offered a little improvement because each
of the huts had a stove to provide some warmth from the
cold desert nights.[8]

Shortly after arrival at Camp Granite Uncle Bob obtained approval for five days of leave. The records reflect
that he was on leave from September 20 through September 25.[9]   Other information is available that leads
me to believe he used this time to travel to the Los Angeles area to visit with his sister Eva and brother Everette
who were both living and working in the area. Eva was

working in a naval shipyard. Everette's type of employment at the time is not known, but it is known that he entered the U.S. Navy a few months later. The piece of information that links the three siblings together at this time is a studio photograph taken of the three family members looking very happy to be together. Uncle Bob looks especially proud to be wearing his army khaki uniform. This appears to be the only time they could have been together during this time frame. Of course, he might have been able to garner a weekend pass into the Los Angeles area sometime over the three months the division remained at Camp Granite. In any event, it is certain that it was sometime during these few months that the photograph was taken.

Everette McHolland, Uncle Bob, and Eva McHolland, taken in California, fall of 1943—courtesy Wiley-McHolland family.

The scarceness of correspondence from Uncle Bob during this period might be a possible clue tied to the intensity of the training being conducted. There are no letters of his available while he was at Camp Granite. This is not to say there were none written during this time as the possibility exists that letters were received from him but not kept. As this was his first assignment with a combat unit he would have been fully occupied with becoming acquainted with his men as well as learning and performing his duties as a machine gun platoon officer in simulated combat conditions.

Another indication that Uncle Bob would have been very busy at this time is based on information contained in the *Battle History of the Third Battalion 358th Infantry*. The history noted "Operating out of the newly constructed Camp Granite, the Division received additional instruction under the burning desert sun, ending up with a month of maneuvers against the 93rd Infantry Division, a colored outfit. In maneuvers the 90th became the first Division to successfully "crack" the Palen Pass fortified defense line."[10]

Since the fighting in the desert lands of North Africa had ended and there were no other desert areas in either of the war theaters, it did not make much sense for the unit to be concentrating on the tactics of desert training. A more logical reason for the selection of this area for maneuvers could be that it offered a vast uninhabited space where large forces could operate with relative freedom in various training activities.

PROMOTION!!!

With about eighteen months on active duty as a second lieutenant and performing very successfully as machine gun platoon officer in M Company since August, Uncle Bob's diligent efforts were about to be rewarded. While at Camp Granite his regimental commander, stating that Uncle Bob "clearly demonstrated his qualifications for the grade of 1st Lieutenant," forwarded on November 15, 1943 to the War Department his recommendation for Uncle Bob's promotion. In just over two weeks the War Department issued the orders allowing him to wear the silver bar of a First Lieutenant to be effective November 30, 1943.[11] Along with a modest pay raise he would no longer be looked upon as just another "shavetail."

Although the official promotion date was November 30, considering there would have been lag-time in receiving the promotion orders from the War Department, Uncle Bob likely received the official notice sometime during the first week or so of December, 1943. He would be wearing the new silver bar for about three weeks before the unit would be packing and loading all personnel and equipment for another long train ride. Although it was the height of the holiday season, the unit would have little time for celebration as they would spend Christmas in the desert preparing for the next big move. By the end of the week they would be on trains headed all the way across the country to Fort Dix, New Jersey.[12] Howard Pemberton remembers the train stopping in Kansas City, Missouri on New Year's Eve. This was a welcome break as the troops were unloaded and able to stretch for a while. Howard recalls making a telephone call home during that stop.[13] I imagine Uncle Bob was also among the many who waited in long lines for a chance to say a quick "Hello" to loved ones before they again boarded the train for the remainder of their cross country journey to Fort Dix.

Chapter 9 Endnotes:

1. Keith D. Dickson, World War II for Dummies (New York: Wiley Publishing Co. 2001), 251.
2. History of the 90th Division in World War II (90th Division Association, 1945) 1.
3. John Colby, War from the Ground Up: The 90th Division in WWII (Austin, Texas: Nortex Press, 1991), 1.
4. Lieutenant Colonel Charles B. Bryan, Battle History Third Battalion 358th Infantry (Pizen, Czechoslovakia: Novy Vsetisk, 1945), 1.
5. Bryan, 1.
6. Telephone interview, Howard Pemberton, 2008.
7. Bryan, 1.
8. Telephone interview, Pemberton.
9. Documents, Official Personnel Filc.
10. Bryan, 1.
11. Documents, Official Personnel File.
12. Bryan, 1.
13. Telephone interview, Pemberton.

Chapter 10
Fort Dix, New Jersey and Beyond

The 90th Infantry Division would spend most of the first three months of 1944 at Fort Dix, New Jersey in preparation for overseas deployment. *The Battle History of the Third Battalion, 358th Infantry* described this time as the "Port of Mobilization" period during which "all companies were reorganized, replacements received and the multitudinous preparations requisite for a long overseas voyage completed." Uncle Bob would be among those taking care of personal affairs such as powers of attorney, wills, and tying up assorted loose ends. Personal effects not essential for a combat mission were packaged and shipped home. With all of the hustle and bustle of getting ready for shipment overseas, many were able to obtain passes over the weekends to see the sights of the Big Apple.[1] Howard Pemberton recalled that it was also during this time that every one was granted ten days leave to return home to see sweethearts, family, and friends.[2]

LAST LEAVE HOME AND A NEPHEW'S FIRST AND LASTING MEMORY

Learning that ten days leave was granted during this period was very significant to me because of the timing of certain events and the things I remember about Uncle Bob. *(Note: this is the period in which none of the personnel change card information is available in Uncle Bob's records.)* It must have been sometime in January or early February of 1944 when he took his ten days leave. Our family (Dad, Mom, my brother Bob, Aunt Mary Lea and me) had just moved in January 1944, into the home in which I spent most of my younger years in Hurley. My mother was over eight months pregnant at the time. My youngest brother, John, arrived on February 8. I point this out because it was not until in a letter Uncle Bob wrote home dated February 24, 1944, that he indicated he had been informed of his new nephew. He offered this humorous take on the occasion, "I guess Johnny Maurice will do for a name but of course Bobby Stan has the best name. I was kindly figuring on being an aunt this time but I can't complain." Consideration of the sequence and timing of the events during this period allow me to reliably confirm my personal memory of Uncle Bob.

My earliest memory in life occurred during this period in early 1944. I recall sitting on a window seat with my brother, Bob, one night at our home in Hurley. I remember Uncle Bob's sister, Mary Lea, being there and I am sure our mother was there, too. As we peered into the darkness Uncle Bob was teasing us saying there were bears and lions out there. I remember having a very scared feeling and starting to cry. I'm sure my brother was crying, too. I recall Mary Lea chiding Uncle Bob about carrying his teasing too far and he backed off and tried to cover up his mistake. I also recall him taking my brother and me with him to buy us ice cream and candy at some point during this period. It very possibly could have been the next day after the teasing episode. Uncle Bob's sister Mary Lea believes he did this to make sure we were back in his good graces. If this was the case, it must have worked because something happened during this time to make Uncle Bob a very special person in the mind of a three year old. I could never have imagined how exceptional an individual my Uncle Bob really was and neither could I know how his memory would be perpetuated and affect me throughout my life.

A SAD FAREWELL

Memories have faded over the sixty years since Uncle Bob's last leave home. His sister, Mary Lea, does not recall many specific details of his last leave, but she does remember having the feeling that he would never return home.[3] A definite answer will never be known whether Uncle Bob had a premonition of death or that he was merely making preparations just in case, but a couple of things he did during that last trip home provide cause for speculation. He gave one of his most prized possessions, his Masonic ring, to his Uncle John McHolland for safekeeping with the instructions that It would be Uncle John's property if he did not return. Another friend, Lynna Box White, tearfully related that he solemnly told her before he left home for the last time, "Lynna, they'll bring me back in a wooden box."[4] No one knew the details of the military planning occurring at that time, but the logical expectation of any informed person was that the Allied forces would be invading the European mainland at some point in the near future in an effort to stem Hitler's quest for world domination. Perhaps it was Uncle Bob's extensive participation in the full range of an infantry unit's activities in combat that led him to prepare his friends and loved ones of the distinct possibility he would not return. Whatever the reason, his farewell must have been a tough time for everyone.

LAST LETTER FROM FORT DIX

Uncle Bob's letter written on February 24, 1944, was mentioned briefly before in establishing the time frame of his last leave home. He had given his "approval" of the name Johnny Maurice and wrote of his feigned disappointment in not being an aunt. The letter was addressed to his sister, "RB Wiley," and opened up with "Dear Folks." He began by covering some practical matters he had to take care of before leaving for overseas, "I have sent some stuff home by express. I want you to take care of those clothes until I will be able to wear them again. I still haven't got all home I wanted to send. I wanted to send a comforter and some shoes too, but I guess I'll just try to take them along with me wherever I go. I lost the key to my lock on the box I sent home so I guess it will have to be opened by force." He added, "I'm sending my check for $30 to you so you can pay for the express on the luggage and repay you what I owe you. I believe I owe Droopy (Mary Lea) $20 and Roxy $5." He wrote about going to see some of the sights of the Big Apple, "I went to New York last week and I visited Radio city. I went on a tour of Rockefeller Center and up Empire State Building but it was so foggy you couldn't see anything not even the street below. I heard Leopold Stokowski and the New York Philharmonic or Symphony orchestra while I was there. I was very fortu-

Uncle Bob "looking mean" in the M Company photo taken at Fort Dix, New Jersey, in February 1944 by David Pond Willis.

nate as the studio has a very limited capacity and there is already a long waiting list. An old lady had two seats reserved for two service men and we were lucky enough to get them. I was also caught in the blackout at New York (a practice blackout) and they did pretty good too." He wrote about how busy things were, "This certainly hasn't been a rest camp after the desert. They work us harder here than they did in the desert. A fellow never knows where he will be next as to the job he is doing." He added another humorous note about his family name, "I looked in New York, Philadelphia, Bronx Philadelphia, Queens and Brooklyn's phone directory and I never found one McHolland so I guess we're a select group." He finished the letter with information about a company picture that was taken at Fort Dix, "I also sent a picture of our company home. I'd kindly like to have it framed. I really look mean in it. I guess I just feel mean anyway." Uncle Bob is in the front row of the photograph along with the other M Company officers. He does not look particularly "mean" but he has more of a solemn look as do the remainder of the company members who seem to be contemplating an uncertain future.

THE COMPANY PICTURE

More must be written about the company picture Uncle Bob sent home. I remember seeing the picture several times at our home in Hurley when I was growing up. The photograph includes the entire M Company in formation standing at parade rest in front of their barracks at Fort Dix. I learned that photographing the company-sized units before they went overseas became a standard army practice. The photograph is about three feet in length and eight inches high. Uncle Bob's wish to have it framed had not been satisfied as the photograph was rolled up and secured with a rubber band. A few years ago I came into possession of the photograph. Over sixty years after Uncle Bob originally expressed his desire, the photograph was beautifully matted and framed. It is proudly displayed in a special place in my home. Through the efforts of my cousin, Tom Hill, I was able to obtain a complete listing of every person in the photograph. Tom obtained the roster from the Historian of the 90th Division Association, Tyler Alberts.

M Company, 3rd Battalion, 358th Infantry, taken at Fort Dix, New Jersey, February 1944 by David Pond Willis.

OVERSEAS MOVEMENT TO ENGLAND

A certain ominous indication that overseas movement was nearing comes from Uncle Bob's personnel file. There was an Emergency Addressee and Personal Property Card signed by Uncle Bob on March 11, 1944, on which he designated his sister, Roxabel, as the person to be notified in case of emergency and to whom personal property was to be shipped. [5]

Lacking any more letters from Uncle Bob and personnel change information for the next few weeks, I must rely heavily on the *Battle History of the Third Battalion 358th Infantry* to report the unit happenings. It records the next few weeks as such:

> "The Battalion moved from Fort Dix on the 13th of March, 1944 to a camp "Somewhere on the east coast," in this case it was Camp Kilmer, N. J. Here the final preparations were made. March 21st the entire Battalion took a train ride to the New York Port of Embarkation."

The Battle History continues:

> "Loading the ship took up the next two days and then came the day when we all bid farewell to the Statue of Liberty on March 23rd. We saw that grand old lady a lot sooner than we had expected when our ship, the SS John Erickson, developed engine trouble about 100 miles out and had to return to port for repairs. While the trouble was being remedied, the troops stood unhappily on the decks, watching the pedestrians in the heart of New York, just a short distance away.

> "Repairs were quickly completed and the boat was on its way again on the 27th. The next 15 days passed with daily boat drills, a limited training program, and inspections helping to while away the time. There were the inevitable submarine alerts, but fortunately nothing ever materialized. The ship traveled in a very large convoy and it was indeed comforting to see aircraft carriers and destroyers

on all sides. After the first few days out, nearly everyone got over seasickness. However, no one ever could get accustomed to eating only two meals a day, and English meals at that. A small library and church services were about the only forms of recreation available and consequently the first sight of land on the 8th of April was loudly cheered."[6]

Jolly Old England

The account of the *Battle History of the Third Battalion 358th Infantry* continues to document the movement, activities and location of the unit:

"The Battalion docked in Liverpool, England on the 9th of April, 1944. On the morning of the 10th, all personnel disembarked and went by train through Warrington, Crewe and Shrewsbury to the little English town of Bewdley. From here, traveling on QM trucks, the Battalion moved about seven miles west of town to some peaceful English fields called Sturt Common. Here pyramidal tents had been setup and this Battalion, plus Regimental Headquarters set up in "Camp A."

"At Camp A the Battalion underwent an intensive training program which included speed marches, calisthenics, close order drill, squad problems and courses on the German army, equipment and language. On Saturdays, there were trips to Birmingham, Ludlow, Kidderminster and other neighboring towns. For those who were so inclined, there were six hour passes during the week nights to visit nearby pubs."[7]

From this report it is obvious the 90th Division was a part of the massive force being assembled to undertake the invasion of Europe with the daunting mission of regaining territories overrun by the Nazi juggernaut. The next available letter from Uncle Bob was written during their stay at Camp A in England. It is a letter to Mary Lea written on April 26, 1944. He gave no hint of where he was or what he was doing:

Dear Droopy and all,

I am fine. Have you been hearing from me any?

Did you and Uncle ever do anything about making a deal with Andrews? I was just wondering. I don't even remember how much money I have in the bank but it should be 6 or 700 by now anyway and I don't think I should let it pile up it should be put at some use.

I guess you should let somebody break Minnie Pearl if Herb is afraid to. I don't want her to grow up to be a mare without the proper education that a mare belonging to a McHolland should have, but be careful who you lend her to and on what terms you lend her on. I would not want to lose her but I don't want a 6 year old mare not broken even if I have to sell her.

Bob

The letter indicates that mail was probably slow in reaching him in England. Since he was not able to spend much money it appears he was thinking about investing it in land and that his Uncle John McHolland was involved in helping negotiate with someone by the name of "Andrews." In the last paragraph he refers to an unbroken mare with the name of Minnie Pearl that his cousin and farm caretaker, Herbert McHolland, is afraid or unwilling to tackle the job of breaking. Noting the difficulty Herbert apparently encountered in handling this animal, it is certain this is the same troublesome horse that Uncle Bob's young friend from Hurley, Gene Anderson, recalled him referring to as "Minnie No Brains."

TWO MORE LETTERS FROM ENGLAND

There is information available from two letters Uncle Bob would have written during his stay at Camp A near Bewdley. One was a short V-Mail letter dated May 1, 1944, addressed to Roxabel. This note was very short and contained little information. He began the letter with "Dear Sis and All, Just a few lines to let you know that I am well and feeling fine." He wrote only one more paragraph in which he related that he had run into someone who he knew from one of the CMTC camps he attended.

The other letter was written to Mary Scott Hair, his dear friend from Hurley. It was dated May 9, 1944, from "Somewhere in England" and provided a sense of the situation and a view from the younger set of the British populace about what was happening. Uncle Bob wrote:

> *"The war cry of this war is 'any gum, chum-Every English kid you see has that on his lips soon as he spots a Yank.*
>
> *"I talked with a ten year old boy about school and fighting and life in general. The boy said he would quit school and go to work in a carpet factory when he reached the ripe old age of thirteen.*

"I asked him who he thought the world's best fighter was—and he said he guessed Hitler was. Anyway, it looked that way to him."

LAST MOVEMENT IN ENGLAND AND FINAL PREPARATIONS FOR BATTLE

Within a few days Uncle Bob would be on the move again with his unit. Time for action was drawing nearer as their next move would take them to a marshalling area in southeast Wales where final preparations would be made for their part in an epic chapter of world history.

The *Battle History of the Third Battalion 358th Infantry* describes the events in this manner:

"On May 12, 1944 the Battalion moved out of Bewdley RR station and boarded another English Train. After passing through Worcester and Cheltenham we detrained at Serern Junction, just East of Bristol. From here, we moved some twelve miles by truck to a marshaling area in SE Wales. The camp was called Llanmartin and was a fairly permanent one with all troops being billeted in Niessen huts. At this camp, we dug air raid slit trenches, held innumerable TE 21's, and went on some twelve mile endurance marches. These endurance marches had to be made while wearing impregnated underwear, full packs and in addition, four hand carts per company had to be pulled. The country covered during these hikes was quite hilly.

"On Sundays, the troops were permitted to visit Newport, Cardiff and Bristol. During the week, only Newport was within pass range. The people in these towns were fairly

friendly, but had a peculiar habit of closing all amusement centers and pubs on Sundays."

It is hard to imagine what was going through Uncle Bob's mind now that the time had come when the tactical "training" situations he had become so familiar with were about to become the real thing—combat. The blank training ammunition would become real bullets that kill and the artillery simulators would become deafening bursts of searing metal fragments that maim and kill. One can be certain Uncle Bob was thinking of loved ones back home, of how he will react under fire, of the welfare and safety of his men, and a myriad of other things as the battle drew near He was a man of faith and I am certain his way of handling all of this was placing his fate in the hands of his God. Everyone knew the cost of this undertaking would be tremendously high, but few could foresee the degree of sacrifice required and the full extent of the struggle ahead.

Chapter 10 Endnotes:
1. Bryan, 4,5.
2. Telephone interview, Pemberton.
3. Personal interviews, M. Brown.
4. Personal interview, Lynna White Box, 2008.
5. Document, Official Personnel File.
6. Bryan, 5.
7. Bryan, 5.
8. Bryan, 5.

Chapter II
Normandy and the First
Month in France

From the time the United States joined the Allied cause in December, 1941, and entered World War II, discussion soon began about an invasion of the European mainland. Given the fact that the Axis forces occupied virtually all of Europe this course of action appeared to be inevitable at some point. Although woefully unprepared for war, the United States had quickly swung into action and produced the greatest war machine ever known. Seemingly impossible manning and material levels were reached in an incomprehensibly short space of time. By May of 1944 the Allies, with considerable United States assistance, had defeated the Axis forces in North Africa, Sicily, and Italy giving the Allies control of the Mediterranean region. The Russians had held their ground on the eastern front and were moving forward against the German armies. Time had come for the Allies to take the long anticipated next step. Months of diplomatic wrangling among the super powers, along with months of detailed planning, had preceded General Dwight D. Eisenhower's decision to implement Operation Overlord on June 6, 1944, D-Day.

PREPARATIONS FOR THE BIG DAY

The *Battle History of the 3rd Battalion 358th Infantry* reported preparations of the unit, which included Uncle Bob's outfit, M Company, from June 1 through the early morning of June 8 in this manner:

> "June 1st and the entire camp was restricted to area for security reasons. Final preparations were made with Battalion being divided into 33 boat groups. On June 4, 1944 the entire Battalion, less motors, moved out to a nearby railroad station. Following an hour ride which took us through Newport, we detrained just outside of Cardiff harbor. Here the Battalion boarded the Liberty ship SS Bienville. That same day the ship moved out into the Bristol Channel and dropped anchor. It was here that on the afternoon of June 6 we were informed that this was it, D-Day. Utilizing huge map blowups and detailed defense charts, the Battalion was briefed on the part it was to play. Everyone was very much excited and eager to land and get this over.

> "During June 7 the SS Bienville crossed the English Channel and moved into position off Utah Beach, arriving there early on the morning of the 8th. Then followed some anxious hours of waiting on landing craft to debark the troops, Some Jerry planes could be seen trying to strafe the beach north of us."[1]

D-DAY AND D-DAY +2

One regiment of the 90th Division, the 359th that was attached to the 4th Infantry Division, landed on D-Day, June 6, at Utah Beach. They were met with stiff enemy opposition. However, there was relatively less action to contend with at Utah Beach when compared to the other invasion areas, particularly Omaha Beach where the U. S. 1st and 29th Divisions and the 2d Ranger Battalion suffered grave numbers of casualties. Two days later on June 8, when M Company made it ashore on Normandy, Uncle Bob and his unit were still faced with treacherous conditions of constant artillery barrages, enemy strafing from the air, and a harbor containing many unexploded mines.[2]

"The Longest Day" and "Saving Private Ryan" are among the many movies that have endeavored to graphically depict the horrible face of war, as well as the enormity of the event at Normandy. But it was an intensely personal event for each individual involved and subject to his own perceptions and interpretation. One of those individuals was Hobert Winebrenner a young farm boy from northern Indiana. Hobert served as a machine gun section leader within M Company and was on the same ship with Uncle Bob, the SS Bienville, as it moved through the mine-infested waters off the Normandy shore on June 8. Hobert did not serve directly under Uncle Bob but he knew him well and wrote very complimentary things about Uncle Bob in his book, *Bootprints: An Infantryman's Walk through World War II*, co-written with Michael McCoy. In the book, Hobert provides his own unique description of his introduction to French soil on that date:

> "*Amid scattered explosions, troop ships and transports continued to consummate their unions. A fixed flow of Americans funneled onto Utah Beach. At long last, our turn arrived.*

> "*We poured over the side. Nervous soldiers awkwardly lumbered down cargo nets. No matter how nimble you might be, those things always made you look like a lummox. We packed the transport tight and cruised for shore. A steady stream of water sprayed over our heads. Scared and loaded down with gear. We chattered little and moved even less.*

> "*Because our packs would take us straight to the bottom, we first worried about being dumped into deep water …..We leapt into less than knee-deep water.*

> "*When that door went down, we scrambled out in a hurry. No one knew what to expect and we weren't about to take any chances. Getting off that beach topped everyone's list of objectives. We ran as fast as drenched clothes and oversized field packs would allow. Only blurred bootprints remained in our sandy wake.*

> "*…..About to leave Utah Beach behind, I took one last look. What a mess! The whole thing resembled a junkyard, mired in tow to ten feet of water. Although the dead and wounded had largely been removed, wreckage was strewn everywhere.*"[3]

Sergeant Hobert Winebrenner, Heavy Machine Gun Section Leader, M Co., 358th Infantry, somewhere in France, 1944— courtesy Hobert Winebrenner.

Granting there could be some exceptions, but many of those participating in this epic chapter of history, including Uncle Bob, would likely agree with the scene and portrayal of events of that day as described by Hobert Winebrenner and Mike McCoy. By the end of this day the whole of the 90th Division would be off the beach and in an assembly area readying for their first toe to toe battles with the enemy.

A BRIEF LETTER HOME

Somehow in the midst of the confusing scenario of June 8, Uncle Bob found the time to write a letter to his sister, Roxabel. It was a short and hastily prepared note that could have been penned on the ship in the hours off shore while preparing for the landing or, perhaps, it was written later in the evening when the unit reached their assembly area further inland. In consideration of inconsistent and delayed mail deliveries, it appeared he wanted to be sure she knew he had heard from her. He wrote, "Just a few lines while I have time. I received a letter from you today." He also mentioned he had received a letter from cousin Raymond McHolland who was an MP in North Africa. He wrote a couple more short sentences in which he was obviously commenting on a couple of items about acquaintances around Hurley that Roxabel had written about in her letter. Following censorship rules of the army, Uncle Bob gave no hint in the letter of where he was or what he had been doing.

A RUDE WELCOME TO FRANCE-- THE HEDGEROWS

During the next few days Uncle Bob would be directing his machine gun platoon in support of the division mission that was to aid in sealing off the Cotentin Peninsula and prevent German reinforcements from being supplied from that area. After moving through the village of Chef-Du-Pont and across the Merderet River, the 358th Infantry Regiment was assigned the mission of taking the small French towns of Picauville and Pont L'Abbe. [4] It was from Chef-Du-Pont to Picauville that the infamous French hedgerows were first encountered. The difficult task ahead was described in *Peragimus, "'We Accomplish": A Brief History of the 358th Infantry Regiment"*:

> "..... *The famous hedgerow country of Normandy raised itself as the ugly, bitter battlefield on which the 358th Infantry was to fight some of its bloodiest battles. Each hedge was another line of defense for the Jerry. Prominent also was the sunken roads where the unforgettable odor of the dark Normandy soil was most noticeable.....This, indeed was a new type of fighting, and for a time the hedgerow proved a difficult obstacle. Soon, however, the Infantry learned to overcome this obstacle and drive the German from his hedgerow home. Normandy exacted its bloody toll and the plodding Infantry moved on, day after day, from hedgerow to hedgerow."* [5]

A TOUGH INTRODUCTION TO
BATTLE FOR THE 90TH

The action to secure Pont L'Abbe began on June 10 and continued through June 14 when after an intensive struggle with many casualties suffered, the Germans finally began to retreat. From June 15 through June 18 the 3rd Battalion of the 358th continued their attack against stiff German resistance through Gourbesville and Le Calais chasing the retreating Germans and halting at Colomby on June 18. Although they had the Germans in their sector on the run, the 90th Division had taken many more casualties. *The Battle History of the Third Battalion 358th Infantry* reported, "By the 19th of June the enemy resistance in front of the Division had decreased perceptively and so the entire Division went into a defensive line across the base of the Cotentin peninsula while Cherbourg was being taken."[6]

I must note that the 90th Division has come under criticism for its performance during the Cotentin peninsula operation. Their division commander was summarily relieved during this period. It is important to note that the mission of the 90th was a very difficult one under any circumstances as it involved a frontal attack on the enemy occupying well-prepared positions. Although high casualty rates were sustained, it was the 90th's perseverance and determination against the German dogged resistance that allowed two other army divisions, the 9th Infantry and the 82nd Airborne, to execute an enveloping action that cut off the Cotentin Peninsula and allowed the 4th, 9th, and 79th Divisions to ultimately take the important port city of Cherbourg. [7] The 90th had done its part in this first major action and would be better prepared for the next one. In fact, as the war progressed, General George S. Patton was "outspoken in his compliments to the (90th) Division and in his belief in our excellence, "when asked to designate one division for a Presidential Unit Citation, he chose the 90th"[8]

A Reflection on The First Days of Battle

I suspect that Hobert Winebrenner spoke for many others, including Uncle Bob and his M Company buddies, as he described the situation during these days, "Today, if given the chance to describe Normandy in one phrase, I'd shout, 'Violent mass confusion!' But back then I never fully grasped the extent of the chaos surrounding me. Lines lay disconnected and flanks, wide open. The Germans not only fought in front of us, but also in back. Opposing pockets waged tiny wars all over the battlefield—all over the peninsula. No one, anywhere, was truly safe."[9] This was their first exposure to such devastation and human carnage. They saw close friends blown apart in front of them and others badly maimed with terrible injuries. This was the brutal reality of war but it was only the beginning—many more tough times were to come.

A Break in the Action and Taking Time to Write Home

A badly needed break in action lay ahead for the 90th Division. From June 18 through June 30, Uncle Bob's parent unit, the 3rd Battalion, 358th Infantry set up a defensive line along the Madeleine River, between Baupte and Appeville.[10] During this period things were much quieter, but patrolling continued to be conducted, much of it behind enemy lines. It was during this period that Uncle Bob took the time to write a couple of letters to Mary Lea and another to his friend Mary Scott Hair.

His first letter was short and expressed relief that he had made it though the first few days of battle. He also recognized the high quality of the men in his unit:

France
24 June 44

Dear Sis,

Just a few lines to let you know I am well after my first tussel with the Hun. I'm not afraid of the Hun but I sure do respect him. He's a lousy shot thank goodness.

I've sure got some fine men in my outfit. A fellow sure can be surprised in a man. I have been several times already. A good soldier is worth his weight in gold.

How do you like school? I guess it is the same old grind. If you need money just draw from mine and your account and keep track of it if you want to. Did you ever get the well started? If I ever get paid again I'll send some more money.

Bro Bob

The second letter, also to Mary Lea (Droop the Drip), written two days later was longer and newsier with his sense of humor still in evidence.

June 26, 1944
France

Dear Droop the Drip,

How's my little sis? Enclosed please find a couple of more chances for a husband that you have now missed. By the way, chances for this type of husband is decreasing every day. They were a couple of "Drips" anyhow. I've got a feeling that them "fellers" don't like us. They act terribly unfriendly toward us. Kindly like "Revenuers and Moonshiners" love for each other,

I don't know whether it is proper for me to send this home but I found it on the battle field with no identification.

What you said about the Ration Office just goes to show you Great Minds runs on the same course. If Madam Curie hadn't discovered radium Dean or I would have, see.

You asked about that $100 that was just my regular monthly allotment. I made my account jointly with you so you could draw from it. If I wanted anything done or you needed anything or if something happened to me you would have the money without probate. There should be around 7 or 8 hundred $s in my account.

I want more land if I can get it. If not I want a barn and have the house fixed up. I'll send the money extra for the well. If I ever get a payday I should have enough to pay for the well without drawing from the account. So let me know just how much money I have to my part of the account. If you need any use it. You are welcome to it but I'd like to know how I stand financially. Be on the lookout *for some land because I save over $100 a month now.*

If we get a good well at the house you can get a pump for it.

Tell Dimp and Bug hello for me. Write soon and often.

I got a letter from Bro and Eva. Everette looked just about as comfortable in his sailor suit as a baby on a briar.

> *Good bye for now,*
> *Bob*

Two German soldiers, this photo was included in Uncle Bob's June 24 letter to Mary Lea—courtesy Wiley-McHolland family.

Along with teasing his sister about the young German gentlemen in the photograph, Uncle Bob passed on information about his pay situation and instructions on how to handle things. After what he had been through he was still thinking about the future as he indicated again that he wanted to invest some of his money in land and to get a new well and pump for the farm.

With regard to his comment about "great minds' it is not known for certain which Dean friend he was referring to, but it had to be either Edwin or Dale "Rip." At the end of the letter he could not pass up the chance to add the comment about his brother Everette. Everette was in his early thirties when he was drafted into the navy. Uncle Bob had earlier indicated his concern about Everette's fitness for duty with a combat unit.

Uncle Bob got very serious in the letter he wrote to Mary Scott Hair and expressed some of his deeply held beliefs. It was dated June 26, 1944 from "Somewhere in France":

> *"I am enclosing some pictures I found on the battlefield. I did not take them from a dead German—the Krauts carry picture of their loved ones, too. Any personal belongings such as letters and pictures are scattered like leaves after a battle.*

> *"I studied these pictures carefully. This one of the little boy and his mother—there will be no swastikas for him. He will have a chance to grow up in a free world where he can think for himself, a free man.*

> *"Not only for Jerry , Bobby, Johnny and Thomas Earl, but for any children and for all people everywhere, will our sacrifices be made—that they may live the 'Abundant Life' due them.*

> *'I firmly believe that peace will triumph over war and that love will rule the world."*

Somewhere along the line the pictures Uncle Bob sent back with the letter have been lost, but even with the tough days he had already experienced he reveals an optimistic view of the outcome of the struggle. It is particularly touching that he specifically mentions his four nephews in expressing his hope for the future.

CONTINUING PREPARATIONS FOR BATTLE

The twelve days along the Madeleine River at the end of June offered some time for the units of the 358th Infantry to regroup, but there was always much to be done and little time for rest. The brief history of the 358th, *Peragimus, "We Accomplish"* described these days in this way:

> *"While in this location, meager comforts were made available to the fighting men. Some were able to use a blanket in their foxholes, the first bit of cover since the landing on the Normandy beach; and some received hot "chow" for the first time. However the gallant and courageous actions did not cease, for many patrols were dispatched to penetrate deep into enemy lines. The patrols that came back were frequently badly mauled, but vital information was obtained, and the great courage of the officers and men who fearlessly entered enemy lines is beyond description. At night there was the familiar drone of "Bed Check Charlie", and frequently – almost always, the chronic harassment of enemy artillery came screeching and screaming overhead and detonated with a loud, terrifying explosion that shook the very earth."[11]*

"Bed Check Charlie" was the name the GIs gave to the German's low flying reconnaissance plane that was heard almost every night in its mission to gain surveillance data.

Award of Combat Infantryman Badge

The first of Uncle Bob's combat awards came after these first few weeks of intensive combat. Records show he was awarded the Combat Infantryman Badge with an effective date of July 1, 1944.[12] This badge is an infantryman's mark of honor and is awarded to an army infantry soldier "personally present and under hostile fire while serving in an assigned infantry or special forces primary duty, in a unit actively engaged in ground combat with the enemy."[13] Given his duties as machine gun platoon leader and knowing what has been documented about the activities of his unit during this period, there is no doubt that he fully met the requirements for the award.

Duty Changes On the Horizon

By late June, 1944, the city of Cherbourg, and more importantly, its port, was under Allied control and the area of the Cotentin Peninsula secured. The Allies would now focus their sights toward the south where they would continue to battle it out with the tenacious German occupation forces, bent on carrying out the Fuhrer's orders to hold their ground at all costs. The 90th Division would be among the units thrust into the middle of this action. As a consequence, the turbulent times ahead would result in some hasty changes in assignments for Uncle Bob within a short period of time.

Chapter 11 Endnotes:

1. Bryan, 5-6.
2. Bryan, 6.
3. Hobert Winebrenner, Mike McCoy, Bootprints: An Infantryman's Walk Through World War II (Albion, IN: Camp Comamajo Press, 2005), 19-20.
4. Bryan, 6-7.
5. U. S. Army, Peragimus, *We Accomplish";A Brief History of the 358th Infantry (Weiden, Germany: Ferdinand NIckl, 1945), 6.
6. Bryan, 7-8.
7. Colby, 85.
8. Colby, 159.
9. Winebrenner and McCoy, 57.
10. Bryan, 8.
11. Peragimus, 7.
12. Documents, Official Personnel File.
13. Website: www.tioh.hqda.pentagon.mil/Badges/CombatInfantryman-Badges.htm.

Chapter 12
K Company--A New Challenge

The Normandy invasion had been a success in the sense that the Allies had established a beachhead from which several divisions, along with tons of supplies, could get ashore and keep moving ahead. However, once ashore, progress was slower than the planners had projected, mainly due to the stiff resistance of the German forces.[1] July, 1944, arrived with more tough days of fighting ahead as the forces turned their attention southward and moved into action through the remainder of the hedgerows and into the marshes of northern France. It would be almost another month before the anticipated "breakout" into more open country would be achieved.

The first two weeks of July, 1944, would bring even more intensive combat action for Uncle Bob along with turmoil regarding his official duty assignments. One familiar with the tactical mission and situation of the 90th Division at this point can readily discern a relationship between these two factors. On July 3, the division was assigned the mission of capturing the Foret de Mont Castre (Hill 122). This hill was the dominant terrain feature in the area and anchored the German's main line of resistance known as the Mahlman Line.[2] The next ten days would be among the toughest times the division would go through in the war.

TOUGH GOING ENCOUNTERED WITH THE SOUTHWARD ACTION

Uncle Bob would have been experiencing the severe conditions encountered by his parent unit, the 358th Infantry. The harsh weather, tough enemy resistance, and heavy casualties suffered from July 3 through July 8 are described in *Peragimus, We Accomplish:*

"On July 3rd, a memorable day in the battle of France, the Division launched an attack southwest against a strong enemy line defended by determined, fanatical paratroopers and SS men. On the first day of the attack, the rains came and the damp dismal weather of the succeeding days made the battle one of the most unforgettable in history. Casualties were heavy and communications and supply were hampered by heavy enemy shelling. The 2nd Battalion charged through to Les Sablons, bypassed it, and continued south, while the First Battalion fought for St. Jores. The Third Battalion, initially in reserve, moved up to Les Sablons to clean out the town and tie in with a Second Battalion. These were days that put a man's courage and strength to the most severe test – days that did not end with nightfall, but dragged on incessantly through daylight and darkness, with rain and mist that apparently would never cease. Hard fighting continued until the Division faced a

*great hill covered with deep woods that rose from the land
like a powerful giant and engulfed all who were so bold to
enter."* [3]

The biggest job was yet to come. The actions during
these five days had merely positioned them for their primary mission—the taking of Foret de Mont Castre (Hill
122).

THE FORET DE MONT CASTRE--HILL 122

The control of Hill 122 was vital to the Allies success because of its strategic position and features. It was a small
mountain that rose quickly to about 500 feet above sea
level. From its top the Atlantic Ocean could be observed
from both sides of the peninsula and one could see all the
way north to Normandy. Not only was the hill very steep
and covered with heavy woods and vegetation, but it was
heavily fortified with well trained, entrenched German
troops.[4] Fighting for control of the hill raged from July
8 through July 11. An example of the fierceness of the
battle is shown in the shocking number of losses suffered
by the 3rd Battalion, 358th Infantry. Battalion strength
in early afternoon of July 10 was 19 officers and 563 enlisted men. By the end of the day the battalion had lost
11 officers and 343 enlisted men, leaving only 8 officers
and 220 enlisted men to fight.[5] One report had it that
only three officers of the 3rd Battalion were not killed
or wounded in the battle.[6] Uncle Bob's first company
commander, Captain John Marsh of M Company, was
among the many brave men that gave their lives to take
this god-forsaken piece of ground. Captain Marsh was
awarded the Army's second highest combat decoration
for his heroic actions in the battle, the Distinguished Ser-

vice Cross.[7] Although the capture of this hill, late on July 11, was a monumental struggle for all battalions of the 358th Infantry, the performance of the 3rd Battalion was deemed so exceptional that it was awarded the highly coveted Presidential Unit Citation for its pivotal part in breaking the German resistance. [8]

MOVEMENT TO THE SEVES RIVER

By July 12 the woefully short-handed 3rd Battalion,358th Infantry had driven the remaining Germans off of Hill 122. At this point the battalion consisted of only four officers, one of whom was Uncle Bob, and 126 enlisted men in the three rifle companies or about one fourth the size of a full strength battalion. Ahead of the battalion lay the Seves River across which the Germans had withdrawn to set up another line of resistance. *The Battle History of the Third Battalion 358th Infantry* reported the battalion's next movement, "Between the 12th and 15th, the Battalion moved up to the Seves River where a defensive line was set up. Finally, on 15 July 1944 this Battalion went into Division reserve in the town of Gorges. Here some very sorely needed replacements were received, showers and new clothes were provided and hot chow was served."[9]

DUTY CHANGES AMID THE CONFUSION OF COMBAT

Given the combat conditions and high rate of casualties in the division during the first days of July, 1944, one might expect much confusion in unit personnel assignments and strength accountability. The extreme circumstances probably account for the duty changes that occurred to

Uncle Bob during this short space of time. According to his personnel records and personnel change data, Uncle Bob was still a part of M Company, 3rd Battalion, 358th as the division operations began on July 3. On July 4 the records show that he was assigned to D Company (like M Company a heavy weapons company), in another battalion, the 1st Battalion, 358th Infantry, with duty as the company Executive Officer. The Executive Officer serves as the primary assistant to the company commander so in a sense this would have been considered a promotion. However, within three days Uncle Bob would be reassigned again. This time he would be assigned back to the 3rd Battalion in one of the line rifle companies; K Company.[10] The casualties being incurred in the fight for Hill 122 would certainly be cause for these rapid changes.

Records reflect that Uncle Bob was officially assigned to K Company on July 8, 1944. This would indicate that he was assigned just as the battle for Hill 122 began. Emmett Boyd, who was the Weapons Platoon Sergeant for K Company cannot pinpoint the exact date that he remembered Uncle Bob becoming the K Company commander, but he believes it was just after the battle for Hill 122.[11] Considering the dire need for replacements, it is possible that he became a part of K Company, first as a platoon leader or executive officer replacement during the battle for Hill 122, and that he would have been named company commander as the company was filled and reformed after Hill 122 was secured.[9]

Assumption of Command--K Company

A document found in Uncle Bob's personnel record confirms that he took over K Company on or about July 15,

1944, in Gorges and further described the dire circumstances he faced with the decimated company:

> *"Company K at this time had just been through the heavy engagement in the Foret de Mont Castre and had lost all its officers and non-commissioned officers as well as over one hundred enlisted men. Upon Lt. McHolland's assumption of command, the company had but fifteen enlisted men, all privates first class and privates. (Author's note: This statement was not completely accurate as Emmett Boyd, the Weapons Platoon Sergeant survived this battle.) None of these men were the original men which landed in Normandy on 8 June 1944. (Author's note: again, not a completely accurate statement.) Within the next few days, Lt. McHolland received five replacement officers and over 100 enlisted men replacements, a handful of whom were non-commissioned officers. With such a meager cadre for an organization, Lt. McHolland set about in a few days time, to train a rifle company which subsequently became the most aggressive one in the organization."* [12]

Much more would be heard from K Company in the coming months under Uncle Bob's capable leadership.

TAKING TIME TO WRITE A QUICK NOTE HOME

Uncle Bob was obviously pleased with being given the command of a rifle company as he wrote about it to his sister Mary Lea. The letter is undated but was obviously written after the battle for Hill 122. It was most likely on or about July 15, in Gorges when the battalion was placed in division reserve. [13] He wrote:

Dear Sis and All,

I've just pulled through another battle and I am O.K. I am now commanding K Company for the time being.

I'll be O.K. but I don't have much time to write. This business of war is never dull but it is oftimes discouraging.

I still haven't ever got paid so I can't send any money home. I haven't been paid for three months. My allotment is coming through I guess.

If you get a good stream of water at the house make a water tank.

As Ever,
Bob

He gives a vague hint of the horrors of war he had experienced and is concerned that he has not been kept informed of his pay situation. He then provides some more instructions about what to do about the water situation on the farm. With more action ahead it would be a while before they would hear from him again.

A ROCK-SOLID NONCOMMISSIONED OFFICER--EMMETT BOYD

The name of a key member of K Company, Emmett Boyd, surfaced in a previous paragraph as the date Uncle Bob assumed command of the company was being established. Emmett would occupy a very important position in K Company; that of Weapons Platoon Sergeant. An

infantry rifle company consisted of three rifle platoons and one weapons platoon. The rifle platoons were made up of the infantrymen armed with M-1 and Browning Automatic Rifles. The weapons platoon consisted of teams with .30 cal. light machine guns and the "artillery" of the company, .60 MM mortars. In the words of Emmett Boyd, "The machine guns were normally attached to the lead rifle platoon and the mortars were used to set up positions to knock out German machine gun nests and concentrations of their troops."[14]   Given the continuing shortage of officers at company level, particularly those who would fill the weapons platoon leader position, Emmett, as weapons platoon sergeant, would find himself serving as weapons platoon leader for much of the time. In that position he got to know Uncle Bob well as he reported directly to him as the company commander. Emmett would serve in one or the other of these positions throughout Uncle Bob's service with K Company.[15]
15

Emmett Boyd was barely twenty one years of age when he was assigned responsibility as K Company weapons platoon sergeant. Emmett was one of the many soldiers sent overseas to fill the units who would be participating in the Normandy invasion. Initially, he understood he was to be assigned to the 4th Infantry Division, which landed on Utah Beach on D-Day, but his orders were changed and he ended up with the 90th Infantry Division. This assignment came during the first week of July, 1944, as preparations were being made for the unit's memorable assault on Foret de Mont Castre (Hill 122). [16]

Born and raised in the green rolling hills of east Texas, Emmett Boyd graduated from high school in Athens,

Emmett Boyd, Weapons Platoon Sergeant, K Co., 3rd Battalion, 358th Infantry— courtesy Captain Emmett T. Boyd, U. S. Army, retired.

Texas, at the age of sixteen. Upon his graduation in 1939, Emmett overcame a couple of minor obstacles to join the Texas National Guard. Conveniently he lied about his age to surmount the first hurdle. The other problem involved his weight. The regulations required that an enlistee weigh a minimum of 120 pounds. Emmett only weighed 110 pounds sopping wet. Emmett relates that a kindly old doctor, administering the physical examination, said that "if he wanted to get in that badly he would show his weight at 120 pounds." With this benevolent gesture Emmett became an underage, underweight member of the Texas National Guard's 36th Infantry Division.[17]

Emmett Boyd entered on active duty with the 36th Infantry Division when it was activated at Camp Bowie, Texas, in November, 1940. Emmett's parent unit within the division was the 144th Infantry Regiment. With the army reorganizing its division structure the 144th Infantry Regiment was pulled from the 36th Infantry Division in on December 8, 1941, established as a separate unit, moved to Fort Lewis, Washington, and assigned the important mission of guarding the northern portion of the west coast of the United States. Emmett moved up the ranks to the position of Technical Sergeant with the regiment while the unit's mission and location changed many times from December, 1941, until April, 1944. Among the duty locations he served were Camp Bowie, Texas; Fort Lewis, Washington; Santa Rosa, California; Wilmington, North Carolina; Key West, Florida; and Camp Van Dorn, Mississippi. It was in April, 1944, at Camp Dorn, Mississippi, where the regiment was virtually stripped of its force—about 1700 of its men were re-assigned as overseas replacements. With D-Day rapidly approaching, the War Department was anticipating the need for many replacements once the ground action began in France. Emmett was among a group of non-commissioned officers in the ranks of Staff Sergeant, Technical Sergeant, and Master Sergeant who were tapped for overseas assignment. He was assigned to Fort Meade, Maryland for overseas processing and would find himself with K Company in early July. [18]

THE SEVES RIVER AND "THE ISLAND"

After the time spent in division reserve at Gorges, Uncle Bob would lead K Company in his first action as commander as it moved to the Seves River on July 19 and set up a defensive line facing the Island of Seves. The "Island" was a marshy area of land between two branches of the Seves River occupied by a substantial number of dug-in German troops .[19] Emmett Boyd remembers moving out to the front of the island "where we dug in, preparing for an assault across the Seves River and marshes to rout the Germans in and around a little village of St. Germain Sur Seves. I was beginning to believe they formed our division as marsh rats to fight in the bogs and marshes."[20]

A document from Uncle Bob's personnel record describes the actions of K Company during the days after he took command of the company in Gorges through the Seves River operation; "After approximately five days of training in the vicinity of Gorges, the 3rd Battalion moved into a defensive position just north of the Seves River near Gomfreville, France, and remained there for approximately ten days. Company K, while well dug in, suffered five to ten casualties per day from heavy German artillery concentrations. With the inexperienced personnel in his company, Lt McHolland was faced with a problem of preventing his men from straggling, a problem which called for very active and aggressive leadership on his part." [21]

Emmett Boyd vividly described his situation during this period by the Seves River, "We were under constant shelling for about three days. Several of our new men were hit and killed there. We would start digging our foxhole at the edge of the hedgerow and dig under it. ... After about three days of this, the whole area was beginning to smell real bad, from the dead. Lt. McHolland, our new Company Commander, a brave but sensitive man, crawled up to my fox hole and asked how things were going. He couldn't believe that my only problem was the smell from the dead lying all around us. I still today wonder why I was so insensitive at the time."[22]   Emmett was impressed with Uncle Bob's leadership from the beginning as he related, "He was always so calm, never excited, like a rock."[23]

HEROIC CHAPLAINS--AN UNEXPECTED TRUCE

Emmett went on to provide his perspective of a surreal incident which occurred at a point in the heat of the Seves "Island" battle that profoundly affected both the

Germans and Americans and ultimately got the attention of the U. S. Press. Emmett saw it this way; "We asked for, and the Germans agreed, to let us have a three hour truce to remove the dead and wounded. It was such a nice feeling to get out of that hole under the hedgerow and walk around a little bit. The medics came up for the wounded and Graves Registration came to pick up the dead. After the truce, we got poised to make our attack across the marshes." [24]

Uncle Bob also noted this event in a letter written a few weeks later to his friend, Mary Scott Hair, in which he hinted that more details would be coming about the part played by the battalion chaplain, Captain Edgar Stohler of the Salvation Army. He told Mary to watch for the chaplain's story in the paper. A while later the story was reported by the Associated Press in this way:

> *"With the Americans in Normandy, July 23 (Delayed) AP: Three American chaplains seeking out wounded under fire in a marshy no-man's land brought a spontaneous cessation of hostilities in this bloody sector for three hours today.*

> *"During the brief armistice the Germans came out and directed the chaplains and the litter bearers to the wounded.*

> *"Principals of the episode were Chaplain Joseph J. Esser, Catholic, Cleveland, Minn.; Edgar H. Stohler, Spavinaw, Okla., Salvation Army; and James M. Hamilton, Ft. Worth, Tex, Disciples of Christ.*

> *"Defying fire from both sides and our strafing planes overhead they went into the marsh holding aloft Red Cross*

flags, succoring a man here, another there.

"The enemy was impressed by the bravery of these men of the cloth and stopped shooting. Soon guns of both sides fell silent except the artillery in the rear.

"The chaplains were met in no-man's land by a German officer and through a German-speaking American removal of the wounded was arranged.

"While the little group was negotiating, a German cam-eraman came out and snapped pictures of them.

"Within a few minutes after the chaplains reached an aid station the deathlike silence was broken over the battlefield. The Germans had started shooting again and the fight was on." [25]

The Germans finally succumbed to the relentless pressure of the 358th Infantry Regiment as they had withdrawn from the "Island" by July 27, leaving their calling cards in the form of mines and booby traps. *The Battle History of the Third Battalion 358th Infantry* reported the next movement was, "across the "Island" through Les Milleries across the Tautel River and on down to an assembly area near Cathelmais, France. It was here that the Battalion saw its first movie and first USO show since landing in France."[26]

It was likely during this short break in the action that Uncle Bob took time to write to his brother Everette who was now in the Navy in California:

26 July
1944

My Dear Bro,

*I am always glad to hear from you and look fwd to get-
ting letters. I am not in a position where I can be prompt
about writing.*

*I now command K Company so I guess you know how
busy that makes me besides the trouble that the Jerries gives
me.'*

I guess you heard about "Dinner" Dean.

*These "Krauts" scares the dickens out of me—but it
sure pays to be afraid at times. As the "Good Book" says
there is time for all things. Don't worry about my nerves
though because look at this hand writing—I am as steady
as the "Rock."*

*My knees kneels only to God but they shake for almost
anyone.*

Good Luck, Good Cheer, Keep the Faith,

Bob

Uncle Bob's reference to "Dinner" Dean, his good Hurley and CMTC buddy from Hurley, Dale "Rip" Dean,
was about the news that he had been killed in action
serving with the 82nd Airborne Division at Normandy.
Along with his humor, he expressed his abiding faith in
the Almighty.

A BREAKTHROUGH IS IMMINENT

After two months of fighting through the hedgerows and marshes of the Cotentin Peninsula area Uncle Bob and K Company would be a part of the breakthrough, and of what the history of the 358th, *Peragimus,* *"We Accomplish"* termed "The Race to Le Mans," "The Normandy defense had been cracked, Jerry was broken and running, and the sky was filled with friendly air power as the tanks of the Third Army rolled toward Avranches. The prison-like hedgerows of Normandy were left behind and before them lay the open, rolling terrain of interior France. The ensuing days brought lightning fast maneuvers, and the 358th Infantry became a leading element in the 90th Division's race across France." [27] K Company of the 3rd Battalion, 358th Infantry, under Uncle Bob's command, would be an integral part of this action.

Chapter 12 Endnotes:
1. B. H. Liddell Hart, History of the Second World War (Old Saybrook, CT: Konecky & Konecky, 1970), 543.
2. Colby, 89.
3. Peragimus, 8.
4. Colby (Falvey), 98.
5. Colby (Lefauvre, National Archives), 117.
6. Colby (Falvey), 117.
7. Winebrenner and McCoy, 86.
8. Colby, 118.
9. Bryan, 11.
10. Documents, Official Personnel File.
11. Telephone interviews, CPT Emmett T. Boyd, 2008

12. Document, Official Personnel File.
13. Bryan, 11.
14. CPT Emmett T. Boyd, World War II Experiences of Emmett T. Boyd, Captain USA Ret (Unpublished), 2.
15. Telephone interviews, Boyd.
16. Telephone interviews, Boyd.
17. Telephone interviews, Boyd.
18. Telephone interviews, Boyd.
19. Bryan, 11.
20. Boyd, 3.
21. Document, Official Personnel File.
22. Boyd, 4.
23. Telephone interviews, Boyd.
24. Boyd, 4.
25. Colby (Indianapolis Star, AP article), 142-143.
26. Bryan, 12.
27. Peragimus, 11.

Chapter 13
Moving Across France--
K Company Becomes a "Force"

It took about a month longer than the planners had en-visioned, but by the end of July 1944 the Allies had at-tained control of the Normandy area of northern France. The British Second Army had taken Caen in the eastern sector of the front while General Omar Bradley's First U.S. Army had overcome the worst of the hedgerow coun-try and Germans and pushed through to Lessay, Periers, and St. Lo in the west.[1]   Significant changes occurred in the Allied forces structure on August 1, 1944, in readying for the push across France.[2]   As a result of these changes, the 90th Division came under control of the newly formed Third U.S. Army, commanded by none other than Lt. Gen. George S. Patton.[3]   On the same day Patton as-sumed command, Uncle Bob's K Company would be on the move southward along with the rest of the division and Third Army toward Avranches and more open country. Rapid movement and quick-hitting action would be the norm of Patton's Third Army for the coming weeks.[4]

Bravery at Ste. Hilaire du Harcouet

The following account by Brig. Gen. William G. Weaver, Deputy Commander of the 90th Division, sets up the situation for the action that occurred on August 2 in Ste. Hilaire du Harcouet in which Uncle Bob and K Company played critical roles:

> *"On this date (1 Aug 44) the division came under orders of XV Corps, Third Army, to move south by motor through the Coutances-Avranches gap. Thence its course would be to block the enemy between the See and Seleune rivers; to protect the dams on the Seleune river from Ste. Hilaire (du Harcouet) to Avranches; to seize and secure the bridge over the Seleune at Ste. Hilaire (du Harcourt); and to capture Lauvigne and connect with the 79th Division to the southwest.*
>
> *"Ste. Hilaire (du Harcouet) and Lauvigne were captured by a task force commanded by Lt. Col. Chris Clarke, 358th Inf. By a tank attack followed by a company of foot troops (K Company, 3rd Battalion, 358th Infantry), Clarke seized the Seleune river bridge before it could be demolished by the enemy...."* [5]

The outstanding performance of K Company was a key determining factor in the success of the operation at Ste. Hilaire du Harcouet. A document from Uncle Bob's personnel record describes the situation encountered by K Company at St. Hilaire du Harcourt and Uncle Bob's profound impact in the resulting action:

> *"... The town was thinly held by one or two platoons of Germans who had fields of fire for 400 yards across an*

open valley. The Germans, in this instance, withheld their fire until Company K men were at about two hundred yards range and then opened up with many machine guns. Under the sudden fire, Lt. McHolland's men reacted with the aggressiveness of veterans and rushed the town, completely overrunning the German force, capturing and annihilating them. Under Lt. McHolland's aggressive leadership, the company then continued on to mop up the town. This first attack of Company K portrays how Lt. McHolland, with but a meager cadre of men, had by his own leadership and aggressiveness converted them into an aggressive and fighting organization." [6]

SILVER STAR--FIRST AWARD

Uncle Bob was awarded the Silver Star for his part in the action at Ste. Hilaire du Harcouet. In a statement recommending the award, the battalion commander, Lt. Col. J. W. Bealke, Jr. stated, "The success of the attack was due largely to the utter disregard of his own personal safety displayed by Lt. McHolland." The citation for the award read:

"1st Lt. Robert B. McHolland, 0-43315, Co. K. 358th Infantry, while serving with the Army of the United States, distinguished himself by gallantry in action. On 2 August at St. Hilaire, France, Lt. McHolland commanded the advance guard company during the advance on St. Hilaire. Finding that the route to St. Hilaire led across a bridge defended by the enemy Lt. McHolland personally led the major portion of his company in a dash across the bridge in the face of enemy fire. The leadership and prompt action of Lt. McHolland was an inspiration to the men of his command and his fast movement resulted in the early capture of the town." [7]

Captain Mac

A QUICK LETTER TO SISTER EVA

Even with the hot and heavy action of that day, Uncle Bob found time to write a short V-mail letter to his sister, Eva. Based on information contained in *the Battle History Third Battalion 358th Infantry,* the town, Ste. Hilaire du Harcouet was secured by 1500 (3 pm) and "the rest of the battalion closed in around the town and prepared to stay for the night. Everyone was fairly well settled when suddenly an order was received to move out at 1800 (6 pm) ...."[8] It must have been sometime during this short break that he wrote this letter:

2 August 1944

My Dear Sis,

I am glad to hear from you so often. I received about three of your letters today so I decided to write.

I really don't have so much time to write in fact it's a full time job with plenty of overtime with no extra pay either. But nobody can pay us for what we do except with kindness and appreciation for what we've done and doing.

Don't worry too much about me. I'll be O.K. no matter what happens. As our Chaplain said "Just because you fail is no sign the Lord wasn't with you." If my soul is safe no harm can come to me at all.

Your baby Bro
Bob

One would never suspect the life and death struggle he had been through merely hours before during that same day. It is apparent the words of battalion Chaplain

242

Stohler were a great comfort to him as he faced the possibility of death every minute of the day.

LONG MARCHES ACROSS FRANCE IN AUGUST

When the battalion moved out at 1800 (6 pm) on August 2, it moved about ten miles through the darkness of night to secure another road center, Louvigne. Louvigne was taken by 1 am the next morning. Because of a bombed out bridge, the battalion remained in this area until August 5 when it began a very long march as reported in *the Battle History Third Battalion 358th Infantry*:

> *"Then on the 5th of August the Battalion began its longest foot march—covering 25 miles the first day, 17 miles the second day, and 20 miles the third day, arriving at St Suzanne by dark of the 7th. This foot march was broken only once because a bridge was out over the Mayenne river, so the troops went swimming there. Enemy action during the three days consisted of about five rounds of tank fire received in St. Suzanne. The entire 62 mile march was made during days of intense heat and over extremely dusty roads."* [9]

BATTLEFIELD MEETING WITH AN OLD FRIEND

The rapid movement of the entire Third Army continued as the 3rd Battalion, 358th Infantry was moved 22 miles to the east by trucks on August 8 to Degre near the Sarthe River. After a bridge was established over the river the unit moved to another assembly area about five miles north of Le Mans where they remained until August 12.[10] It was sometime during this period that Uncle Bob and an M Company friend, Sgt. Hobert Winebrenner, a Machine Gun Section leader, had a chance encounter in the midst of the constant activity and movement. Hobert recounted the story of this meeting in his book, *Bootprints: An Infantryman's Walk through World War II* in this manner;

> *"I took charge of a machine-gun section on our battalion's right flank. On one memorable occasion, we stopped at a T-road intersection. Per orders, I fanned out my crews and positioned their guns with excellent fields of fire. But due to our ceaseless movement, I chose not to dig them in. It was a decision I'd shortly come to regret.*

> *"1st Lieutenant Robert McHolland pulled up in a jeep. I'd known him a long time and liked him much. Everyone did. Respected and well-loved by the troops, he was a man's man, who didn't play games or put on airs—just took care of business....*

> *"Maybe more than anything else, McHolland had a quiet charisma about him. While many officers clamored just to hear the sound of their own voices, he chose his words sparingly. Consequently, when he spoke, everyone listened.*

> *"I assumed that he wanted to talk of our next objective. To orchestrate movements between heavy weapons sections and the rifle units, the officers in our battalion often straddled platoon and company lines.*

> *"Yet on that occasion, I was wrong. For not digging in my guns, McHolland read me the riot act. I privately wondered if I had a sign attached to my ass reading, 'Chew here!' Between him and Patton (who had dressed him down earlier in the day), they left little for anyone else."* [11]

Hobert tried to explain that everyone was moving too fast to dig in, but Uncle Bob would have nothing of it telling him, "Anytime we stop, I want your men digging in! This is a standing order that I expect to be followed! It's for your own good! Got it?" [12]

About that time an explosion occurred in their area that both men quickly reacted to investigate. After doing all they could to check things out Hobert and Uncle Bob returned to the intersection. Hobert explained, "There were no hard feelings. That wasn't the first time, nor would it be the last that he straightened me out. I probably needed it. And in some ways, I'm sure his advice helped me survive." [13]

Northward Movement to Encircle the Enemy--Closing the Falaise Gap

On August 12, the 90th Division would be swinging back to the north to be a part of the Third Army's enveloping movement to trap the German divisions that remained in northern France. The 3rd Battalion, 358th Infantry moved 20 miles by foot to Alencon where it remained until August 15. They moved out by motor on the 15th and traveled north about 20 miles to Chailloue. No specific details were provided, but the *Battle History Third Battalion 358th Infantry* pointed out that K Company ran into some enemy at Chailloue that were dealt with in "Kraut Killer" style. On August 17, K Company was preparing to attack Exmes when orders were changed that moved the entire battalion in the area of Michelot. It was during the night of August 18, that the "battalion was employed on the Division right flank with the mission of seizing the high ground NE of Chambois and establishing road blocks on the two main roads leading east and northeast of Chambois. The roads constituted the last remaining routes of escape for the German units still left in the Falaise pocket." The battalion would be heavily engaged for the next three days in the momentous action to close the Falaise pocket and trap the remaining elements of the German army. [14]

K COMPANY'S EXQUISITE PERFORMANCE AT CHAMBOIS

It was during this action in Chambois that K Company distinguished itself again and became known throughout the 90th Division as the "K Kompany Kraut Killers." In a document from Uncle Bob's personnel record, K Company's part in the action is described by Lt. Col. James S. Spivey:

"Company K, on the Battalion left, moved north until they ran into a German radio car, a command car and a tank, which they promptly and aggressively knocked out with small arms and bazookas.

"They then moved north and onto the objective with one rifle platoon on each road and one in between the two roads ... About the time the Battalion arrived in this position, a large German column with tanks, trucks, half-tracks and motorcycles, all loaded with personnel came down the northeast road and was viciously engaged with complete surprise by Companies K and L. The meeting was as much a surprise to Company K as to the Germans. Immediately, Lt. McHolland called for his bazooka teams and went to work on the column, knocking out tanks, trucks, and half-tracks.

The Germans dismounted from their vehicles and made uncoordinated attacks in numbers that exceeded our men by ten to one. It was only the boldness and aggressiveness of Lt. McHolland and his Lieutenants, that turned the situation into a rout and slaughter of the Germans. It was on this occasion that one of the Company K bazooka teams knocked out four tanks with five rounds of bazooka fire.

"For three days the Battalion remained in this position, capturing 951 prisoners, and knocking out 15 tanks and 40 miscellaneous half-tracks, trucks and vehicles. By far, the majority of these vehicles and prisoners were accounted for by Company K as inspired by Lt. McHolland....

"At the time of Chambois, Company K had had one month's training all together including approximately ten days on the defense and a few small engagements. The confidence, boldness and aggressiveness of this newly formed outfit was entirely due to the leadership and training of Lt. McHolland. His personal aggressiveness in moving out with his men and fighting the Germans himself was an inspiration and example to his new men." [15]

A SECOND SILVER STAR FOR UNCLE BOB

Uncle Bob would receive his second Silver Star, an Oak Leaf Cluster, for his part in the Chambois action. In his recommendation for the award, the battalion commander, Lt. Col J. W. Bealke, described Uncle Bob's actions were "with complete disregard for his own safety even though he was under heavy artillery, small arms and tank fire. As a result of his extraordinary heroism Lt. McHolland's Company was inspired to repel the enemy counter-attack." Uncle Bob would be promoted to Captain by the time the award was presented, thus, the citation for this award read:

> *"Captain Robert B. McHolland, 0-433315, Inf, then 1st Lt, Company K 358th Infantry, United States Army. On 19 August 1944 in the vicinity of Chambois, France, Capt McHolland's company was given the mission of capturing the initial objective of his battalion. After rapidly and aggressively leading his troops to this objective, Capt McHolland personally supervised the destruction of an enemy Mark V tank and armored half-track and arrived on the final objective. At this point he placed a road block on the enemy escape route, ambushed a German armored column and inflicted heavy casualties upon the enemy with rifle grenades and small arms. When subject to a heavy counterattack, Capt McHolland repeatedly exposed himself, directing and controlling his company. His outstanding leadership kept the escape route closed despite strong resistance and resulted in the capture of 300 prisoners."* [16]

THE K KOMPANY KRAUT KILLERS

The reputation of K Company as one of the best fighting outfits in the theater began to spread as a result of its outstanding performance at Chambois. Not long after this action, it was reported in documentation contained in Uncle Bob's personnel record that a special form of recognition for K Company members was created. Lt. Col. James S. Spivey describes the KKKK badge of honor:

The "K Kompany Kraut Killer" patch—courtesy Captain Emmett T. Boyd, U. S. Army, retired.

"Shortly after Chambois, Lt. McHolland and Lt. Short, one of his platoon leaders, instituted a badge to be worn on the left breast pocket of all K Company men who had killed five Germans. The badge consisted of a red heart upon which was a black K. The red heart was to symbolize the red blood of the men. The black K stood for the new official company title "K Kompany Kraut Killers." A white streak of lightning running diagonally through the center of the badge stood for the terror and speed with which K Company descended upon their enemy. These badges were made up from captured German cloth and issued to men of the Company who had achieved five verified kills. They caused continuous discussion and pride to the men who had won theirs and the rest of the company worked hard to win and wear "Their Badge." Upon winning the badge, a soldier was pronounced a full-fledged Kraut Killer." [17]

Captain Mac, far right, somewhere in France, 1944 with his K Kompany command team. Note "K Kompany Kraut Killer" patch on left breast pocket—U.S. Army Signal Corp photo, courtesy National Archives.

EMMETT BOYD--A PROUD MEMBER OF THE KKKK FRATERNITY

Emmett Boyd, weapons platoon sergeant of K Company, expressed his pride in being a part of this select group:

"Under him (Uncle Bob), and his encouragement we became the street fighters for the Division. No town was too small or too large for us to enter and go down the street, shooting up the town and getting the Krauts out of town. We became known as "K Kompany Kraut Killers." Capt Mac arranged for a special award, and got a French seamstress to fabricate, to wear on our left breast pocket that was shaped like a heart with a K and lightning strike through the K. Any soldier in the company that killed five Krauts got the award. I still have mine that I got a medic to cut off my fatigue jacket and Combat Badge when I got wounded on January 31, 1945 during the Bulge. Capt Mac wanted recognition for his troops and we would never have received it if he hadn't let everyone up the ladder of command know just what kind of soldiers he had in his outfit." [18]

Emmett Boyd who went on to serve twenty years in the army, retiring as a Captain in the Finance Corps, called Uncle Bob "the best soldier I ever had the privilege to serve under." He went on to say that "Every man in the Company was so proud to be under his command. He was quiet, considerate and kind to everyone. He expected the very best from everyone in his company and got it. I remember that he never settled in after a day of fighting until all of his troops needs were taken care of. He would listen to our bitching but never participated in our idle griping." [19]

INTO RESERVE AND TIME TO WRITE

After its impressive performance at Chambois, the 3rd Battalion, 358th Infantry was relieved on August 22 by the 50th British Infantry Division. The battalion moved into reserve in an area near Surdon, France for a welcome break in the action. The next three days were spent in this area where the usual inspections and drill were conducted. Hot meals were served and the battalion was visited for the first time by the American Red Cross Clubmobile. [20] Uncle Bob took advantage of the lull to get off another short letter to his sister, Eva:

France
22 August 1944

Dear Eva,

I am still well, whole and hearty thanks be to God.

I actually believe that the prayers of my friends and relatives are sure holding me up, too.

I just got your letter and thanks a million for writing even tho I can't write you very often.

I don't think it's very noble of Nellie quitting her job a riveting. I don't like my job and many others don't either and many are dying doing a job they hate. I don't care whose toes I trod on any more. I can never get over some things I have experienced and it burns me up people quitting comparatively easy jobs because it is not to their liking.

Bob

Again, Uncle Bob affirms his faith in the Almighty, but it appears he also is beginning to show the effects of some of the unspeakable things he has experienced. This is the first point in all of the available letters written by him that he touches on negativity. His displeasure with Nellie, his brother Everette's wife, quitting her job is clearly evident.

THIRD ARMY BYPASSES PARIS IN ITS CHASE AFTER NAZIS

With the German army on the run to the east back toward Luxembourg and its homeland, Patton's Third Army would be in hot pursuit until a fuel shortage slowed things for a while. The *Battle History Third Battalion 358th Infantry* reported the rapid movements of the last few days of August 1944:

> *"Early on the 26th of August, the Battalion moved out on its longest single day trip. In all, the Battalion moved some 225 miles passing through Sees, Mamers, La Fert-Bernard, Chateaudin, Pithiviers and Malasherbes. Troops stopped at 1800 in the Foret de Fontainebleau just 25 miles south of Paris B which regrettably was the closest the Battalion got to that famed city. At 1830 the troops loaded up again and after passing through Namours moved across the Seine river at Montereau where we relieved a Battalion of the 10th Infantry, 5th Division. As the Battalion passed through Namours it saw for the first time the way the French treated women who consorted with Germans. These girls made a spectacular sight as they paraded dejectedly down main street, dressed in their nightgowns and completely shorn of their locks. Civilians lined both sides of the street and loudly booed each girl as she passed.*

"At 1400 27 August, the Companies moved out again, this time to the town of Donnemarie en Montise .... all companies promptly settled down. That night the towns-people threw a street dance in our honor. It was one of those spontaneous affairs of a populace desiring to show their joy and appreciation to the soldiers who had freed them from the oppressive yoke of German slavery.....

"Then between the 28th and the 31st, the Battalion moved mainly by motor some 60 miles ending up in the town of St. Masmes. En route we crossed the Marne river. At St. Masmes, the entire division was immobilized by lack of gasoline." [21]

General Patton, whose Third Army had played a major part in the Allies taking control of northern France and was on the move toward the German homeland, was furious with being held up because of a fuel shortage. Patton attributed the shortage to the fact that it was being diverted to Field Marshal Montgomery's slower moving forces. [22] Nonetheless, progress was temporarily slowed for Uncle Bob and his K Company. However, they would soon be busy again clearing small French villages, one-by-one, of German troops as they moved ever closer to Germany.

Chapter 13 Endnotes:
1. Colby, 168-9.
2. Bryan, 13.
3. Colby, 171.
4. Colby (Weaver), 172.

5. Colby (Weaver), 172.
6. Document, Official Personnel File.
7. Document, Official Personnel File.
8. Bryan, 13.
9. Bryan, 13.
10. Bryan, 13.
11. Winebrenner and McCoy, 101.
12. Winebrenner and McCoy, 101.
13. Winebrenner and McCoy, 101-2.
14. Bryan, 13-14.
15. Document, Official Personnel File.
16. Document, Official Personnel File.
17. Document, Official Personnel File.
18. Letter, Emmett Boyd to Tom Hill, December 20, 2006.
19. Letter, Boyd to Hill.
20. Bryan, 15.
21. Bryan, 15.
22. Hart, 562-3.

Chapter 14
K Company–The Reputation Grows, a Promotion for the Commander

The slowing in late August and early September 1944 of the Third Army's rapid advance across France allowed the German troops who had escaped through the Falaise gap to receive reinforcements, reorganize and continue to present stiff resistance. Much of the fighting for K Company in September would involve tedious struggles in small French villages. The Germans were desperately defending their ground in these villages to prevent the Allies from moving on and gaining a foothold on German soil. Intense house-to-house fighting would often be a normal part of the day's work for Uncle Bob's K Company in its push toward the heavily fortified area of Metz, the Moselle River, and its ultimate destination, the German homeland. By the end of September, logistics shortages would cause a virtual halt in movement of the Third Army. However, word would continue to spread about the exploits of the "K Kompany Kraut Killers." This would even include coverage by a national media source.

ON THE MOVE AGAIN-EASTWARD

September, 1944, would begin with K Company remaining a few more days in the St. Masmes area in France.[1] This break afforded them the opportunity to enjoy hot meals and some movies. The S-1 Journal of the 3rd Battalion, 358th Infantry documented two of the movies shown during this time. One was "Song of the Open Road" starring Edgar Bergen, Charlie McCarthy, W.C. Fields, and Jane Powell. The other was "Follow the Boys" starring George Raft and Vera Zorina.[2] The lull ended on the 5th of September as the battalion moved on foot for about 15 miles before stopping around 6 pm for a hot meal. After the meal the battalion was loaded on trucks and moved eastward about 64 miles passing through the World War I battlefield area of Verdun and Etain, places Uncle Bob had heard about from Hurley World War I veteran, Ernest Hair. They arrived at Dommary Baroncourt well after midnight on the 6th of September. After getting some rest, the day would be spent in planning and preparation for confrontation with the Germans occupying the villages that lay ahead. [3]

OBJECTIVE--FONTOY

On September 7, the 3rd Battalion, 358th Infantry moved out of Dommary Baroncourt on foot with the town of Fontoy as its objective. [4] It would soon become clear to K Company and its rifle company counterparts that a type of warfare, termed street fighting, which also included house-to-house fighting, would become the usual procedure as they cleared each small French village of German troops and made their way ever closer to the

Metz fortifications. On the way to Fontoy, and beyond, there would be other small towns that required the Kraut Killer treatment of K Company. Uncle Bob's Weapons Platoon Sergeant, Emmett Boyd, further described a typical operation of K Company in this way:

> *"We would move in and sweep through every street and building in the village, eliminating the German main forces and those stragglers and snipers left behind. We would go down each street in single file throwing grenades in the windows or door of each house along the way, and then spray each one inside with our M-1, carbine, .30 cal machine gun, or burp gun before we went in. If the Krauts would surrender when we went into a town we would take them as prisoners. If they dug in they signed their own death warrants. We became experts at 'Street Fighting'."* [5]

As the battalion made its way toward Fontoy the area around Mont was cleared. Next along the way was a mining town, Tucquegnieux, which K Company assisted in clearing. Just outside the town they faced machine gun and mortar fire. Along with the battalion they dug in just outside Fontoy and remained in this position on September 8. The towns of Mairy and Trieux had to be cleared on September 9, and the battalion reached the edge of Fontoy by dark. The battalion attacked Fontoy on September 10, and cleared the town by noon.[6] K Company played a crucial role in this action and was the subject of an article in Warweek, the feature portion of the very popular Stars and Stripes magazine, concerning the company's part in the sweep through Fontoy.

K Company Makes News in Stars and Stripes

The Warweek article about K Company was in the October 7, 1944, edition and was entitled "Doughboys Learn About Street Fighting." It was written by Paul V. Conners, Warweek Combat Correspondent, who had accompanied K Company during the Fontoy operation and interviewed several company members after the action. Among those mentioned in the story was Lt. Max Short, one of Uncle Bob's top-notch platoon leaders and fighters. Lt. Short commented on the commando tactics that were required to clear the towns and was credited with knowing the business of street fighting. Conners went on to further describe the action in Fontoy and give credit to Uncle Bob's sterling leadership of the company during this action:

> *"Lt. Robert B. McHolland, Hurley, Missouri, tough, bearded commander of the company had woven light machine guns and bazookas into his pattern of fire. Some of the men fired rifle grenades. Others threw hand grenades.*

> *"The machine guns, fired from the hip with the operators changing every three or four minutes, cut down the Krauts who exposed themselves in windows. When a Heinie sniper was spotted in a church steeple at the far end of the street Sgt. James C. Livingston, New Kensington, Pa., with the front bipod of his machine gun removed, and the weapon resting on another man's back, gave the Kraut a burst of lead and quieted things in the steeple. Grenades and bazooka fire made things miserable for the enemy who was shooting from deep inside houses. The bazookas had*

no trouble penetrating the walls of buildings.

"The company bowled down the street working in platoons, one covering one side of the street, another the other side. Each covered the other. A mopup squad followed, wiping out Krauts who were not killed or dug out of buildings by the forward elements. The men who mopped up didn't knock politely on doors. They kicked them in or blew them open with bazookas and grenades. They poked their rifles around corners before entering rooms. They shot Jerries who showed treachery while surrendering.

"The fight had been well planned. Lt. McHolland, in his pre "game" fight talk, had directed that the men sweep into town and on down the main drag with the utmost speed practicable, their weapons pouring hell into the Heinies. The fight went as planned ....

"'Fire and movement' had been the theme of the company commander's instructions. His men carried them out. Almost miraculously not a doughboy was killed though half a dozen were shot up. The enemy had 25 dead, 60 wounded and a half a hundred had yelled 'Kamerad' (Surrender) (sic)." [7]

K COMPANY--FAVORED STATUS

The reputation of Uncle Bob's K Kompany Kraut Killers would continue to grow. Commenting on the special status the company maintained, Emmctt Boyd wrote:

"K Company was a favored group by commanders up the line throughout the Division for getting things done. Every third day one of the line companies in the Battalion would

*go into reserve. On our push across France we were always
out front. Once we took our objective and moved on so fast
that we captured a railroad tunnel and found ourselves five
miles in front of the front lines. It was such a good feeling
to go inside the tunnel and get out of the rain and cold.
It was our turn to go into reserve for the day. We talked
Captain McHolland into calling Battalion Headquarters
and let us stay in place and not pull back. It probably was
the first time for a unit to go into reserve five miles in front
of the lines. We set up defensives positions in front of the
tunnel mouth and took turns of keeping dry and warm
during the night." [8]*

Hobert Winebrenner in his *Bootprints* account gave high
praise to Uncle Bob and K Company, "Past heroics had
not only earned him charge of "K" and a promotion to
the rank of captain, but also two Silver Stars. Known as
the "Kraut Killers," his rifle unit numbered among the
best in the business of war. They had become almost
legendary for their courage under fire—a true reflection
of their CO." [9]

A Break at Ste. Marie Aux Chenes

Once Fontoy was secured, the battalion moved on to
clear the next objective, the industrial town of Algrange.
The battalion was met with fierce enemy resistance, but
by dark on September 10, the high ground on both sides
of Algrange had been secured. This gave them observation to the next important objective, Thionville, as well
as a view of the Moselle River. By September 12, Thionville was secured. The next couple of days were spent
in regimental reserve. On September, 15 the battalion
was moved south by motor to Ste. Marie Aux Chenes.[10]

They would spend the next eleven days here in Division reserve during which time they would enjoy hot chow, GI shows, and movies. One of the movies they saw was "And the Angels Sing" starring Fred MacMurray, Dorothy Lamour, Betty Hutton, and Raymond Walburn. They likely also saw Marlene Dietrich star in one of the most popular GI shows. [11] There would also be the usual inspections and some serious training in preparation for another lengthy effort to take the fortress Metz. The German homeland was getting tantalizingly nearer, but more intensive struggles lay ahead before the battalion would set foot on German soil.

LETTERS TO HOME

Two of Uncle Bob's letters, written while the company was in reserve, are available along with excerpts from a third. The first letter was written to his Aunt Zona (McHolland) and Uncle Arthur Singleton in Ava, Missouri. Zona was his father Stanley's youngest sister:

France
16 Sept 44

Dear Aunt Zona and Uncle Arthur,

I just received your letter and was very glad to hear from you.

I have been in France for a long time now and I am very anxious to get this over with and get back to the states. They are the best place in the world for my money.

I never did hear how the elections turned out in Missouri. I did hear that Carter never carried his job.

I am now commanding K Company and I should be a Capt. Before long. Several of the others have received their Captaincy so mine should be on the road. At least I hope so. I'll let you know when I get it.

Write to me.

Your Nephew
Bob

Evidence of the strenuous physical and mental strain on Uncle Bob after three and a half months of fighting across France began to emerge in this letter. He displays his interest in politics as he obviously refers to the Missouri primary elections held in August. "Carter" could possibly be the same Carter that was Webster County Superintendent of Schools when he taught school at High Point. He expresses his pride in being K Company commander and is looking forward to being promoted to Captain.

CAPTAIN MAC

What Uncle Bob did not know when he wrote this letter was that the orders promoting him to Captain had already been issued and his effective date of promotion was September 13, 1944. In typical army fashion the records indicated it would be a few days later while the company was still in Division reserve in Ste. Marie Aux Chenes that he would receive his coveted Captain's silver bars.[12]

The second letter from Uncle Bob during this period at Ste. Marie Aux Chenes was written to his sister Mary Lea (Droopy):

France, 1944
September 25, 1944

Dear Droopy,

A long time I haven't heard from you. I would like for you to consider letters to you also to Roxy and vice versa.

I have seen many interesting sights. I had business that allowed me to see the place that I am sending you a post card of. It is most beautiful but it is not colored as the picture shows it. I was also through many of the World War I battle fields but we had considerable less trouble on them than the old timers did. But I would not begrudge them their fun though.

I have one of the best companies in our division and up at regiment we are known as "K Company Kraut Killers." We made quite a name for ourselves during one action. You'll probably read about two of them in the papers by the name of Giebelstein and Caldwell. They have been interviewed by almost every press but it's probably old by now because many of the clippings have already drifted back from the States. I understand that I am in for a decoration for that action, too. I always told you I'd get it, ha.

I never did get to see Paris. It looked for a while we would be one of the first there but we didn't make it. I was in the forest of Fontainebleau where Napoleon had his famous Chateau where he courted the beautiful Josephine. Oh Boy what a place. It reminded me of the song "A Lovely Way to Spend an Evening." I can't explain that one.

I must close for now.

I thought you said Edwin was in Arkansas.

Bob

The post card picture to which Uncle Bob referred was not with the letter but it must have been something he had seen on his interesting journey across France. He wrote solemnly of the World War I battlefields they had motored quickly through in early September. He seemed to be disappointed at missing out on seeing Paris firsthand. But he was impressed with the forest of Fontainebleau area where Napoleon and Josephine carried on their affair. He wrote with pride about his K Company and two of his PFCs, Caldwell and Giebelstein, who had distinguished themselves by knocking out four tanks with five rounds of bazooka fire in the action to close the Falaise gap at Chambois. [13] Their exploits at Chambois had made the national newspapers. It was also for his performance at Chambois that Uncle Bob was awarded his second Silver Star.

The third letter, written to his Hurley friend, Mary Scott Hair, was dated September 27, 1944. The excerpt from the letter was a part of Mary's tribute to Uncle Bob, Rosary for Remembrance. In the letter he wrote about youngsters from the villages, "These French kids sure are cute. Many of them speak three and four languages.

They call me "Captaine Robaire." And they make more noise than a full-fledged attack. You can't help loving them." The break in the action had allowed him time to reflect on those who always had a place in his heart—kids.

ON TO VIONVILLE--MOVING CLOSER TO METZ

On September 27, the battalion moved on foot out of St. Marie Aux Chenes to Vionville positioning them ever closer to the Metz area and its many heavily fortified positions.[14] The continuing problems of fuel and material shortages required General Patton to begrudgingly slow his army's movement as it approached Metz and to "assume a defensive posture."[15]

Chapter 14 Endnotes:
1.   Bryan, 15.
2.   S-1 Journal, 3rd Battalion, 358th Infantry, September 1944.
3.   Bryan, 15.
4.   Bryan, 15.
5.   Boyd, 5.
6.   Bryan, 15-16.
7.   Paul V. Conners, "Doughboys Learn About Street Fighting," Stars and Stripes (Warweek Feature), October 7, 1944.
8.   Boyd, 5.
9.   Winebrenner and McCoy, 150.
10. Bryan, 16.
11. S-1 Journal, Sep 44.
12. Documents, Official Personnel File.
13. Bryan, 14.
14. Bryan, 16.
15. Hugh M. Cole, The Lorraine Campaign (Washington D.C.:Historical Division United States Army, 1950), 13.

Captain Mac

Chapter 15
October--A Pause in Offensive Operations

The strategy for the European Theater of Operations was decided upon in late September, 1944, by the top Allied commanders. Their decision would directly impact the actions and speed of movement of General Patton's Third Army. Priority would be given to Field Marshal Montgomery's Army Group to secure the port area of Antwerp, Belgium. This would be critical to the Allies main effort which was to be a drive from the north to the Ruhr and on to Berlin. Thus, priority for supplies and equipment would go for this undertaking rather than to Third Army's push in the south through the Metz and Moselle areas to the Saar basin. Patton was not happy with the "defensive attitude," but would try to keep moving forward by taking advantage of local attacks. One of his priorities was to drive a wedge into the complex and heavily fortified Metz area.[1]

The so-called "Fortress Metz" consisted of several forts

surrounding the city. It was important because of its strategic location in the vicinity of the border between France and Germany. As many as seventeen forts in two separate belts around the city had been constructed over hundreds of years to deter attackers. The forts were located in positions with good observation. They were fortified with vaulted areas for artillery and bunkers connected with trenches. Some were also surrounded by a moat. [2]   As part of the Third Army plan, K Company and the 3rd Battalion, 358th Infantry, would spend much of October in training for an attack on Metz.

VIONVILLE AND GRAVELOTTE

The battalion remained in Vionville until October 11 except for one company which would be positioned on line at Gravelotte. From Vionville, K Company would take its turn on line in Gravelotte, rotating every four days with the other companies in the battalion. Gravelotte was close enough to some of the Metz forts to receive constant shellings from German artillery. At the same time, the company would conduct regular probing patrols. [3]

When the company was back at Vionville intensive training was being conducted in reduction of fortified areas in preparation for the anticipated attack on the heavily fortified Metz complex. There was also time for movies, clubmobiles, and PX rations during this time.[4]   With reserved fondness, Technical Sergeant Emmett Boyd, K Company Weapons Platoon Sergeant, remembered Vionville as the first place he was able to sleep in a building since he had left England in early June. The building he slept in was a barn. [5]

MORE TIME TO WRITE HOME

The days at Vionville provided the opportunity for the army postal personnel to deliver mail and time for Uncle Bob to try to catch up with answering some of it. Three more of his letters home are available for this period. The first one was written to his brother Everette:

France 28 Sept 44

Dear Brother,

I received your series of 5 letters dated August 29, 1944 and the address seems to keep changing so I have to write just now.

I enjoyed your last letters OK.

You really are more optimistic about the war than I am. From where I sit it looks like a tough row ahead and I have a front row seat for the show and have for some time.

I have been through some of World War I battle fields being—Chateau Thierry, Verdun and Argonne. I didn't have as much trouble getting through as the boys did 25 years ago.

I suppose you know by now that I have made captain?

Things isn't so rough now but I look for it to get rough any day now.

I never did find out why you were in the hospital. Is it your old ailment?

One of the saddest parts of this war is generally the good men are the ones who gets hurt. These no good bastards won't ever do anything to get hurt. But sometimes even they get it. Just plain luck keeps me alive and Divine Guidance.

Your Bro

Bob

Uncle Bob's thoughts about the war take on an ominously more pessimistic tone. Reading and hearing the news reports of the war back in the States, Everette and others were being informed of the Allied advances and were becoming hopeful the end of the war was coming into view. But Uncle Bob knew first-hand what was required to make the advances and knew the road ahead to victory would not be easy. He envisioned tough times immediately ahead for his unit. His reference to "these no good bastards" in describing the men who would not fight is the strongest language found in all of the letters he wrote.

The second letter from Vionville was a short one written two days later to sister Roxabel:

France
30 September 1944

Dear Sis and All,

I was presented a Silver Star medal for action in

France on 2 August. It was presented to me by the assistant division commander. In fact I believe him to be the one who recommended it because he was right there when I received it and when the action was too. I am sending it home. I suppose it will be a little late in getting there because it takes packages a lot longer.

Has anyone heard from Delmar?

Is little Ray in France? I have a sneaking idea he is but I don't remember what outfit he is in so I don't know how to figure out how to find him. Ask S.B. his address.

Don't forget to write to me. When I'm busy I don't mind not getting letters but when there is a lull in the fighting I miss them.

Your brother
Bob

In this letter Uncle Bob refers to the first Silver Star he earned at Ste. Hilaire du Harcouet. The person who presented the award was Brig. Gen. William G. Weaver, the Assistant Division Commander, 90th Infantry Division. He asked about Delmar Bowyer, his friend from Hurley who was serving somewhere in France. The "Little Ray" he asked about was his cousin, Raymond McHolland. He had been in North Africa and was in Italy at this time. Uncle Bob let it be known that letters from home were always welcome, especially when he had time to enjoy them.

Uncle Bob wrote this third letter to sister Mary Lea while at Vionville:

France, 4 October

Dear Droopy,

Just a few lines to let you know that I am well.

I'm sending home a Extract copy of the order that authorized the award of my second Silver Star. When you are awarded a second Silver Star all you get is an Oak Leaf Cluster to the Silver Star. I have the cluster to be pinned on the medal but I won't send it home as yet because I've loaned it to another officer to wear on his ribbon. I have three stars on my Theater of Operations ribbons. One for the Normandy Campaign, one for the Northern France and one for the Battle of Germany.

There isn't much news I guess election news is hot and furious.

Today I will draw a complete month of Captain's pay and in January I will draw 3 years foggie for 3 years service. That will be 5% of base pay or about $10 more per month.

I will close for now.

Your Brother Bob

The Oak Leaf Cluster, to signify his second award of the Silver Star, was for his part in the action at Chambois on August 19. He had received the orders for the award. He was formally presented the awarded on October 15 by Brig. Gen. James A. Van Fleet, who had just been named Division Commander, 90th Infantry Division. This is the same General Van Fleet who commanded the U. S. Forces in the Korean War. At the same time, Uncle Bob was also formally presented the Combat Infantryman Badge he had earned in July. The War Department provided a picture of the awards ceremony with Brig. Gen. Van Fleet pinning the medals on Uncle Bob in full combat uniform. The picture appeared in the Joplin, Missouri, Globe newspaper and Uncle Bob was incorrectly identified as Captain Robert McDonald.

Uncle Bob receiving his second Silver Star and the Combat Infantryman Badge from BG James A. Van Fleet, 90th Division Commander, October 1944—U. S. Army Signal Corps photo.

ST. HUBERT

On the afternoon of October 11, the battalion loaded up and moved to St. Hubert where they de-trucked and relieved another battalion of the 357th Infantry that was maintaining a defensive line. For the next week the battalion would be aggressively patrolling in and around the towns of Bronvaux, Marange, Silvange, and Ternel. [6]

With the unit in a primarily defensive posture, Uncle Bob took advantage of the opportunity to write more letters. Two of his letters and an excerpt from another are available from October 15 and 16.

The first of the letters was addressed to sister Roxabel:

France 15 Oct 44

Dear Sis,

I'm in a writing mood. I was wondering where Howard Inmon was enlarging his store at. What were his plans? His idea of hiring Maurice sounds as if Income Tax was getting higher. I have completely lost out on mine.

Is Inez still home? If so give her my best regards and I would like to know what outfit Homer is in. I see different Armored outfits once in a while. I might keep an eye open for the Major. Is he still a Major? He's probably a Lt Col by now.

Did anyone ever find out about the Andrews property anymore? I have often wondered about the Potter's place. Where the old Snodgrass people lived. I'd like to have a little more to lean on when I get home because I'm figgering on doing more leaning than pushing. That's for sure.

How many more hours does Droopy need to graduate? I've forgotten. I believe she has about 85 or 90 now. I figger on finishing on my War Bonds if necessary.

> *As Ever,*
> *Bob*

Howard Inmon, who had provided a character reference letter for Uncle Bob in his commissioning effort, owned and ran one of the general stores in Hurley. Apparently Howard was considering hiring my father, Maurice Wiley. If he was hired he could not have worked there very long as he was drafted into the army within a couple of months. He asked about his Hurley singing friend, Inez Inmon Bowman and her husband, Homer, who had made Lt. Col. and was assigned to an armored unit somewhere in France. Optimism returns as Uncle Bob asks about property around Hurley in which he can invest and indicates that he plans to finish college when he gets back home.

The second letter was written to Hurley friend Mary Scott Hair dated October 15. An excerpt of the letter from her "Rosary for Remembrance" tribute to Uncle Bob read:

"Today is Sunday. If the situation is favorable we may have some kind of service this afternoon.

"I am sending you a pressed flower. I found it in a German officer's medical manual.

"If the Lord is willing, I'll be seeing you all, someday."

Mary noted that the flower was a beautiful pansy, carefully protected by two folds of waxed paper. Sadly, this was the last letter she received from Uncle Bob.

 Uncle Bob wrote to sister Roxabel again the next day from the St. Hubert area:

France 16 October 44

Dear Sis,

I sent you an article about your brother's company. I sent it free mail so it may take it longer to get to you. It was the War Week the weekly feature of our overseas paper the Stars and Stripes which is incidentally a pretty good paper. But I wouldn't believe all that stuff they wrote about me because I haven got a beard. I just hadn't shaved for two days. I do have a cookie duster. Which I think is pretty smooth. While we're on the subject that document is not for public consumption. It is just for the family to read. I don't want to hear about it from anyone else.

Guy Peters must have had some advance notice on the Wheeler Branch Dam.

I don't need anything for Christmas. But I do enjoy newspapers. I've begun to get the Crane paper again.

Too bad about Millard Israel, but I wouldn't worry too much until they get another report.

Kindly address future correspondences as Captain. I sure went through a lot for that recognition.

Bob

The Warweek article Uncle Bob sent was the same one previously mentioned that was written by Paul Conners about K Company's participation in the action at Fontoy. He clarified the part about having a beard, but did admit that he had grown a mustache. His admonition to keep it within the family did little good as word about the K Kompany Kraut Killers quickly spread among his family and friends. Guy Peters was a family acquaintance from Hurley who apparently had gained some information about a proposed dam in the Wheeler Branch area of the James River that would potentially flood Hurley and the Spring Creek valley. It cannot be determined from Uncle Bob's letter what that information was, but more will be revealed in a later letter. Millard Israel was another Hurley boy serving in the army. Word had been received from his family that he was missing in action and Uncle Bob was offering hope, although the family later learned that he was killed in action. Even though the official War Department orders officially promoted Uncle Bob to Captain on September 13, and another document indicated that he received his new rank insignia at Ste. Marie Aus Chenes in late September, this is the first time he has mentioned it in a letter. NO ONE could really know just how much he had gone through to earn his silver bars.

Return to Vionville and Gravelotte

The battalion moved on foot from the St. Hubert area back to Vionville on October 19. They stayed in billets where they had stayed a few days before. In the afternoon of October 19, the battalion relieved another battalion occupying defensive positions around Gravelotte. The weather conditions were miserable. It was cold and would rain almost every day. Two companies would be on line conducting vigorous patrolling with one company in reserve. Companies would rotate frequently in an effort to help keep the troops dry. [7] Uncle Bob found time to write when K Company rotated back into reserve. There are two more letters he wrote during this period.

Letter to Home--Another Warweek Article

The first letter was written on October 20 and addressed to Mary Lea:

20 Oct 44, France

Dear Folks at Home,

I haven't much to say only that I hope that infernal dam doesn't go through and I'll be voting against it. It would ruin the value of the land around home and also ruin a lot of good farming land. I don't believe it will ever go through. It would be silly.

Besides they are already laughing at me for fighting for a home that will be under water when I get home. Oh,

278

*no anything but that. I must be a popular fellow because
I am quoted again in the War Week but don't believe the
part about me growing old because I'm not older than I
ever was, except I'll be 26 come Dec 10.*

*Delmar is close to me but I haven't seen him yet. I'll
be seeing him before long. I believe I saw elements of his
Division next to mine. So I'll be looking him up.*

I hear from Eva quite often nowadays.

I will close, lots of love

Bob

Information Uncle Bob received about the Wheeler
Branch Dam must have sounded bad to him as he clearly
stated his position. *(Note: the dam was never built.)* His com-
ments indicate Lt. Short along with others were ribbing
him pretty hard about it. The Warweek article he referred to was in the October 14, 1944, edition of Stars
and Stripes where the correspondent, Paul V. Conners,
again quoted Uncle Bob and Lt. Max Short in a story
about the adverse effect rumors had on the morale of
the men. He was still hoping to see his friend Delmar
Bowyer, but it is believed he never caught up with him.
Finally, he mentioned that sister Eva was being faithful
with her correspondence.

THE LONGEST LETTER HOME--
FRUSTRATION SHOWING

The second letter was a long letter to Roxabel in which he
touched on a variety of subjects. The miserable weather

conditions plus his four solid months of hellish combat began to show as he vented some of his frustrations:

France, 27 October (44)

Dear Folks,

I received a letter from you dated the 16th of September and I have received several letters dated since then. I have no idea whatever about the letter I wrote to you in which wasn't a letter. I guess maybe I just forgot to enclose in it any message whatsoever. Those were pretty busy days when I wrote those letters.

I hear from Edwin quite often in fact he is the only fellow that does write to me very often at all. I hear from Johnny Alfrey about once every three months but Edwin writes more often than that.

There is a little French girl I would sure like to bring home with me. Her name is Eugene Marie. There are eleven in her family. She is ten years old and speaks both French and German well but her folks are French. She is getting where she can talk some English and she is teaching me French. I can now say "Wee", "Pom Joor", and "Se voo play" and she can write Shakespeare's 18th sonnet verbatim, which I would say was "reverse English." Her father was a miner but the Germans closed the mine so their living is quite skimpy. I don't get to see them very often but next time I will have some pictures of my girls from France. Oh yes, the kids call me Captain Robaire. Just one look at them and you can see why we are fighting. Even the Willis Sipo family has a good living to lots of these people. I doubt the "Liberation" will be so welcome after the new wears off because our occupation in combat areas sure upsets their routine living. When people are hungry they don't think too much of liberty. In the long run they will profit, but it looks like a tough proposition until then. A speedy victory would certainly aid the cause as far as the common people are concerned. After all, those are ones that will suffer.

Just a matter of opinion but I believe that if Germany doesn't give up soon she is committing racial suicide.

Thanks for sending me the pictures of the boys and the old ones of me. I've been showing the fellows the picture of me by the big post and telling them that was me as a civilian which was long ago. Also the one of me and you.

Some very much talked of American ingenuity is represented. I am writing this letter under the light of a candle made from Bee's Wax which we have robbed from a bee-hive and a wick from a shoe string. No, I didn't think it up, it was my armorer Articificer who is a Dutchman from Minnesota.

I thought I had told you but I guess I haven't so I tell you now. But I told Herbert to put the engine from the well on the new well.

I have been sending about $50 a month to Droopy through what is known as P.T. A. In August I sent $100 and every month since then at least $50. I figgered she'd put it in the bank for me. But I haven't heard whether she got any of it at all or not. It takes from 6 weeks to 2 months for it to go through so I was wondering. In your last letter you said something about a bond allotment going *to the bank. I haven't any bond allotments going to any banks at all. I have a $100 allotment that should have been going through for over a year now. I know it should be there. I don't know how much money I have in the bank in fact I never hear anything. I don't know whether the taxes are paid. How much the lambs brought. If any calves have been sold or anything. Then on top of all that they claim this whole town is going to be flooded. Such a life.*

But the best ever yet is Vena wrote two letters in which the sole contents was about the ball game when I heard them all the same time you did because the game time over her was 0800 o'clock at night and every company has a radio on their kitchen truck so I was able to hear every single game. Another example, if one person has written to me about Dale Dean fifty has and I knew about it long before any of you did. What I'm trying to get at I'd like to have news from home that concerns me. I don't want no one to feel sorry for me because I'm part of the best fed, best paid, best equipped army in the world and that's all a soldier can hope for or ask for.

Let me know how much money I have in the bank, how may bonds and let me know how much it cost for electricity. Any what has Billy Box done to pay rent if anything and why didn't he?

When do they propose to build a dam at Wheeler? I don't believe the Missouri Pacific Railroad will let it go through. It doesn't look as if it would be worth that much money to me.

I also believe they will sell the old Doctor's building cheaper when that dam project doesn't go through. It's just near election time and some congressman wants some campaign talk to bolster his vote getting capacity.

I will close this long letter now.

> *As Ever,*
> *Bob*

The weather was cold and damp when he wrote this letter with the light of a bee's wax candle with a shoestring wick. Some of the frustration of being so far away for so long emerges as Uncle Bob feels in the dark about his financial situation and how his farming operations are being handled. He had heard from Vena, but appeared to be disappointed that all she wrote about was the ball games (St. Louis Cardinals/Browns World Series) which he had heard himself. He continued to voice his concern about the proposed dam and made it clear he wanted to know more about his financial and farming situation.

THE LITTLE FRENCH GIRL-- A ROSARY FOR UNCLE BOB?

The little French girl, Eugene Marie, Uncle Bob wrote about opens the intriguing possibility that she might be the person responsible for the beautiful rosary he obtained while he was in France. Mary Scott Hair in her Rosary for Remembrance tribute to Uncle Bob noted that "the ever-grateful French people were known to give their liberators many prized keep-

The beautiful rosary that was among Uncle Bob's returned personal effects—Courtesy Wiley–McHolland family.

sakes and heirlooms. While it is merely supposition it seems logical that little Eugene Marie (sic) gave this love-ly string of carved wooden beads to her hero, Captaine Robarie (sic)." [8] *(Note: We will never know for certain how he came by the rosary. To extend the mystery further, Technical Sergeant Emmett Boyd, K Company Weapons Platoon Sergeant, offered the possibility that the donor of the rosary could have been a sweet little girl by the name of Rosie whom they had befriended while in Vionville.)* [9]

A LETTER TO COUSIN DORLA--
UNCLE BOB LIGHTENS UP

Another letter of a much lighter nature was obviously written sometime during this period. Although it does not show the day he wrote it, the envelope was post-marked November 2, 1944. The letter was written to one of his young cousins, Dorla Dean Milliken who lived in Claremore, Oklahoma, and who Uncle Bob was known to tease mercilessly. Dorla's mother, Uncle Bob's Aunt Elva, was his mother, Nancy's, sister:

France, Oct 44

Dear Dorla,

Mon, petite cherez, how are you? Has Oklahoma ever joined up with the other 48 states yet? If it don't hurry up and join up I don't believe it ever will get another chance. I hope the state will be able to make it through the winter this year because I heard that Missouri is sending most of her food and water to the soldiers overseas. I read in the paper where they are sending food from France to help the

Oklahomans.

Tell the Mayor of Claremore I have a very antique French pistol I'm saving for his collection of guns. I've carried it all over France, but I can't mail it home because you can't mail firearms, even if it is too old and rusty to fire anymore.

I suppose you have grown some but I'll bet you still have plenty of freckles. I would appreciate a picture of yourself. But I'll bet that Missouri boy will already have my picture. Those Missouri people are all right if you ask me.

How's Aunt Elva and Uncle Jim? Why didn't Billy join a good outfit—like the army? My brother Everette has joined the navy and has completely disgraced the McHolland name because all of the McHollands have been army people. Oh, hum. It looks as if I'll have to win the war for both of us now. The navy never wins wars.

I'm proud to hear that Leon is in school. I reckon as how that's about a fine a thing as a fellow can do being as how he was rejected for the armed forces.

That "swell hunk of human" sounds like a Frank Sinatra fan and Sinatra in my opinion is worse than anybody from Oklahoma I know of.

Take care of yourself and may the Lord help that poor defenseless Missouri boy. He'll need it, Redhaid!

Forever,
Bob

Dorla was barely in her teens when this letter was written. Uncle Bob had visited with her and her family in Claremore, Oklahoma and Dorla had visited with her relatives in Hurley. He never let up in his teasing of Dorla. Uncle Bob had apparently made the acquaintance of the Claremore mayor, a gun collector, during one of his visits with the family. The antique pistol to which he referred was sent back with his personal effects after the war. The pistol never made it to the mayor's collection as the family decided to keep it. The gun was beyond restoration to operating condition, but was framed and mounted on a velvet-like background making a very nice presentation.

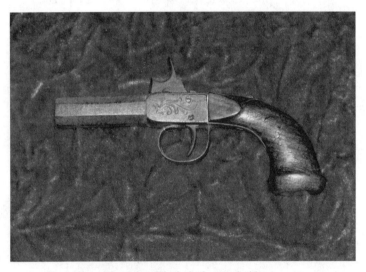

The antique French pistol returned with
Uncle Bob's personal effects—courtesy Sheila Wiley.

GOODBYE TO VIONVILLE AND GRAVELOTTE

The days of rigorous patrolling and occupation of defensive positions in Gravelotte ended for K Company on November 1 as the 63rd Armored Infantry Battalion of the 10th Armored Division relieved the 3rd Battalion, 358th Infantry, from their positions around Vionville and Gravelotte. [10] The Battalion would begin preparations for another crucial maneuver—the crossing of the Moselle River. After which, the Battalion would play a critical role in the final capitulation of "Fortress Metz."

Chapter 15 Endnotes:
1.   Cole, 258-9.
2.   Cole, 126-9.
3.   Bryan, 16.
4.   Bryan, 16.
5.   Boyd, 10.
6.   Bryan, 16.
7.   Bryan, 16-17.
8.   Hair, 6.
9.   Email from Emmett Boyd, December 4, 2007.
10.   Bryan, 17.

Captain Mac

Chapter 16
The Moselle River, Fortress Metz and into the Fatherland

As November, 1944, began Third Army plans for the long anticipated attack on Metz were being finalized. A risky and improbable crossing of the swollen Moselle River would be accomplished by the 3rd Battalion, 358th Infantry. It would also play a critical role in the mission to secure Metz and to continue the push toward the German border.

PREPARATION FOR A PERILOUS RIVER CROSSING

After the Battalion was relieved on November 1, attention focused on their next important operation; that of crossing the Moselle River. *The Battle History of the 3rd Battalion 358th Infantry* describes the activities of K Company and the Battalion through November 6: "Moving by motor, the troops passed through Mars Le Tour and Briey, finally stopping in Filliers. Here for the next five days the Companies went through a rigorous training program with river crossing exercises predominating. A few movies, church services and hot showers afforded some relaxation."[1]

The Unit Journal of the 3rd Battalion, 358th Infantry records that while much of the training was directed toward river crossing operations the training schedule for these days in Filliers included care and cleaning of equipment, inspections, close order drill, physical training, bayonet drills, attack on pillbox (concrete defensive fortifications of the Germans) tactics, and patrolling. There was time set aside on Saturday night, November 4, for a movie, "What a Woman," starring Brian Ahern and Rosalind Russell. Troops were paid during this period and church services were held on Sunday, November 5. It is interesting to note that on Saturday afternoon, the 4th, one officer and one non-commissioned officer from each company were permitted to attend a meeting at Division headquarters to hear General Patton speak. Names of those attending were not included, but it is likely Uncle Bob would have been the K Company officer in attendance. [2]

A GLOOMY LETTER TO BROTHER EVERETTE

While training for the river crossing consumed much time during these days, Uncle Bob used some personal time to write to his brother Everette:

France
3 November 1944

Dear Brother,

I received your air mail letter. I was glad to hear from

you, but I have decided that the navy didn't gain much by drafting you but I guess you are getting more done for your physical condition than you could have afforded in civilian life. Maybe the reason they messed your back up was that they were probably practicing on you.

I see you don't know much about infantry combat, as we Captain's have just as dangerous a job as any 2Lt even if it wasn't so. I seem to always get mixed up where the action is hottest anyway. But the danger is always in relation to the job you have and a rifle company commander percent of casualties is the highest percent in the battalion or any other one job. Discouraging aren't I?

I don't care much anymore. Sometimes I think I want to return to civilian life again. I'll have to let Uncle Sam take care of me. I don't know what I would do otherwise.

I was very much disheartened to hear that you were having domestic troubles. It is always a trying time when a woman is in a family way so I would advise you to be as considerate as possible during the trying months. There was surely something attractive about Nell or would you have ever married her. I don't see how such solemn things can be discarded so easily. I believe I'd sure give it a better try than that. Unless, of course, you already have, I will not make an assertion because I don't know the details. Well I will be waiting to hear from you.

Your Bro,
Bob

Signs of excessive stress continue to be reflected in the negative tone of his letter. Everette was drafted late, probably in 1944, apparently suffered from some type of back problem and was in the hospital or under treatment during much of his time in the navy. Uncharacteristically, Uncle Bob did not show much sympathy toward his brother's back problem. Everette must have thought his promotion to Captain would get him farther away from the battlefield. Uncle Bob explained his chances for survival still were not very good. The really disturbing part of the letter is when he says he really doesn't care much anymore. This represents a definite sign of battle fatigue. He ends the letter giving advice on some personal difficulties Everette and his wife were experiencing. He offered a telling statement about his beliefs in the sanctity of marriage when he wrote "I don't see how such solemn things can be discarded so easily."

Nell and Everette McHolland, U. S. Navy, 1944—courtesy Dr. Sharon McHolland.

ANOTHER SHORT NOTE HOME

Uncle Bob got at least one more letter off before the next action started. He wrote a short note to "Folks" which meant the letter was addressed to sisters Roxabel and Mary Lea:

France 7 Nov 44

Dear Folks,

I'm sending a money order home for $60. I've been sending the money home by P.T.A. but it takes about 60 days. I sent a $100 in August, $50 in September about $50 in October and none in November. They should come as government checks to Mary Lea Mc. I want the money to be put in the bank.

Well today is election day and I suppose that all you folks will be voting. I expect to be hearing the returns sometime tomorrow. I have a guess that it will be who it has been for the last twelve years. I didn't vote.

I will close for now as I have some work to do.

Bob

Uncle Bob had just been paid and was taking care of some personal finance business. The date of the letter, November 7, happened to be Election Day in 1944. With his interest in the political scene and the ability to vote absentee, it is unusual that he would not bother to vote. This is possibly another indication of the toll his participation in the war was taking on his mental welfare. His closing to the letter was probably an understatement as the Company was preparing for a treacherous river crossing and an attack on one of the heavily defended Metz forts.

ARRIVAL AT CATTENOM

The weather was rainy and cold when the Battalion was alerted on the afternoon of November 7 to be ready to move, Around 1400 hours (2 pm) the troops were loaded on trucks and moved about twelve miles to the town of Ludlange where they unloaded and ate supper. After supper the troops were loaded again to be taken about five more miles to Soetrich where they were unloaded. They then made a foot march for eight more miles through heavy rain and pitch darkness arriving at their new location in the Foret de Cattenom at 0300 hours, November 8. On that day the Battalion was informed that on the next day at 0300 hours they would make a crossing of the Moselle River. Their objective would be to take Fort Koeningsmacker, one of the heavily defended fortresses to the northeast of Metz.[3]

OBJECTIVE FORT KOENINGSMACKER AND OTHER METZ FORTRESSES

Actions to secure Fort Koeningsmacker and the surrounding area would take the better part of the next eight days for K Company and the Battalion. This operation would number among the toughest experiences of the entire war for these units. The constant rain continued to swell the Moselle river to record high levels and made the crossing during the darkness of night even more perilous. The swollen river would delay the engineers' efforts to build bridges resulting in serious problems with re-supply of food and ammunition for three days. Enemy artillery and machine gun fire from densely covered defenses was an ever-present danger. [4] The capture of Fort Koeningsmacker itself was a daunting undertaking. Dr. William M. McConahey, a battalion surgeon for the 357th Infantry described Fort Koeningsmacker as "one of the most formidable forts I've ever seen. It was a series of steel and concrete strong-points built into the top of a commanding hill, and so well concealed that little could be seen of it above ground. Underground passages, dozens of machine-gun emplacements, anti-tank ditches, four disappearing 150mm artillery pieces and so forth made it an extremely strong fort."[5]

Spanning the Swollen Moselle

The *Battle History Third Battalion 358th Infantry* described the Moselle River crossing:

> "*Beginning at 0115 on the 9th November 1944, the Battalion moved on down to the river bank carrying assault boats they had picked up at Cattenom. By 0330 the leading elements had reached the river and were preparing to cross. Enemy activity was remarkably absent. By 0347 both L and K Companies were across—with no opposition reported. At 0409 the assault Companies had reached the railroad tracks about 2 kilometers in from the shore … (Around 0500) the Germans woke up and began throwing artillery all along the river and up and down all approaches to it. By 0720 the crossing site was under heavy machine gun fire from a by-passed pillbox as well as intense artillery fire.*" [6]

A Personal Account of the Crossing-- T/Sgt Emmett Boyd

Technical Sergeant Emmett Boyd, K Company Weapons Platoon Sergeant, gives his first-hand experiences of the river crossing operation at Cattenom and the difficulties encountered in the approach to Fort Koeningsmacker:

> *"It was raining and cold and miserable weather. The engineers brought up assault boats for us to cross over to the high banks across from Cattenom. The bridges had been blown so there was no way over at that point to the assigned attack areas. About the middle of the night we started our assault and, after surviving the crazy currents in the river that the combat engineers masterfully took us through, we landed on the other side of the river. The banks were straight up at that point. We moved up on top of the hill and there was a large long ditch there that we moved into. Within a few minutes there was a barrage of artillery that traversed the ditch from one end to another. Many of our troops were killed at this point. The artillery finally quieted down and the rest of the night was quiet. Early the next morning, we looked back and saw that the river was twice the size as the night before. We could see the engineers trying to build a pontoon bridge, but the Germans would zero in and knock out everything they built. The rain and cold kept the river rising. The engineers could not build a pontoon bridge at that time. We spent three days and nights waiting for supplies to reach us. We could look back and see our people on the other side but knew there was nothing they could do. We were pinned down in our ditch and the Germans in front of us were laying in the mortar shells ... We sat there in the cold and rain without ammo or rations for three days ..." [7]*

K COMPANY--REACHING A PEAK IN FIGHTING EFFICIENCY

In the face of food and ammunition shortages, miserable weather conditions, constant enemy artillery strikes and the stiff German resistance to hold Fort Koenings-macker, K Company along with the Battalion continued to move forward on the objective. Then Captain James S. Spivey, the acting Battalion Commander, stated that "...in the attack across the Moselle River near Koenigs-macker, France, K Company reached its peak in fighting efficiency." [8]

1 LT. MAX SHORT--LOSS OF A BRAVE AND TRUSTED OFFICER

During this operation the actions of K Company and, in particular, Uncle Bob's Company Executive Officer, 1 Lt. Max Short, were recognized on two separate oc-casions. Captain Spivey wrote:

ILT Max Short. (from K Company command team photo)-- U.S. Army Signal Corp photo, courtesy National Archives.

"On 10 November 1944, Lt. Max Short counterat-tacked with his platoon against two German rifle companies and assaulted them, even engaging them in hand-to-hand fighting. With his one rifle platoon, Lt. Short, by his audacity and will to close with the enemy, completely routed over a hundred Germans, killing approximately 25 and capturing around twenty. This type of rout was typical of the aggres-sive fighting of all elements

of K Company. The Company always succeeded in taking its objective as ordered and on time." [9]

The next day in the continuing action to take Fort Koeningsmacker, 1 Lt Short made the ultimate sacrifice and was posthumously awarded the army's second highest combat award, the Distinguished Service Cross, for his extraordinary heroism. The official citation read in part:

" .... On 11 November 1944, the 358th Infantry met intense resistance during an attack against strong enemy positions near Koenigsmacker, France. Lieutenant Short, a platoon leader of Company "K" quickly reorganized his depleted platoon into an effective fighting force and daringly led them through intense fire in a bold assault. When the enemy retreated to prepared positions on the crest of a hill, Lieutenant Short and his men followed in pursuit and engaged them in a fierce hand-to-hand fight. Lieutenant Short killed one of the enemy with his gun butt and another with his trench knife before he fell, mortally wounded. Inspired by his heroic actions the platoon continued on and completely routed the enemy forces, killing and wounding many of them. ..." [10]

T/Sgt Emmett Boyd's Recollection of Fort Koeningsmacker

Technical Sergeant Emmett Boyd, K Company Weapons Platoon Sergeant, recalls the actions that let to the capitulation of the enemy holding Fort Koeningsmacker: " ... We were receiving a lot of artillery from Fort Koeningsmacker that was a part of the Metz fortress complex. A patrol from our company decided that they could enter the fort from our side of the entrance. ... The patrol dropped grenades down the air shafts then got into the fort and started the downfall of that defensive position. ... We finally got a a bridge across the river and got some ammo and rations. We then started to move forward from the top of the hill." [11]

THE BREAKTHROUGH AND CAPTURE OF THE METZ FORTIFICATIONS

By the end of the day on November 11, the German's main line of resistance had been broken. There was still work to be done in clearing more of the small towns beyond Fort Koeningsmacker. From November 12 through November 17, Uncle Bob's K Company would be doing its part in clearing the stiffly defended towns of Elzange, Distroff, Inglange and Metzervisse. K Company was particularly involved in the action at Inglange where they were fiercely counterattacked by the Germans. The Kraut Killers tenaciously stood their ground and finally secured the town taking thirty prisoners, one anti-tank weapon, and three pillboxes. After taking Luttange on November 17, the entire Regiment was placed in division reserve. K Company along with the 3rd Battalion remained in Luttange for the next three days where they would take some time to recuperate from the river crossing and heated battles of the past week. It is interesting to note The *Battle History Third Battalion 358th Infantry* reported that several officers and enlisted men were able to return to Cattenom for 48 hours at the division rest camp. [12]

A Break at Luttange--The Last Letter Home

During this break at Luttange the upcoming Christmas season was on Uncle Bob's mind. There would be time for him to send out Christmas greetings. It was while he was here that he wrote his last letter home. It was addressed to Roxabel and, as usual, gave no hint of the week of hell he had just been through:

Friday Nov 17, 1944

Dear Sis and All,

Just a few lines to let you know I'm OK.

I can't say as I was satisfied for the way the elections came out.

I understand that Donnell is having a close race again this time.

Well you can tell Ernest Hair I must have met one of his old girls. We were going through cleaning out a town and one old lady about 40 years old run out in the middle of the street and yelled "Good by, Darling" that is all the English she knew and I guess that was the last word the jilted Mademoiselle heard as our old GIs left her. She had a child but it looked a little bit young to be a Hair. She must have been very pretty when she was young.

Also tell Mary Hair that I got her package but it was

*under very difficult conditions and I was only able to sal-
vage the eating stuff. I lost the book of Xmas carols and
the harmonica.*

*I lost the bracelet from the Droop but I got your birthday
greetings. I can't imagine where I lost the bracelet.*

I will close this letter now

Bob

After Uncle Bob let them know he was okay he commented on the election. He was obviously disappointed
that Roosevelt had been re-elected for a fourth term. His
comment about Donnell referred to the Missouri gover-
nor's race. His sense of humor seemed to return as he
referred to his Hurley friend, World War I veteran, Ernest Hair, as he related the story of the French woman.
Ernest's wife, Mary, had sent the package of goodies and
the songbook and harmonica that had been lost. Sister
Mary Lea (Droop) had sent a birthday card. Regretta-
bly, he would not live to see his twenty-sixth birthday on
December 10. It is only conjecture but it is possible the
songbook, harmonica and bracelet ended up somewhere
at the bottom of the Moselle. Along with supplies, rations, and ammo many personal effects were lost in the
swift waters during the first three days of the operation
as they were being ferried across.

TWO CHRISTMAS CARDS

On his Christmas card to sisters Roxabel and Mary Lea,
Uncle Bob wrote the following:

19 November 44

Dear Droop & Roxy & family,

Here I go with the Merry Xmas and the Happy New Year and I hope you get it by Xmas as I'm sending it air mail in hopes anyway.

I'm hoping and praying for the day that Peace on Earth reigns and Goodwill towards men is a reality. But I guess that is like Delmar's Army.

Well, I have a lot to be thankful for this is nearer Thanksgiving. We're figuring on having a big Thanksgiving dinner and I'm preparing a special address for the occasion. Pray for me.

Your Bro

Bob

Uncle Bob was afraid if he sent the card by the free V-mail it might not reach Hurley by Christmas so he bought an air mail stamp just to be sure. Although he expresses his hopes for peace what he has seen for the past six months has left him discouraged. One can only guess what he meant by "Delmar's Army," but with this reference to his old Hurley buddy, he must have had unrealistic expectations of what army life would be. He ends his message on a positive note. Again, one can only suppose that when he wrote he had a lot for which to be thankful. And, he was thankful to be alive after what he had been through.

He also sent a Christmas card to Mary Scott Hair in Hurley with two short lines:

I received your last two communications and Hair was right on my location

RBM

A very Merry Xmas and a reunion for the New Year

Capt Bob

In the first line he was confirming to Mary that her husband, Ernest Hair, had figured out where Uncle Bob was in France.

The second line pulls on one's heartstrings as by the time this message was received Uncle Bob had been reported as missing in action.

With the strategic Metz area secured, the last major obstacle standing in the way of an advance to the German border had been cleared. K Company's next operation would take them into Germany for the first time where the enemy resistance would increase as they tried to prevent entry onto their native soil.

Chapter 16 Endnotes:
1.   Bryan, 17.

2. Unit Journal, 3rd Battalion, 358th Infantry, November 1944.
3. Bryan, 17.
4. Bryan, 17.
5. William M. McConahey, M.D., Battalion Surgeon (Rochester, Minnesota: published privately, 1966), 95.
6. Bryan, 17.
7. Boyd, 9.
8. Document, Official Personnel File.
9. Document, Official Personnel File.
10. Winebrenner and McCoy, 143-4.
11. Boyd, 11.
12. Bryan, 17-18.

Chapter 17
Into Germany--More Heroic Actions and a Final Stand

Once the Metz fortified area was secured, the next plan for Patton's Third Army was to push through the Saar-Moselle triangle area into Germany with the ultimate objective of reaching the Rhine River. The German forces had begun their withdrawal from the Metz area on November 17. They withdrew across the German border to a long line of defensive positions termed the Orscholz line. These positions were made up of large anti-tank ditches, reinforced concrete pillboxes, bunkers, dragon's teeth, barbed wire and other field works. They were formidable obstacles that had been carefully planned and constructed by the Germans to deter attacks from enemy forces, particularly armor. [1]

The initial advances by Third Army armored cavalry forces from November 19 through November 22 had been met with fierce resistance. They had been unable to pierce the Orscholz line positions. Determined to crack

the German defense a special combat team, termed
Combat Command A (CCA) was formed. Although the
358th Infantry Regiment was seriously under strength at
this point, it was attached to the 10th Armored Division
to form CCA. ² The tough task of the infantry would
be to clear the way for the tanks to break through the
Orscholz line. For their part in this operation, Uncle
Bob and K Company would face their toughest test in an
ultimate struggle for survival.

COMBAT COMMAND A (CCA)--MOVEMENT INTO GERMANY

The welcome and needed days of rest at Luttange came
to an end on November 21, when the 358th Infantry
Regiment was attached to the 10th Armored Division
and became a part of Combat Command A. Just after
noon on the 21st the battalion was loaded up and moved
by trucks to the town of Rettel, still just inside France,
where they spent the night. They remained in Rettel
on the 22nd where they were served a hot Thanksgiving
dinner with turkey and all the trimmings. This was probably where Uncle Bob gave the Thanksgiving message
he mentioned in his Christmas card. The 22nd was an
unsettled day for the Battalion as they were alerted and
de-alerted for movement at least two times during the
day. They ended up spending another night in Rettel
and would load up and move out at 0730 on November
23. They crossed the German border for the first time
at 0745 and unloaded at Perl, Germany. From here they
moved on foot to an assembly area near Wochern. ³

CLEARING THE CAMPHOLTZ WOODS

The *Battle History Third Battalion 358th Infantry* described the ensuing actions of November 23:

"Following a ground reconnaissance with all the company commanders [which included Uncle Bob], *Captain Spivey (the acting Battalion Commander) decided that the initial objective—Tettingen—could not be taken frontally because the commanding ground in our zone was off to the right of town and was studded with pillboxes which commanded the approaches to town from that direction. Consequently it was decided to attack the pillbox area from the right and then advance on the town from the right rear.*

"This plan was approved by Regiment and the Battalion moved up a dirt road toward Borg. About one mile up the road the companies cut off and turned due north crossing an AT (anti-tank) ditch by means of ladders, and advancing into the Campholtz woods. Amazingly enough, although the Battalion was forced to move across open and high ground, it drew no fire up to the time it actually reached the woods. As the Battalion entered the woods about 1300 (1 pm), Captain Spivey called for a bulldozer to move up and fill the AT ditch so as to have a supply route and route of evacuation behind the troops. The dozer was promptly sent up and did the job.

"With I on the left and K on the right, the Battalion moved through the woods for about 300 yards when they drew fire from Germans in well prepared trenches with barbed wire in front of them. The woods at this point were quite dense and contact between units was difficult to maintain. I

307

and K Companies attacked the enemy and although forced to crawl through barbed wire fences, quickly captured the German positions, reorganized and drove on.

"Again these two companies found the enemy dug in at the edge of the woods but routed them out in a vigorous attack. Eighty-four prisoners were captured during the day.

"Upon reaching the far side of the woods, it had become too late to move out and attack the defenses in the open, so Capt. Spivey ordered the companies to dig in at the edge of the woods.

"The enemy shelled the woods after dark, causing a few casualties. It also commenced raining and everyone was pretty wet and miserable. Ammunition, rations, water and litters were brought up by driving jeeps to the AT ditch and carrying them from there to the companies by hand. It might also be added that during this entire operation, most of the men and officers in the Battalion were suffering from a mild form of dysentery." [4]

K Company in the Campholtz Woods

Lt. Col. (then Capt) James S. Spivey, acting Battalion Commander, described K Company's actions on November 23, "Company K, under Captain McHolland, was the right assault company of the Battalion … his Company very aggressively cleaned out the Germans from a dense wood (Campholtz.) This action required bold fighting at hand grenade range. Also the Company knocked out two pillboxes on this date." [5]

T/Sgt Emmett Boyd--Clearing a Pillbox Along the Way

Technical Sergeant Emmett Boyd, K Company Weapons Platoon Sergeant, was responsible for knocking out one of those pillboxes. He wrote of his part in this action:

> " .... *while crawling through the dragon's teeth (tank traps) a large pill box loomed directly in front of me. Through the small slits I could see a large artillery piece and machine guns moving from side to side zeroing in on us ... We had a satchel charge so Capt. McHolland told us to crawl up to the base of the pill box and see if I could get it into the slit. My platoon started firing into the slits, keeping the Krauts away from the opening, and we crawled up to the side, laid the charge in the slit, set the fuse and ran like hell away from there. I heard the explosion, then in a few minutes the Krauts came crawling out of the trenches from behind the pill box, with bloody ear drums, noses, and eyes trying to surrender.*" [6]

Uncle Bob's Day in the Campholz Woods

Lt. Col. (Capt) Spivey went on to specifically describe Uncle Bob's personal involvement in the action on November 23:

> *"On the afternoon of 23 November 1944 in the vicinity of Tettingen, Germany, Company K, 358th Infantry had attacked through the Campholtz Woods and the First and Third Platoons were fighting on the north edge of the woods when Captain McHolland, the Company Commander, noticed a machine gun tracking his men from a well camouflaged fort to his right rear in the woods.*

"He ran back to his Second Platoon, which was in reserve and protecting the right flank of the Company. From here he took the Platoon Sergeant, four men from the Second Platoon, and five Engineer demolition men through the woods on the right flank of his Company to knock out this enemy fort.

"Leaving these men in the rear of an anti-tank ditch, Captain McHolland went forward fifty (50) yards by himself to reconnoiter the fort before bringing his men up. He came back in a few minutes, borrowed a carbine anti-tank grenade, and told the Platoon Sergeant to work his men around to the rear of the fort and cover that side. He took the five Engineers with him and worked his way through the woods and out into the open beyond the woods and in front of the pillbox. He fired his anti-tank grenade at the machine gun, which was mounted on a large steel ball turret, causing the gun to cease firing. The Engineers could then work their way up to the embrasure (opening in the pillbox.)

"He personally took the Engineers up to the turret and placed a sixteen pound charge of Composition C2 and backed away. The charge knocked the German machine into the pillbox but didn't crack the turret.

"Again Captain McHolland went with the Engineers to place a second sixteen pound charge. This charge also had no effect on the ball turret.

"Captain McHolland went around the fort across the front of the 88MM gun and found a door in the fort. As he reached the door, it opened and a white handkerchief was stuck out by the Germans. Twenty-two (22) Germans came out of the fort to surrender to him. He called for the

Platoon Sergeant to come help him take care of the prisoners. One German was found dead by the machine gun in the fort.

"By his initiative, boldness, and aggressiveness and with utter disregard for his personal safety, Captain personally captured the fort which was endangering his men from the rear." [7]

A WRETCHED NIGHT IN THE CAMPHOLTZ WOODS

After an action-packed day of clearing the Campholtz Woods, Uncle Bob and K Company would suffer through another long, cold and rainy November night in this wooded area waiting to move on their next objective—the small town of Butzdorf. The already under-strength company had suffered several more casualties during the action of the day. Artillery rounds from German positions would continue pound them through the night. Trench foot (potentially disabling condition caused by overexposure of the feet to cold and damp conditions) was an ever-present danger and, along with the intestinal problems of many of the soldiers, added to the misery in the cold darkness. [8]

Staff Sergeant Howard Pemberton, Uncle Bob's old Missouri friend from M Company, was leader of a heavy machine gun squad supporting K Company in the operation. He remembers talking with a battle weary "Captain Mac" in the woods that night. Howard recalled his conversation with "Captain Mac," "That night before we went to Butzdorf, we walked through the woods together. … I could see the fatigue in his eyes. I tried to get him to go back for a rest, but I knew he would never

do it. … He was one of the finest people I ever met."
[9] Of course, Uncle Bob did not heed Sergeant Pemberton's advice and would be there the next day to make the
ultimate sacrifice while leading his beloved Kraut Killers
in their costly effort to secure Butzdorf.

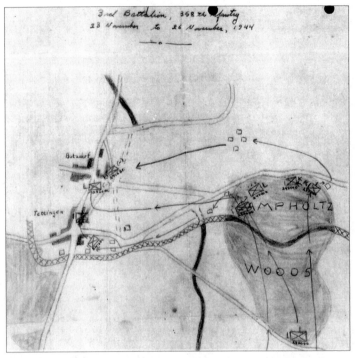

*Sketch of Butzdorf-Tettingen, Germany area, 23-26 Nov 44. Note Campholtz Woods
on right. Small squares are pillboxes. The larger boxes with an "X" through them
indicate the infantry unit. K Company is shown in the upper right area of the Campholtz
Woods—courtesy Tyler Alberts.*

OBJECTIVE--BUTZDORF

The *Battle History Third Battalion 358th Infantry* chronicles
the titanic effort of Uncle Bob and K Company as they
had to fend off an early morning German counterattack

in the Campholtz Woods before their fateful advance on the small town of Butzdorf on November 24, 1944:

> *"Shortly after dawn on the 24th, Company K was coun-terattacked by approximately 40 Germans of which they captured 18 and killed or drove off the rest. The company was then re-supplied with ammunition by Company L. It was also necessary for K Company to knock out a pillbox which would endanger assault companies from the rear if they attacked out over the open terrain.*

> *"At about 1300, I and K Companies jumped off into the at-tack in the open while L Company moved up into the woods. On this afternoon, Company I knocked out six pillboxes and Company K three. The plan of attack was for K to take Butzdorf while I was to take Tettingen (a very short dis-tance separated the two small towns.) The pillboxes were encountered en route to the towns. Both companies were under harassing machine gun and artillery fire as they ap-proached their towns.*

> *"Company K was abreast of Company I for about 400 yards out of the woods. Then leaving one rifle platoon and the mortar platoon upon a ridge short of the town, the 1st and 3rd platoons of Company K with a section of heavy machine guns from M Company attacked the town of Butz-dorf.*

> *"In order to reach Butzdorf, it was necessary for K Company to cross a wide open valley covered with cross fire from ma-chine guns. Captain McHolland thereupon ordered his men to run for the town, get in the buildings and reorganize there. The majority of the three platoons made the town in spite of the heavy machine gun fire ...*

"Upon reaching Butzdorf, the Kraut Killers took cover in the first three houses they reached and reorganized. They then proceeded to mop up the town until an influx of (the enemy) forced them back into the three houses after dark. The Germans were all around the buildings and it was impossible to leave any of them without being subject to German machine pistol fire." [10]

UNCLE BOB'S PART--NOVEMBER 24 IN THE CAMPHOLTZ WOODS

Lt. Col. (Capt) Spivey specifically described the personal actions of Uncle Bob on November 24 while still in the Campholtz Woods, and, later that day, his courageous leadership of the decimated K Company's attempt to secure Butzdorf:

"On 24 November 1944 in the vicinity of Tettingen, Germany, at about 0900 Captain McHolland had his Company CP (Command Post) in a concrete fort when he was informed by his outposts that there were fifteen or twenty Germans coming up a communication trench from one of the forts the Germans still held. Capt McHolland had only about six men around the fort. These men and the Captain engaged in a fire fight for about an half hour, when Sgt. Livingston shot a German who was carrying a flame thrower. The Germans then began to throw hand grenades. The Captain then went back to his mortar section nearby and brought up some of his mortarmen, who were armed with M-1s to assist him.

"Then Captain McHolland saw the Germans start to withdraw down the trench, he took Sgt. Livingston and the Engineer Sgt. with him, climbed over some dragon's

teeth, and went up the trench about 15 yards past seven wounded Germans. The trench was about five feet deep. Captain McHolland asked the Engineer Sgt. how to use the German egg grenades which were strewn all around the wounded. He jumped out of the trench, threw one grenade, and jumped back in. He saw a lot of Germans farther down the trench. With the two sergeants he moved down the trench throwing German concussion grenades at the fleeing Germans.

"Meanwhile a platoon of the 10th Armored Division was knocking out a pillbox in the open abut 100 yards down the trench and about 25 yards to the left of the trench. The three men forced the Germans to run right into the 10th Armored Platoon. Sixty-four (64) Germans whom Captain McHolland had been chasing surrendered to the 10th Armored Platoon. Fourteen (14) surrendered to Captain McHolland and his two sergeants. These three men also killed 14 men and wounded 7.

"The aggressiveness, initiative, and boldness of Captain McHolland was instrumental in this instance in completely thwarting a German attempt to infiltrate back into the fort which he had captured the previous day. A PW later stated that these Germans were ordered to infiltrate back into the pillbox and into the trenches in the woods behind our troops. The Germans were armed with a flame thrower to take back the fort from Company K and had great quantities of concussion grenades for fighting in the woods. The PW stated that here were one hundred men in the unit which attempted to infiltrate up through the communication trench. Captain McHolland, with but a handful of men, had stopped this force." [11]

Uncle Bob's Part--Attack on Butzdorf

Lt. Col. (Capt) Spivey continued in describing Uncle Bob's actions in the assault on Butzdorf:

"On the same afternoon, Captain McHolland was ordered to attack and capture the town of Butzdorf, Germany, while Company I took Tettingen.

"Captain McHolland jumped off across the open at about 1300 (1 pm) with two assault rifle platoons of his company and a section of machine guns from Company M. Half way from the woods to the town, Company K came under very heavy machine gun fire from both sides of Butzdorf and from two German half tracks in the center of town. German tank fire from two thousand yards from the right front was also firing on the company. Company K was suffering heavy casualties. He ordered his men to run for the town of Butzdorf, get into the buildings, and reorganize there. He then led the men across the open with machine gun bullets coming from every direction.

"All but nine men, who were casualties, succeeded in reaching Butzdorf and got into three houses which became besieged from every side for twenty-four hours, until the rest of the Battalion was able to get up to them ..." [12]

Sgt. Hobert Winebrenner's Account of the action at Butzdorf

Due to the boldness and tenacity of their brave leader, what was left of Uncle Bob's Kraut Killers, along with the attached M Company heavy machine gun section, reached their objective. Sergeant Hobert Winebrenner, a machine gunner from M Company gives his eyewitness account of the "Bad Day in Butzdorf" in his *Bootprints* book. As the day started in their position overlooking Butzdorf, Hobert expressed his feelings about K Company and Captain Mac:

> *"I was in a group of machine gunners attached to K Company, now commanded by our old friend and former mate, Captain Robert McHolland. Past heroics had not only earned him charge of "K" and a promotion to the rank of captain, but also two Silver Stars. Known as the "Kraut Killers," his rifle unit numbered among the best in the business of war. They had become almost legendary for their courage under fire—a true reflection of their CO ..."* [13]

Hobert continued with his account of the action to take Butzdorf:

> *"As we set our sights on Butzdorf, Company I was assigned to Tettingen and "L" waited in reserve. By this stage, we had lost all radio contact, with anyone—period. We were truly in it alone. But with no red flags from intelligence, we assumed our objective to be manageable.*
>
> *"First, we had to traverse a wide-open valley into the village. Rather than rumble forward en masse, we trickled into town, a few at a time. It was a shrewd move by McHolland and most of us made it safely into three or four of the outlying houses.*
>
> *"Structure by structure, we began to fight our way through Butzdorf. Our biggest problem lay in our heavy machine guns. I think parts of only two made it, and neither worked worth a damn ...*

"That night, German reinforcements trotted into town, and began to push us back. We soon worked from only a handful of houses at the village's outer edge. However, these structures happened to occupy both sides of the main road running from Butzdorf to Tettingen ...

"A very bad situation turned even worse when two Kraut tanks arrived, and they weren't shy about deconstruction. The enemy armor dismantled one building after another. We were left with only three houses." [14]

T/SGT EMMETT BOYD'S ACCOUNT OF THE BUTZDORF ACTION

Another account of the Butzdorf operation was offered by the K Company Weapons Platoon Sergeant, Technical Sergeant Emmett Boyd. He related:

"Late in the afternoon we started down the hill toward Butzdorf, and as we moved into the town we encountered small arms fire. We thought that the tanks from the 10th Armored Division ... would come in and help us wipe these pockets out. We later found out they would not come in because they were afraid of drawing anti-tank fire ... Our company occupied the first two houses on one side of the main street and another house on the other side. All night long the German half tracks would patrol up and down the streets trying to find us." [15]

K COMPANY--CUT OFF IN BUTZDORF

The German infantry and armor counterattack had left Uncle Bob and the remnants of his unit faced with a grim state of affairs. I company, the assault company to their left, had been held up by the enemy and did not make it to their objective of Tettingen. Uncle Bob had lost all communications back to the Battalion and the darkness complicated things even further. The constant heavy fire from machine guns and machine pistols (burp guns) of the counterattacking German forces kept his men holed up in the houses they had reached. Uncle Bob was not sure how many of the men had made it safely into the town and where they were located. He desperately wanted to locate and account for his remaining force and it is possible he had daringly slipped outside his house to check on his men. It is also possible that he would have been unable to get outside because of the heavy enemy fire and the German patrols.

UNCLE BOB'S LAST FIGHT

Following are two personal accounts of the events that occurred during the long, fateful night at Butzdorf that ended the short but wondrously productive life of my Uncle Bob. There are differences in the accounts that are no longer possible to reconcile completely. The first account is a first-hand eyewitness report from close friend and M Company soldier, Sergeant Howard Pemberton. The second account, provided by Lt. Col (Capt) James S. Spivey, the Battalion Commander at the time, is a compilation of information gathered by his staff after the ill-fated action at Butzdorf.

SGT HOWARD PEMBERTON, M COMPANY MACHINE GUN SECTION SERGEANT

Sergeant Howard Pemberton was in the same house with Uncle Bob and about a dozen others. Fully aware of his dependability, Uncle Bob tapped Sergeant Pemberton to lead a patrol with the mission to go back to the Battalion for help. Sergeant Pemberton had picked a couple of soldiers and was preparing to depart.

He explained, "I was just getting ready to leave. Captain McHolland was the doorman. Then we heard a guy trying to yell quietly, but still be heard, 'K! K! K! K Company!' as he ran alongside the shed toward the door. When McHolland opened it to let this guy in, an enemy machine gunner cut the Captain down, right in front of me. There was nothing we could do for him. McHolland was dead and I never made it out the door." [16] Sergeant Pemberton related to me that Uncle Bob was hit by a burst from a machine pistol or burp gun. [17]

LT. COL. JAMES S. SPIVEY, BATTALION COMMANDER

In a Battalion report, Lt. Col. James S. Spivey offered this version of the events:

> *"After dark, two wounded men from K Company tried to get into Captain McHolland's house, but the door was stuck. Captain McHolland with utter disregard for his personal safety, ran out the rear door of the house and assisted the wounded men around to the rear door. As he was entering the house after the wounded men, he was shot down from behind and killed by a German machine gun. He probably saved the lives of the two men but lost his own."* [18]

A DISTINGUISHED SERVICE
CROSS FOR UNCLE BOB

Portions of Lt. Col Spivey's account were included in the citation that accompanied the Distinguished Service Cross Uncle Bob was awarded for his extraordinary heroism on 23 and 24 November, 1944. It read:

> *"For extraordinary heroism in connection with military operations against an armed enemy. On 23 November 1944, during an attack by the 358th Infantry against strongly fortified enemy positions near (Butzdorf, Germany), Captain McHolland, commanding Company 'K', fearlessy lead a group of his men against a concrete machine-gun emplacement, destroyed it with a demolition charge and forced the occupants to surrender. The following day he again distinguished himself by breaking up a strong enemy attack against his command post. When the enemy force retreated, Captain McHolland and two enlisted men boldly pursued them, killed fourteen of the attackers with hand grenade fire, wounded seven and forced the remaining seventy-eight to surrender. Later, Captain McHolland was fatally wounded while evacuating two wounded men to the safety of a building. His conspicuous heroism, courage, and supreme devotion to duty exemplify the highest traditions of the military service."* [19]

K AND M COMPANY SURVIVORS RELIEVED

The remainder of the night in Butzdorf was hell for K Company and the attached M Company survivors as they continued to fight for their lives. The Germans kept firing their machine guns and pistols at the houses and even demolished one of the houses with bazookas and a Mark IV tank. Seven of the ten men in the house made it through heavy machine gun fire to another house. Sergeant Howard Pemberton of M Company could not figure out why they were not completely overrun, killed, or captured. He thinks the reason might be that the Germans thought there were more U. S. soldiers in the town than there were. [20] This very well could be the reason as the K and M Company soldiers put up a terrific fight. It was sometime during the day on November 25, that a platoon of L Company with two attached tanks reached Butzdorf. The Battalion was relieved by elements of the 10th Armored Division on November 26, and moved back to Rettel, France. [21] Suffering from a high rate of casualties the entire regiment was placed in division reserve. The 10th Armored Division would also be pulled back later and Butzdorf would not be secured for a few more weeks.

CONFUSION AT BATTALION ABOUT K AND M COMPANY

The furious action around Butzdorf and Tettingen resulted in much confusion at Battalion headquarters over the status of K and M Company personnel. There is no record of the daily morning report for K Company from November 24 through November 26. Uncle Bob was officially reported as missing in action on the morning report of November 28. To illustrate the confusion, the Unit Journal of the 3rd Battalion, 358th Infantry shows a brief entry logged at 0300 on November 26, "Capt McHolland is reported KIA." It was also reported that five other lieutenants were listed as either killed or injured, but did not identify their Company. Further evidence of the uncertainty existing at this time was another entry in the Unit Journal at 0930 on the same date stating, "Lt Elwell is going to all companies to check strength figures and especially K Co. Evidently quite a few of K Company men had been taken PsW by the Jerries and the wounded evacuated by German medics in Butzdorf."[22] No mention was made regarding recovery of bodies of U. S. soldiers—something that would lead to much consternation and many continuing questions of Captain Mac's family.

WHAT WENT WRONG AT BUTZDORF?

Recall that the trademarks of General George Patton's Third Army were rapid movement and mobility. The infantry units cleared the way for the armored units to occupy and firmly secure captured territory. Combat Command A had been formed on November with this strategy in mind as the entire 358th Infantry Regiment was attached to the recently arrived 10th Armored Division. The plan for the Butzdorf-Tettingen operation called for the Third Battalion, 358th Infantry, to take these two nearly adjacent towns and thus clear the way for the armor to move in and secure the area. With sparse intelligence regarding the enemy strength and positions, the attack began in the early afternoon of November 24 with K Company moving on the right to take Butzdorf and I Company on the left advancing to take Tettingen. L Company was held in battalion reserve.

Both I and K Companies were faced with the task of moving a few hundred yards down a slope dotted with pillboxes manned by determined German troops. Progress to neutralize each pillbox was slow. I Company encountered more of the pillboxes than K Company and, late in the afternoon, was ordered by the battalion commander, Captain Spivey, to postpone the assault on Tettingen until the next morning. K Company never got the word to postpone the assault. Just as K Company had knocked out the last of the pillboxes in its area, the company came under heavy machine gun fire as it moved toward Butzdorf. At that point Uncle Bob ordered his men to make a run for Butzdorf where they would reorganize. Most of his men and two attached heavy machine gun squads from M Company made it to Butzdorf and took cover in three or four houses on the edge of town. It was almost dark by the time they had reached Butzdorf. They were holed up in these houses when shortly after dark a German infantry company reinforced with tanks made a furious counterattack with grenades and small arms fire on the village. K Company and its attached members of M Company were surrounded by German troops and left without communication to their own headquarters. It has been reported that approximately thirty of the men held on until sometime on November 25 when L Company, reinforced with two tanks, was able to move through Butzdorf.

Many questions came afterward about the disastrous results suffered by the Third Battalion, 358th Infantry, at Butzdorf. Why was the intelligence information so lacking? Why did they not know the town was heavily defended and there were German infantry and armored units at close proximity in reserve. How did the communication lines between Third Battalion and K Company get cut off? I Company was aware that the commander had ordered postponement of the attack, but K Company did not get the word. Why did K Company not get the word? In fact, K Company kept moving and reached its objective. Why was the reserve company, L Company, not committed sooner? I Company had been held up and apparently needed help. At some point, it had to be obvious that K Company was in trouble. Why wait until the next day to send help? And the most burning question—WHERE IN THE HELL WAS THE ARMOR? K Company cleared its zone and made it to the objective. The armor was supposed to come after K Company had done its part of clearing the way. What was the armor waiting for now? If the armor had moved into Butzdorf, the German counterattack possibly could have been repelled. Why did it take until the next day for the reserve company, L Company, REINFORCED WITH ARMOR, to provide the help K Company so desperately needed the night before? These questions and more will always remain for many of those who were there and for the families of those who were lost in the Butzdorf action.

An alarming shortage of accurate intelligence information, an incomprehensible lack of a decision to commit the battalion reserve company to reinforce K Company in Butzdorf on the afternoon or evening of November 24, and an equally puzzling hesitancy to commit the tanks of the 10th Armored Division to secure Butzdorf led to the decimation of the Third Battalion, 358th Infantry, during this operation. On the evening of November 25, no longer able to continue the attack, the 358th Infantry Regiment was relieved by the 10th Armored Division, returned to 90th Division control, and placed in division reserve.

Uncle Bob--Offficial Status, Missing in Action

One thing appears certain at this point. Although Uncle Bob would be initially reported as missing in action, the eyewitness report of Sergeant Howard Pemberton and the Unit Journal entry lead one to suppose that they were reasonably certain that he had been killed. Most likely the hesitancy of reporting him as killed is because his body was not recovered and there might still be the possibility that he was a prisoner of war.

The Regiment and Battalion Salute the Loss of a Great Officer and Gentleman

There are two particularly powerful statements from his unit that magnificently describe the impact my Uncle Bob made on the officers and enlisted men with whom he served. The first comes from the Regimental History, 358th Infantry:

> *"On this night, the Regiment mourned the loss of a brilliant officer. Captain McHolland, who came overseas with the Regiment, formed his company in the heavily shelled woods of the Foret de Mont Castre—out of a handful of replacements and a few old members of the company. From that time on, he became one of the most outstanding commanders in the Regiment—instilling in the men the finest qualities of a soldier. If there was a tough job to be done K Company took it and liked it. The story of Captain McHolland already had become a legend and his name will long be remembered by every man who knew of him."[23]*

The second statement came from his Battalion Commander, Lt. Col. (Capt) James S. Spivey, who wrote of him:

> *"Captain McHolland's extraordinary heroism … was a common occurrence in every battle in which he engaged. His boldness and battlefield leadership was a shining example to the men in his Company. The courage, aggressiveness, boldness, and audacity of every man in Company K, 358th Infantry, reflects the brilliant and superior leadership of this great soldier and officer."* [24]

Fellow soldiers Hobert Winebrenner, Howard Pemberton, and Emmett Boyd have all voiced their admiration and respect for Captain Mac as a person. Ironically, both Howard and Emmett expressed the similar and very poignant sentiment that they knew he would never make it all the way to the end because "He cared too much about his men." [25]

Mary Scott Hair, in her beautiful tribute, "Rosary for Remembrance," to Uncle Bob most aptly illustrated the depth of care, concern and consideration for his men, family, and friends with the verse she used from the apostle John, "Greater love hath no man than this, that a man lay down his life for his friends." [26]

Chapter 17 Endnotes:
1. Cole, 487.

2. Bryan, 18.
3. Bryan, 18.
4. Bryan, 18-19.
5. Document, Official Personnel File.
6. Boyd, 11-12.
7. Document, Official Personnel File.
8. Bryan, 19.
9. Winebrenner and McCoy, 155.
10. Bryan, 19.
11. Document, Official Personnel File.
12. Document, Official Personnel File.
13. Winebrenner and McCoy, 150.
14. Winebrenner and McCoy, 151-2.
15. Boyd, 12.
16. Winebrenner and McCoy, 153.
17. Personal interviews, Pemberton, 2007-8.
18. Document, Official Personnel File.
19. Document, Official Personnel File.
20. Personnal interviews, Pemberton.
21. Bryan, 20.
22. Unit Journal, 3rd Battalion, 358th Infantry, November 1944.
23. Daily Regimental History – 358th Infantry, 25 November 1944, 2.
24. Document, Official Personnel File.
25. Personal Interviews, Pemberton, Boyd.
26. Hair, 8.

Chapter 18
A Telegram Arrives– The Wait Begins

From its onset in December, 1941, hardly a person in the United States was spared the effects of World War II. Gasoline and food rationing, scrap metal and paper drives, planting of victory gardens, encouragement to buy war bonds and other means of supporting the war effort were widely promoted. News of the war dominated everyday conversation. Every adult had become familiar with the War Department notification procedure, informing the next of kin of service members missing, captured, wounded, or killed in action. The folks in Uncle Bob's home town of Hurley, Missouri, were no exception. As the conflict in the European and Pacific theaters continued to rage, the tranquility of the peaceful Spring Creek Valley community was shattered numerous times with bad news of loved ones serving. Several local families had been the recipients of the dreadful, unwelcome telegram from the War Department.

Unwelcome Telegrams

The nearest telegraph office to Hurley was located about six miles away at the Missouri Pacific Lines railroad depot in Crane. Still in his first few years of what turned out to be a long career with the railroad, Vance Shipman was a young telegrapher at the Crane depot during World War II. He recalled, in particular, the wires received at the depot from the War Department during the war years. Those telegrams were delivered personally to families living in the immediate Crane area. However, when a telegram was received for someone with a Hurley address, the usual procedure was to put it in the mail pouch for delivery on the next train to Hurley since the Hurley depot did not operate a telegraph service.[1]

The Missouri Pacific Lines made a regular run twice daily through Hurley, Monday through Friday. The train passed through about seven thirty in the morning on its way to Springfield and returned through Hurley around eleven o'clock on its way back to Crane. In the afternoon the train would return through Hurley around one o'clock, on its second daily run to Springfield. It would pass again through Hurley about four o'clock in the afternoon, on its way back to Crane. The train stopped at Hurley if it had freight cars to drop off or pick up. It would also stop if there were passengers or smaller freight items to drop off or to pick up. If the train stopped, the conductor would hand deliver the paper work for the freight and any other items, such as telegrams received in the telegraph office at Crane or Springfield. If there was no need for the train to stop in Hurley but there were telegrams or paper work to be delivered, they would be placed in a mail pouch and thrown off at the depot as the train passed by the station.

Numbered among those in the Hurley area who had received the bad news of loved ones serving during the war were the families of Herbert and Paul Thomas, Dale "Rip" Dean, and Millard Israel. Uncle Bob's sister, my mother, Roxabel, was the Hurley depot agent. During this time Roxabel took it upon herself to personally deliver telegrams from the War Department to the families of service members living in and around Hurley. [2]

Mabel Alice Thomas Redwing, a younger sister of Paul and Herbert Thomas, related her memories regarding the receipt of the tragic news about her brothers. The telegram with news about her brother Paul came first. Mabel Alice recalled that Roxabel personally delivered the telegram to her father, Herman, whom she located working on the farm for local resident, Fred Steele. The wire informed Herman Thomas that his son, Paul, who was serving in Nebraska with the Army Air Corps, had died in a swimming accident.

The receipt of the War Department telegram about her brother, Herbert, involved a poignant set of events. Mabel Alice related that her father, concerned about not hearing from Herbert for some time had encouraged her mother, Mabel, to write a letter to him. Mabel wrote the letter and took it to the Hurley post office to mail. Unbeknownst to her, a telegram for the Thomas family had arrived that morning at the depot. Roxabel located Mabel at the post office as she was mailing the letter to Herbert. In a highly emotional situation, with tears streaming down her face, Roxabel informed Mabel that there would be no need to mail the letter. [3] In a cruel twist of irony, Roxabel would also be the recipient of a similar agonizing and tortuous message from the War Department.

THE UNWELCOME TELEGRAM ABOUT UNCLE BOB ARRIVES

On Monday, December 11, 1944, the Missouri Pacific train rumbled through Hurley on its regular morning run to Springfield. With no passengers to board or debark and no freight cars to spot or pick up, in accord with usual practice the conductor tossed the mail pouch off at the depot. It was possible the train crew did not realize the pouch contained a telegram from the War Department addressed to one of their fellow employees and the Hurley depot agent. Nevertheless, this seemingly innocent action was perceived somewhat differently by Roxabel and remained a sore point with her throughout her life. [4]

Mary Lea recalls her sister, Roxabel's, hurt feelings about the method in which the mail pouch was delivered on that occasion. Going about her normal duties as depot agent, Roxabel opened the pouch to find a Western Union telegram from the War Department addressed to her. Because she had personally received and delivered the all too familiar communication to close friends before, she knew immediately that the news contained inside could not be good. The telegram was dated December 9, but that date fell on a Saturday in 1944. Since the depot was closed on Saturday and Sunday the telegram did not arrive at Hurley until Monday, December 11. Not only did the telegram deliver the heartbreaking news that Uncle

Bob was reported as missing in action on November 24, 1944, but Roxabel was also deeply hurt by the apparent insensitivity of her fellow railroad coworkers with the manner in which the horrible news was delivered. She maintained they should have had the decency to stop the train and personally deliver the telegram to her. *NOTE: In defense of the coworkers who tossed the mail pouch that day, I can look more objectively at the circumstances surrounding this situation. I believe it is quite possible her friends did not realize the horrible news contained within the pouch.*

For the record, the message read:

THE SECRETARY OF WAR DESIRES ME TO EXPRESS HIS DEEP REGRET THAT YOUR BROTHER CAPTAIN ROBERT B MCHOLLAND HAS BEEN REPORTED MISSING IN ACTION SINCE TWENTY FOUR NOVEMBER IN GERMANY IF FURTHER DETAILS OR OTHER INFORMATION ARE RECEIVED YOU WILL BE PROMPTLY NOTIFIED

> *DUNLOP ACTING THE ADJ*
> *GENERAL* [5]

Although my mother never shared her thoughts or feelings about this heart rending news, it had to be utterly devastating to her. The same could be said for her siblings, close family, and friends. A pall was immediately cast over the entire community and the normally happy and anticipatory emotions associated with the Christmas season.

A Bewildered Child and Lingering Memories

In the Prologue I expressed the situation regarding the telegram experienced through the eyes of a small child. I vividly remember the phone call my mother made to her sister, Anna, in Texas, with the telegram in her hand and, especially, my mother's extremely uncharacteristic emotional reactions. Mary Lea was teaching at the Hurley High School during this time. She recalls receiving the shocking message from the superintendent's wife, who had received a telephone call from Roxabel. Mary Lea, like many others, experienced the numbness of unbelief and unreal feelings that, "This could not be happening! Maybe it is all a bad dream!" [6]

While ever so slight, there remained hope that Uncle Bob was still alive, maybe as a prisoner of war. The fact he was reported as missing gave everyone a small glimmer of hope that he was alive. Many expressions of support and encouragement to Roxabel and Mary Lea came during the days and weeks to follow. Those who resided in and around Hurley offered their best wishes, personally, through their prayers, hugs, and telephone calls. And, cards and letters with messages of optimism began coming from family and friends.

Letters of Hope and Encouragement Pour into the Family

One of the first letters came from sister Eva, in California, in which she wrote:

My Dear Sisters;

I can never express in words, just how your letter struck me. It tore me up so for in the same mail delivery, I received a Xmas card from Robby himself dated Nov 24. A sweet little message and a short letter written in his own hand. It's such a precious letter-I shall copy it and send it to you all so you can hear from him:

"Dear Sis: Just a few lines to let you know I'm still OK. I guess the prayers of somebody is keeping me alive. It shore takes a heap of praying and I suppose plenty have been praying for my safety.

Give Uncle A.G. my regards. I got his letter but I didn't get to save his address. So I can't write, but tell him I'm OK. And to keep writing.

It looks as if this may not last too long from now on out or at least I hope it doesn"t.

So long for now,

Bob"

On his Xmas card the message reads thus: May the true meaning of Christmas be reflected throughout the coming year. Signed: From Bro Bob

Wasn't that sweet? I love every word. It burns deep in my heart for the poor dear darling.

So girls please let's don't give up and let our light of hope go out for him. As long as the message says "missing" only. He may still be in this Land of the Living, only wounded or held prisoner, and will escape death, bad as it seems. As long as life lingers there is still hope. So don't be so downcast. He wouldn't want us to be. I can hear him say: keep courage, Sis, "life is still sweet to me." Don't give up. I can't feel he is killed. The living death may be too terrible for words that he is enduring even tonight. But he says it will soon be over. Let's believe him for he is in a position to know.

How's the babies? I can't seem to find anything for little Johnny's Xmas.

Tabby [Everette] *is in a bad shape. His operation has left his back in very bad shape. He is in a terrible frame of mind now, too. This news will sure hurt him, maybe will collapse him.*

Uncle A.G. [Green] *is in a terrible broken up state of mind, too, over Raymond* [Uncle Bob's cousin who was killed in Europe] *Now Robby's missing is too sad for words. Uncle says let's not give up and still trust he will be spared.*

Kids do write to poor Tabby. He is in a bad shape, I tell you. His address is this:

Everette T. McHolland S2/c
USN Training and Dist Center
Treasure Island Calif
San Francisco

Now write to him he would so appreciate hearing from you all. He may be the bro we have left. Let's cherish him and hold a hope for dear Robby's safety.

> *Good by now*
> *Love always*
> *Your Sis*
> *Eve*

In a letter dated December 12, 1944, brother Everette wrote to Mary Lea:

Dear Mary Lea:

Received your letter, it almost floored me when I read it. In fact when I opened it and seen it was so short, I knew it wasn't good news. I was afraid something had happened back there at first, but I have prayed and prayed for Bob's safety. And we must pray more and more that God has his guiding hand over him.

I received a letter from Bob in the same mail your letter came in on that was written Nov 5th and I opened his letter first and read it. And he wrote very discouraging in it. Something different from him. And when I opened your letter I was afraid something was wrong back there, or with Bob, one.

I'm so upset I can't hardly think. I'll keep his letter until we see each other, and I'll let you read it. Please keep me posted on what you learn from the govt. I'll hop and pray that God is by him and is protecting him from any danger. Write me soon.

> *Love Your Brother*
> *Tabby* [Everette]

NOTE: The "discouraging" letter received from Uncle Bob referred to by Everette is included in Chapter 16 under the heading "A Gloomy Letter to Brother Everette."

Another letter dated December 12, to Mary Lea came from Uncle Bob's Texas lady friend, Francis Wilshire (Shahan), in Fort Worth, Texas. She had apparently received the news about Uncle Bob from his sister Anna.

> *Dear Mary Lea,*
>
> *I just found out about Bob this weekend when I went home, and somehow I wanted to write you. I wish I knew just the right words to say. If a message had to come, I'm glad it was "missing" rather than "killed," for missing always means hope. It is a hard situation to take but there is one thing for which to be thankful—the Germans treat their prisoners better than do the Japs.*
>
> *I know all of my ramblings sound trite to you, but perhaps this little poem by Grace Noel Crowell will help you to more fully understand what is in my heart.*
>
> ### Hope
>
> *This would I hold more precious than fine gold,*
> *This would I keep although all else be lost:*
> *Hope in the heart, that precious, priceless thing,*
> *Hope at any cost.*
>
> *And God, if its fine luster should be dimmed,*
> *If seemingly through grief it may be spent,*
> *Help me to wait without too much to spare,*

To great astonishment.

Let me be patient when my spirit lack
Its high exuberance, its shining wealth,
Hope is a matter, often God, I know
Of strength, of health.

Help me to wait until my strength returns,
Help me climb each difficult high slope,
Always within my heart some golden gleam,
Some quenchless spark of hope.

> *With all my love and prayers,*
> *Frances Wilshire (Shahan)*

A third letter dated December 12 was written to Mary Lea from John and Travis Brown's sister, Laura Mildred (Bug) Brown Layman of Niangua, Missouri:

Dear Mary Lea,

I received your letter today. We were so sorry to hear about Bob. I hope and pray that he is all right. I have prayed lots for his safe return. I had a Christmas card from him yesterday dated Nov 22 but you have heard since then.

We have just finished packing boxes for Tom and Alfrey (John Brown.) Alfrey is in Calif now but he thinks he will be sent overseas before long. His address is:

Lt. John A. Brown
Hq. Co 2d Bn, 342 Inf

Camp San Luis Obispo, California

You have a larger school than I. I only have 15 pupils. I like teaching my home school very much.

Write and let us know if you hear anything more from Bob. Come and see us when you can.

Thanks a lot for sending the word about Bob.

Love,
Laura Mildred

A fourth letter dated December 12, was written to Mary Lea and Roxabel from cousin Margaret McHolland Gastineau of Ava, Missouri:

Dear Mary Lea and Roxie,

I just heard your heart-breaking news. Need I say that I am sorry. All that we can do is just hope that he will come back.

Forrest (Margaret's brother who was on a navy submarine) has been missing a year the 4th of December. We received a letter from the Navy Department saying that he had been continued on the missing list for another period of time. They seem to have hopes for him.

We would appreciate any news that you might have from Bob.

Sincerely,
Margaret

Another cousin, Ava Lee McHolland Terry of Purdy, Missouri, wrote to Mary Lea and Roxabel on December 13, 1944:

Dear Roxie Belle and Mary Lea,

Girls, I received a letter from Dad yesterday telling me the dreadful news of Bob. I just can't refuse to write and tell you that I am so sorry I can't even express any thoughts. Words are too small, but I am thinking of you and I really hope that you have found or will find soon some measure of consolation. Bob was so good the memory of him is so fine that it just makes it twice as hard to bear.

But maybe somewhere his mind is turning and turning trying to think of some way to have you hear from him. The uncertainty of not knowing is an awful strain, I know. I guess you know my brother, Forrest, is in Germany? Jerry's brother, Claude, is in General Patton's Third Army, too. So you know the days and nights are dimmed by worry for us, too.

I will close hoping to hear that you have received some better news from Bob soon.

And wishing all of you a Merry Christmas and a Happy New Year.

Your cousin,
Ava Lee Terry

NOTE: Ava Lee's dad was Uncle Bob's Uncle John McHolland from Hurley..

In a letter dated December 15, 1944, Uncle Bob's closest friend, and a dear friend of the family, offered words of encouragement tempered by personal experience and a realistic sense of caution:

Dear Roxabel,

This is a hard letter for me to write. I don't want to build up false hopes but I don't feel as if Bob has been killed. Bob is the best friend I ever had and I think I know him better than anyone. I have always been certain that he would come back just as I always knew Rip wouldn't. He is just the kind of guy that pulls through.

It's not only this feeling I have but I've been keeping up with his unit and they have advanced several miles since November. If he had been killed they would know that by now. I hope and feel the next time we hear the worst will be that he's a prisoner.

I have been in the hospital for a month now and yesterday I had another attack of malaria so guess I'll spend Christmas here.

Keep your hopes up.

Edwin

A friendly rival of Uncle Bob for the affections of Laura Mildred (Bug) Brown from his days of teaching at High Point School, Carl Layman, wrote a very nice letter to Mary Lea on December 16, 1944 from where he was stationed in Camp Cooke, California:

Dear Mary Lea,

I had a letter from Laura Mildred today saying you had received a telegram from the War Dept stating Bob was missing in action. I am very sorry to learn of this as Bob was one of the best friends I have ever had. I shall never forget the good times we have had together, taking in the movies, baseball games, singing, and going to Church. Bob used to enjoy the church services and sacred songs very much. I'm sincerely hoping that you have received word before now that he is safe but if the worst has happened I'm sure he was ready to go. Death has it's sting regardless, but if we have to give them up it's great consolation to know they were prepared to go.

I feel that you will hear from him even though it may be a while before you do.

How are things going with you and the rest of the folks? As far as I know everyone at home is OK and personally I can't complain. I weigh a measly 198 now so I guess army life agrees with me even if it does get disgusting at times.

If things had gone according to plans we would probably have been on our way over by now but orders were cancelled and I'm anticipating a furlough in Jan or Feb.

I'm in a field artillery battalion and since it's the army I like it pretty well.

Alfrey (John Brown) is stationed at Camp San Luis Obispo which is only 50 miles from here. I talked to him last week but haven't heard from him the last few days. I spent last week end with my nephew who is stationed at Moffet Field near San Jose. We went into San Francisco Sunday afternoon and crossed the Golden Gate Bridge just as the sun was setting. It was a very fine view but I would just as soon be seeing the sun set in Missouri.

It's rather cool of a morning out here but is usually very nice later in the day. The rainy season will start soon and that usually means plenty of water and mud.

I was in Camp Roberts last winter and it really was sloppy during the rainy season. That's about 75 miles from here so I imagine it will be the same story here.

I was at Camp Callan near San Diego for 30 days before we came here. During our stay there we had a 7 day cruise in the Pacific which was very interesting.

Well I must close as I have to write L.M. (Laura Mildred.) Be sure to notify me as soon as you receive any news about Bob.

> *Your friend,*
> *Carl Layman*

A Missouri Pacific Railroad official from Springfield, Mr. L. H. Ellison, who had a son missing in action (later confirmed as killed in action) wrote a letter to Roxabel dated December 16, 1944:

Dear Roxeybell:
I have just learned that you brother has been reported missing in action in Germany.

I am so sorry to hear of this report. There is nothing that can be said that will in any way relieve your anxiety, but believe me I can truthfully sympathize with you and your family. The best thing I know to do is to keep up your hopes and worry as little as possible. So long as they are only reported missing, this is the chance that they will show up later or be reported as prisoner of war, especially the ground forces.

We have had letters from three different parties who have visited the Air Base where J. D. was stationed and they have all given us a lot of encouragement that he may yet show up as a prisoner of war, although we have a report from the War Department stating that he was killed in action. All we can do is wait and see what the future brings.

Very respectfully,
L. H. Ellison

These are but a few of the many sincere gestures of promise received by the family during these days and weeks of anguish, agony and uncertainty. One can be certain there were other notes, as well as a constant flow of telephone calls and personal greetings offering prayers and thoughtful consideration for the family's painful plight.

CHRISTMAS 1944--A SOMBER TIME FOR THE FAMILY

The usual sense of anticipation and celebration of the Christmas season had been dampened by the unfortunate turn of events involving Uncle Bob's status. Added to this was the fact that my father, Maurice, had received a notice from the county draft board to report for duty at Jefferson Barracks, Missouri on January 17, 1945. Personally, I do not remember any details of this Christmas. However, with three small boys, myself and my brothers Bob and John, expecting Santa Claus, even with dark and ominous clouds hanging over the festivities I am certain that our dad and mom made sure the old fellow with the beard completed his expected stop at the Wiley home in Hurley on Christmas Eve, 1944.

Chapter 18 Endnotes:
1.　Telephone interview, Vance Shipman, 2008.
2.　Personal interviews, M. Brown.
3.　Personal interview, Mable Alice Thomas Redwing, 2008.
4.　Personal interviews, M. Brown.
5.　Western Union Telegram from War Department, 12-9-44.
6.　Personal interviews, M. Brown.

Chapter 19
The Bad News Arrives--
Expressions of Sympathy Flow

In late December, 1944, Hitler launched his great counteroffensive on the western front resulting in what became known as the Battle of the Bulge. At the same time, the community of Hurley was enduring a subdued Christmas season hoping and praying that the missing in action news about one of their favorite sons would have a favorable outcome. The three weeks following receipt of the infamous War Department telegram must have been a tortuous period of uncertainty for Uncle Bob's family and loved ones desperately holding on to the remote expectation that he would somehow beat the seemingly obvious odds. The sad news came in an expected form; another abhorrent Western Union telegram addressed to Uncle Bob's sister, Roxabel, from the War Department. The mundane message tersely read:

*THE SECRETARY OF WAR ASKS THAT I AS-
SURE YOU OF HIS DEEPEST SYMPATHY IN*

*THE LOSS OF YOUR BROTHER CAPTAIN ROB-
ERT B MCHOLLAND WHO WAS PREVIOUSLY
REPORTED MISSING IN ACTION   REPORT
NOW RECEIVED THAT HE WAS KILLED IN
ACTION TWENTY FOURTH NOVEMBER IN
GERMANY CONFIRMING LETTER FOLLOWS*

DUNLOP THE ACTING ADJ
GENERAL [1]

THE DREADED TELEGRAM ARRIVES

I cannot be certain when Roxabel actually received this
telegram. However, based on information from correspondence contained in the scrapbook maintained by
Mary Lea and Roxabel, it may be reasoned that she received the telegram sometime in the afternoon or evening
of New Year's Eve, December 31, 1944. This is based on
the fact that the telegram was dated "105PM 12-31-44."
New Year's Eve, 1944, fell on a Saturday. This made it
likely that the telegram office at the Crane depot would
probably have received it sometime that afternoon. Entered in the scrapbook is a Western Union telegram from
Uncle A. G. (Green) McHolland, Long Beach, California, to Mary Lea dated 5:30 PM, January 1, 1945. The
telegram contained the short message, "SORRY THAT
BOB HAD TO GO." For Uncle "Green" to have known
on January 1 that Uncle Bob had been killed, it is concluded that Roxabel received the telegram on Saturday
evening or, at the latest, on Sunday morning. That being
the case, when they received the information, Roxabel
and Mary Lea would have immediately notified close
family members of the news by telephone or wire.

MESSAGES OF SYMPATHY AND COMFORT

Uncle A. G. (Green) McHolland's telegram was the first of many words of sympathy offered to the grieving family. Within a few days other family members and friends of the family would provide their words of comfort through cards and letters. The content of several of the letters provided further insight into Uncle Bob's character and personality. Those letters, or excerpts from them, are included in the following paragraphs.

Letter from cousin Reba (Uncle John McHolland's daughter):

Richmond, Calif
Jan 4, 1945

Dear Roxie and Mary Lea,

Girls, I've just heard about Bob. I wish there was something I could say or do to console you in your grief, but there is nothing, I guess, but at least I want you to know that my heart is with you, and you are not alone in your grief.

To me he didn't get to be a grown man, he was always the babe I fell down the stairs with. I loved him like that, kids, so you can guess how I feel about it, too.

I know Bob wouldn't want us to grieve like we are. All we can do is say "God rest his soul." And pray that it is a "big mistake" and some day he will come back to us.

Stranger things have happened you know.

But darlings, just remember that every one who knew you kids know you had a swell baby brother. And I know he had two fine brave sisters who are not afraid to face life as it comes and not apt to crack up in time of trouble. I think that is what I love about you so much. You can take it on the chin and keep fighting.

I have one consolation. I've put a few little pieces of steel together that's making big battle ships that are going to avenge those three graves! (Forrest, Raymond and Bob) And all the Forrests, Raymonds and Bobs!

How are the babies? Kiss them for their old big no good cousin.

Is Anna still there? Tell her Hello for me if she is. I see Tabby quite often.

Girls, go over and see Dad every once in a while. He loves you. Will you?

> *Lovingly,*
> *Your cousin,*
> *Reba*

Letter, in part, from Mrs. Joe Layman, mother of Carl Layman, to Mary Lea dated January 4, 1945. She knew Uncle Bob from his teaching years at High Point school:

Niangua, MO
Jan 4, 1944

Dear Friend,

On receiving news of Bob's death I wish to take this way of extending my sympathy. Surely there are many sad hearts in this community as the word goes into the homes of the pupils of High Point School where he taught the children to lead upright lives. Surely his teaching will go with them through all the trials they meet. I think Carl has lost one of the best friends he ever had, seemed he could not believe Bob was dead. But many as Bob had to go.

I think he got to fulfill his ambition. He told me when he was here if he had went on he would have been Captain there. It seemed he wanted to go over, but I don't think all of them that is the case. But I don't think any of them that is Carl, Alfrey or Bob ever wanted to go. But their country called and they answered. He was so much company to Carl and myself. You see Carl's father had just died. Found him dead in bed on Thanksgiving morning. No one here but Carl and myself when I saw he was dead. So you see we know the sting of death in the family. I also lost Carl's baby brother. He would have been about 20 now. I have a great nephew now assigned to Patton's army just one day's difference in his and my baby's age. So if mine had lived he would probably be facing what Bob, Carl and thousands of others have faced.

Carl and Bob would sing together when Bob would come up after supper. He was the first I ever heard sing "Hide you in the blood of Jesus." They would also sing "The Wandering Orphans" and surely they have lived that life since this awful war......

Hope Roxie Belle and kiddies are OK. I am not personally acquainted with her but I have heard Bob talk of you all so much seems I know you all. Wish you could come up and visit.......

So Good Bye,
Mrs. Joe Laymen

Letter, in part, from Aunt Elva Brown Milliken (Nancy Brown McHolland's sister) to Roxabel:

Claremore, Okla
Jan 7, 1945

Dear Niece,

Your letter rec'd telling the sad news. I know that your heart is heavy and Maurice having to go away too. But maybe the Good Lord took Bob because he wanted to spare him the things that are to come and maybe everything is for the best and we just can't see it that way.

I think that he was a good boy and that God will receive his soul. That should be a great consolation to us.

I know that I should have done more for him than I did, but it is too late to think about that now.

I know that Mary Lea misses him so much and will feel so alone now.

Do hope that you, she and babies are OK……..

Love, Aunt Elva

An undated letter from dear family friend and classmate of Roxabel, Inez (Sukey) Inmon Bowman, she had also included a portion of the Longfellow poem, "Resignation":

Roxy and Mary Lea,

    For two days I've tried to think of something I could do to lighten your grief. Nothing I can say will actually help but it may if you know besides Homer there is not another on the front that would have hurt more to receive such news of. That's why I wish I could help in some way. The thing that will comfort you most is knowing Bob was ready to go--though I'm aware even that can't fill his vacant place with you.

    With part of Homer's Christmas money I bought a picture for the church—Christ on the Battlefield. With your permission I want to place a plaque under it in memory of Bob. I'll talk to you about it when I'm able to get out.

With love,
Sukey

Letter from Edith Brown, mother of John and Travis Brown, dated January 8, 1945, who wrote of her family's deep affection for Uncle Bob and the fact that he was at peace with his God:

Niangua, MO

Jan 8, 1945

Dear Mary Lea,

We received your letter telling us about Bob. We are so sorry. I tried every day to write and it seems that I cannot.

We loved Bob dearly, these children thought as much of him as of each other. I am so sorry. It doesn't seem possible that he will not be back.

We kept a young boy four years. He came here while Bob was staying with us. He thought so much of Bob. Last March he went to the Navy. We had a letter from him last Friday asking for Bob's address as he had lost it, but Saturday morning he called out from Marshfield he had received an unexpected furlough. We were so glad to see him, but he is so sad over Bob, he can't quit talking about him.

I heard Travis tell Tom yesterday that he was with Bob like he was his father, that he felt like he would come back.

Alfrey wrote last week that he was going to write to Bob's First Sergeant and see if he could tell him anything regarding Bob. Alfrey knew this man when he was at Ft. Wood. Of course he may never hear from him either.

How is Roxiebel and Maurice and how are the little boys? I would like to see them. We might some day.

How is Herb's family? I believe Bob told me their baby was a girl. It seems to me that he said Everette was in the Navy.

I suppose school is in progress in Hurley again. These children are all back in school after their holiday. Laura Mildred said what a blessing every one had more work than they could do, or we would all go crazy these days.

Bob wrote one time not to worry about him that whatever God saw fit to do would be all right with Bob. It seems that difficulties could be settled without this awful killing and so much suffering.

Write sometime. I will surely be thinking of all of you.

With Love and Sympathy,
Edith Brown

Letter of heartfelt sympathy from another dear family friend and classmate of Roxabel, Betty Steele Hall, dated January 11, 1945:

Joplin, Mo
Jan 11, 1945

Dear Roxie and Mary Lea,

I have put off writing you because I can't find words to express my sympathy of the news about Bob. He was such a grand person. Although it had been several years since I had seen him, I remember him vividly in school.

Words are so meaningless at a time like this, but I believe as it had to happen this way, that he would have preferred it.

How are your boys? My little girl has had a cold but is better today. She is growing. Sondra is gong to be as tall as I.

When Ruth gets back with her big boy why don't we all— you, Suk, Mag, Ruth and I all get together with our kids.

I just wanted you to know I am thinking of you and you have my heartfelt sympathy.

Love,
Betty

Letter, in part, from cousin Ava Lee McHolland Terry, dated January 29, 1945:

Purdy, Mo
January 29, 1945

Dear Roxy Belle,

I received your letter and was awfully glad you wrote. How are the boys? I would love to see them. Where is Maurice stationed and does he like the army? There aren't many that do but Forest always pretended he did. He is in Belgium now. Mary Jo wrote me that Bob died trying to save one of his men. Roxy, such a sacrifice is unusual to say the least. Bob was unselfish but I never thought he would be called on to display such courage........

Affectionately,
Ava Lee Terry

A FORMAL LETTER FROM HIS UNIT

The telegram from the war department was followed up with a letter that provided the formal notification that Uncle Bob had been killed in action. The letter was dated December 27, 1944, and was likely received some time during the first week in January, 1945. That letter from Captain Charles G. Brandt, Personnel Officer of the 358th Infantry Regiment addressed to Roxabel follows:

Dear Mrs. Wiley:

I am sure you have received notice from the War Department that your brother, Captain Robert B McHolland, 0-433315, was killed in action in Western Germany on 24 November 1944.

Robert was commanding Rifle Company "K" in Germany, when the Germans attacked in an effort to overrun the 3rd Battalion's position. Exhibiting great courage and coolness, Robert ordered his company to advance and then preceded them in a counter-attack against strong enemy emplacements, pill-boxes, and well fortified terrain. It was during this action, when Robert tried and did succeed in obtaining a place of safety for one of his men, that he lost his life.

By his aggressive and determined leadership, and by his all-out effort in this battle, as in everyone in which he has participated, Robert successfully took his objective with very few casualties among his men. Robert was known as an officer of courage with the utmost devotion to duty. His loss is felt by the entire Regiment.

Any effects that Robert had will be forwarded to you through the Quartermaster General, Washington, D. C. If you do not receive them within several months, I suggest you write to that address.

With Deepest Sympathy,

CHARLES G. BRANDT
Capt., Infantry
Personnel Officer [2]

THE FAMILY GRIEVES TOGETHER

The days and weeks that followed receipt of the tele-gram, along with the letter confirming that Uncle Bob was killed in action, were filled with indescribable sorrow and pain for his family. With the initial phase of the in-evitable grieving process begun, the solid support of close family members and friends was an invaluable source of comfort for Roxabel, Mary Lea and their siblings. It helped that Mary Lea was kept busy with her teaching job at Hurley High School. With Roxabel's husband, Maurice, reporting for duty with the army, she would be even busier caring for their three small children and holding down her job as depot agent. A few short weeks after the confirmation of Uncle Bob's death brother Ev-erette was granted leave and made the long trip from his Navy duty station in California to visit with Roxabel and Mary Lea in Hurley. During the same, period sister Anna journeyed from Texas for a visit with her brother and sisters. Sister Eva, working a "Rosie the Riveter" job in the Naval shipyard at Long Beach, California, could not make the trip home but continued to keep in close communication with her brother and sisters.

RECOGNITION AND
UNANSWERED QUESTIONS

As must eventually occur, life went on for the family but the struggle to deal with Uncle Bob's death continued. The coming months would bring much deserved recognition from the War Department for the bravery and heroism displayed by Uncle Bob. However, questions began to smolder about the specific circumstances regarding Uncle Bob's death and the location of his remains. Written inquiries from family and friends about these events would continue with inadequate explanations provided, particularly those about the recovery of his remains. It would be several years before information would be obtained that would finally answer many of these questions.

Chapter 19 Endnotes:
1.   Western Union Telegram, War Department, 12-31-44.
2.   Letter, Hqs, 358th Infantry, 27 December 1944.

Captain Mac

Chapter 20
After the War--Striving for Closure

May 8, 1945, V-E Day, marked the date of Germany's unconditional surrender to the Allies. About three months later on August 15, 1945, V-J Day, Japan's Emperor Hirohito, tendered that country's unconditional surrender to the Allies. The world's most costly conflict by any standard had officially come to an end. However, pain and suffering caused by the six protracted years of devastation, destruction, and death would never be over for countless numbers of families who lost loved ones. Virtually every community in the United States experienced the loss of young men in the prime of their lives in this monumental struggle against the satanic forces of inhumanity, tyranny, and evil. Like so many others, the Hurley community gave much more than its fair share toward the lofty price of freedom and in the protection of our precious liberty and way of life.

A MEMORIAL TO HURLEY'S HEROES

A small haven from the cares of the world, Homestead Park, lies in an idyllic setting in Uncle Bob's home town of Hurley, Missouri. Situated along a small meandering spring that feeds into the clear running waters of Spring Creek, several tall trees provide shade over the picnic tables placed for visitors who frequent the site for community and family outings. The land for the park was generously donated by Uncle Bob's close friend and Hurley's most revered citizen, Mary Scott Hair, in the early 1980s. The highlight of the dedication ceremony for the park in July, 1981, was the placement of a memorial to honor the local heroes who gave their lives in the service of their country in World War I, World War II, the Korean War and the Vietnam War. Inscribed on the monument are the names of those brave men who made the ultimate sacrifice in World War II: Robert Barnett, Joe Coffer, Dallas Daum, Dale Dean, Millard Israel, Junior Laney, Donald Merritt, Bruce Parsons, Milford Spears, Billy Steele, Curtis Wolf (brother of Byron Wolf, student of Uncle Bob at Inmon school,) Lyle J. Roy, Herbert Thomas, Paul Thomas, Elton Wright, Frank Wright, Harold Bell Wright, and Robert McHolland. It was previously noted that the Herman Thomas family lost two sons in the war, Paul and Herbert, Also, to be noted among the names inscribed on the monument are three young men who bore the last name of Wright. Those three men, Elton, Frank, and Harold Bell came from the Henry Wright family. A hollow ring sounds with the statement that the war never ended for the families of these eighteen noble men. The grief and suffering for these families would never end.

Hurley Homestead Park Memorial to the town's servicemen killed in World War I, World War II, Korean War, and Vietnam War—courtesy Sheila Wiley.

ARRIVAL OF UNCLE BOB'S PERSONAL EFFECTS

In the wake of the war among the many mundane administrative requirements to be accomplished by the War Department was the return of the possessions of the soldiers missing or killed in action. For months after the fighting ceased, one of the events that evoked reminders and memories of their loved ones was the receipt of their personal effects. There is something hauntingly melancholy about sorting through the last earthly possessions of loved ones. By letter, dated August 8, 1945, from the Army Effects Bureau, Uncle Bob's sister, Roxabel, was advised that a footlocker bearing his personal effects was shipped to her address in Hurley. The footlocker arrived sometime later in the month. A copy of the inventory that accompanied the footlocker listed many items of clothing along with brushes, pens, books, letters, and photos.

Two more cartons containing the remainder of Uncle Bob's personal effects arrived the next month. The first of the two cartons contained all clothing items. Along with several more clothing items, the inventory of the second carton listed a sleeping bag, a pair of glasses, souvenir beads (a rosary), religious material, a sewing kit, ID tags, and a souvenir flint pistol. Interestingly, the rosary provided the centerpiece for Mary Scott Hair's tribute to Uncle Bob, Rosary for Remembrance. The flint pistol is the same item Uncle Bob referred to in the letter to his cousin Dorla Milliken in late October 1944.

A SISTER'S WAY OF COPING

Those few years after the war were undoubtedly difficult for all of Uncle Bob's loved ones, but his sister, Roxabel (my mother), had her own way of dealing with any of life's problems. Although very young and innocent I was lastingly affected by the manner in which my mother struggled to cope with the tragic loss of her beloved brother. Always taking care to hide her emotions, I am certain she shed countless tears for her brother out of the sight of her family. Ultimately, she chose to deal with the pain by not talking about Uncle Bob. A few years ago I became aware that some of the men who had served with Uncle Bob had called to speak with my mother about him. I am sure they only wanted to share with her their cherished memories of Uncle Bob. I cannot pinpoint the exact times and dates of the calls, but I suspect that she had received calls from the 1950s into the 1970s. As I delved further into gathering information for this tribute, I often lamented those lost, albeit unknown, opportunities to speak with persons who had served with Uncle Bob. Apparently my mother made it known to the callers that she did not want to talk with them. I believe the suppression of her feelings about the loss was directly linked with behavior she exhibited for many years after Uncle Bob's death. At risk of sounding like a Freudian disciple, I think other of her actions were often the result of displaced emotion, i.e., displacing her anger for the loss by sometimes directing it toward unrelated actions of her loved ones.

NEPHEWS PRESENTED UNCLE BOB'S COMBAT AWARDS

In the months after his death many tributes were offered to honor Uncle Bob's memory, war service, and exceptional heroism. I clearly recall the formal presentation of the combat awards he earned in the five months he served in combat. The ceremony was held at O'Reilly General Hospital in Springfield, Missouri in the fall of 1945. Like the good mother she was, our mom meticulously dressed my brothers, Bob and John, and me for the very special occasion. Sisters Mary Lea McHolland and Anna McHolland Hill were in attendance. Anna's son, Thomas Earl, had traveled with his mother from Burleson, Texas, to participate in the ceremony. The hospital commander, Brigadier General George B. Foster addressed a gathering of family and friends, "I am particularly honored today to present four high awards for the actions of one officer..." Quoting from the citation for each award, Brig. Gen. Foster then presented Uncle Bob's combat medals to his nephews: the Distinguished Service Cross to Thomas Earl, The Silver Star with Oak Leaf Cluster to me, and the Bronze Star to my brother Bob. [1] My brother John was only about a year and a half at the time or would possibly have received

Uncle Bob's Purple Heart which was presented to the family. Although all attendees are not known, those in attendance at the ceremony included family friends Travis Brown and Vena Custer Berglund. I was almost five years old when I was presented with Uncle Bob's medal, but I can still remember sensing that there must have been something extra special about my Uncle Bob.

John, Bob, and Jerry Wiley, 1945—courtesy Wiley-McHolland family.

A LASTING TRIBUTE BY MARY SCOTT HAIR

As mentioned, Uncle Bob's dear friend, Mary Scott Hair, and close friend of his family, from Hurley, applied her exceptional literary talent in composing a touching tribute to Uncle Bob. Mary's Rosary for Remembrance was published in the "Crane, Missouri, Chronicle" on January 10, 1946. In this moving tribute Mary masterfully used an item of Uncle Bob's returned personal effects, a beautiful hand carved rosary, to Illustrate the essence of Uncle Bob's character and personality.

RECOGNITION IN THE CONGRESSIONAL RECORD

Mary Scott Hair sent a copy of the Rosary for Remembrance to the Congressman for the Seventh District of Missouri, the honorable   of Galena, Missouri. Uncle Bob had been acquainted with Congressman Short from the beginning of his political career in the early 1930s and greatly admired him and his political philosophy. The congressman was so stirred and moved by Mary's tribute to Uncle Bob that he decided to offer it for entry into the Congressional Record. With his unique oral talent, the "Orator of the Ozarks" eloquently introduced the entire passage of the tribute to the second session of the 79th United States Congress on May 21, 1946, with the following remarks:

> *"Mr. Speaker, under leave to extend my remarks, I include a beautiful and touching tribute paid by my cousin, Mary Scott Hair, to one of my most loyal and ardent friends and supporters, Capt Robert McHolland of Hurley, Mo.*
>
> *"Much as I would like to say, I cannot mar this magnificent tribute to one who gave his last full measure of devotion to a great cause. All I can do is to shed a tear to read the following tribute….."* [2]

The entire text of Mary's extraordinary work can be found in the Appendix.

Continuing Questions about
Uncle Bob's Death

From the moment the first telegram arrived from the War Department informing the family that Uncle Bob was missing in action, many questions about his situation immediately arose. Concern about Uncle Bob would continue to intensify as another three weeks passed before the family received the second tersely worded telegram confirming he had been killed in action. The letter from the unit personnel officer that followed shortly after the second telegram contained a brief statement regarding the events that led to his death. [3] However, it omitted important specific details of the circumstances surrounding his death. From the beginning there were unanswered questions regarding whether Uncle Bob's body was recovered. The family's concern continued to grow and was fueled by a perception of confusion and uncertainty within the War Department regarding the subject.

Various inquiries from family and friends about Uncle Bob and the details of his death were made to the War Department during the early months of 1945. Uncle Bob's Official Personnel File contains copies of correspondence from Anna McHolland Hill, Lt. Alvin T. Wiley (brother of Maurice serving in Germany), and Mary Scott Hair. Each of these requested information regarding his death. Copies of the responses to Mrs. Hill and Lt. Wiley are part of the Official Personnel File. Both letters supplied the basic information that was provided to Roxabel in the initial letter from the personnel officer of the 358th Infantry Regiment. There was no copy in the file of a response to the letter written by Mary Scott

Hair. However, it is believed her inquiry was probably a key factor which ultimately led to the locating of Uncle Bob's remains, and thus, the provision to some of the lingering questions. [4]

THE INFLUENCE OF A
DEAR FRIEND'S INQUIRY

Uncle Bob's personnel file contains a faint copy of the letter dated January 18, 1945, from his friend Mary Scott Hair. It was addressed to the "Regimental Chaplain, 358th Infantry." Mary was aware of Uncle Bob's close acquaintance with Chaplain Stohler of the 358th and hoped to obtain more information directly from him about Uncle Bob's death. Only parts of the copy of the letter Mary sent are legible. However, it is apparent she had requested any information the chaplain could provide about the events when Uncle Bob was killed. As noted, there was no copy in Uncle Bob's personnel file of the specific response to Mary Scott Hair's request. However, in comparing the set of information contained in Uncle Bob's official personnel file with the different set of information contained in his Individual Deceased Personnel File, and closely examining the timeline of certain events, it appears highly likely that Mary's inquiry ended up in the Headquarters of General Patton's Third Army. Her inquiry about the details surrounding Uncle Bob's death apparently struck a nerve within the Third Army office of the Quartermaster. Among various other supply and logistical responsibilities, the Quartermaster was responsible for accountability and disposition of soldiers' remains. Discovering there was no record of having recovered Uncle Bob's body, on March 12, 1945, the Third Army Quartermaster ordered the 90th Infantry

Division to conduct an investigation and report on the circumstances of Uncle Bob's death and the recovery of his body. [5]

SPECIAL REPORT BY 358TH INFANTRY REGIMENT REGARDING UNCLE BOB'S DEATH

In accordance with the usual "army way" of doing things through channels, the 90th Division Commander directed the 358th Infantry Regiment to investigate and report its findings regarding Uncle Bob's death. The initial report of the 358th was submitted to the 90th Division in correspondence dated April 8, 1945. After review by the Third Army Quartermaster, the report was returned to the 90th Division for additional information which included sketches of the area where Uncle Bob was killed. It took almost another month for the division to complete and forward the report with the added data back to Third Army Headquarters. The correspondence containing the final report was dated May 5, 1945. Following are the contents of that report:

1. In compliance with basic communication the following information is submitted: Robert B. McHolland 0-433315 358th Inf Regt.
2. An isolated burial was not made.
   a. It was impossible to evacuate remains because of tactical situation.
   b. Death occurred in the vicinity of Butzdorf, Germany. Map coordinates are WL 0403 Nord de Guerre. No permanent landmarks are known.
   c. It is believed machine gun fire was the cause of death.

d. The deceased died almost immediately and was not evacuated to hosp.

e. The deceased was not killed in a vehicle.

f. Pertinent facts concerning the deceased are as follows: Clothing sizes – shirt 16 x 32; trousers, 32 x 31; field jacket, 38R; and shoes, 8 1/2D. The deceased's height was 5' 10', weight, 160; his eyes were blue and hair, brown. He had a scar on face below cheek bone; friends are unable to specify which cheek bone. The deceased was not married.

3. On 24 Nov 44, Capt McHolland was inside a house in the vicinity of Butzdorf, Germany. Two enlisted men from one of the platoons had been directed to contact Capt McHolland for tactical purposes. They tried to gain entrance through the front door but were unsuccessful as door was locked. Capt McHolland directed that they enter house by rear. As a result of intense sniper fire they were pinned down. Capt McHolland advised them he would contact them and would leave by rear door. He made his exit from rear door and as he was about to make turn to go to the front of the house where men were being subjected to sniper fire, he was seriously wounded and died almost instantly. It is believed that machine gun fire was directed at him.

4. Since Co "K" was forced to withdraw from their positions around Butzdorf almost immediately after the death of Capt McHolland and since they did not return to that sector, the officer's body was never recovered by this orgn. [6]

Following established procedures, the Third Army Quartermaster on May 8, 1945 (V-E Day), forwarded the report about Uncle Bob to the Chief, Graves Registration and Effects Division, Office of the Quartermaster General. Along with the information was the official request of the Third Army commander for the search to locate the remains or isolated grave of Uncle Bob.

GRAVES REGISTRATION SERVICE—— A NOBLE MISSION

An article published in the May/June, 1946, issue of "Quartermaster Review" will aid the reader to better understand the scope and depth of the search and recovery operations conducted by the Graves Registration Service of the Quartermaster General after World War II. The article began by stating, "The most intensive search in history is being conducted on the far-flung battlefields of World War II. Identification and proper burial of unknown American servicemen who died overseas is a work which will go on indefinitely as America bends every effort to pay fitting tribute to those who gave their last full measure of devotion." The writer then pointed out the painstaking efforts of the graves registration search teams to locate and identify the remains of our servicemen:

> *"In attempting to locate the graves of service dead, search teams entering a town or territory seek out all available records of burial. Clergymen who may have officiated at burials, and people who took part in the actual burial, are sought out in an effort to determine the location of graves. Bodies thus located are sent back to a collecting point where an effort is made at identification. Then the bodies are*

placed in a temporary cemetery to await final disposition.

Identification tags worn by service personnel, or papers found on the remains, will in most cases serve to identify the body. A record is then made giving the exact location of the temporary grave in which the remains are interred .... A form known as the Report of Interment provides for the recording of every physical detail which may be used as a means of identification, and is used in all cases. This is done to eliminate any possibilities of error." [7]

It was this type of thorough effort and dedication on the part of those conducting the investigative operations that eventually led to the location and recovery of Uncle Bob's remains.

As the weeks and months passed without more information forthcoming from the War Department, family members began to lose hope that Uncle Bob's body would ever be recovered. However, they could not have known the extensive efforts underway by the graves registration personnel as they fanned out across France and Germany in their committed pursuit of the remains of fellow Americans.

UNCLE BOB'S BODY FOUND--GRAVES REGISTRATION REPORT OF INVESTIGATION

It was through the persistence and dedication of the 606th Quartermaster Graves Registration Company that Uncle Bob's remains were located in a German Military Cemetery in Kastel (Castel), Germany on or about February 21, 1946. Enclosed in the Individual Deceased Personnel File for Uncle Bob is a completed

Graves Registration Form No.10, Report of Investigation – Area Searching. This form included the following detailed information regarding the recovery of Uncle Bob's remains:

1. Was investigation preceded by advance publicity? Yes
2. Name of deceased: McHolland, Robert B. Rank: Unk ASN: 0433315 Org: Unk
3. Means of identification: One I.D. tag on body
4. Location of isolated grave, nearest town: Castel, Germany; Map1:250000, sheet K-80 Trier, Ger, coord WL 1508
5. Full name of cemetery: German Military Cemetery, Castel, Germany, Grave No. 8
6. Approximate or established date of death: 28 November 1944 from Burgermeister's report
7. Approximate or established date of burial: 28 November 1944 from Burgermeister's report
8. Manner in which grave was marked: Wooden board with grave number
9. List personal effects found: All personal effects were taken by German officers when the body was buried
10. Information concerning place and particulars surrounding death and burial: The body of this man was picked up near the town of Castel, Germany by German soldiers and taken to the cemetery where it was buried by the caretaker. A German chaplain was at the burial but his name is not known. Name of caretaker: Alois Leuk, Castel, Germany, No. 18. [8]

This report was signed by the Investigating Officer, William H. Zerhan, 2d Lt, Infantry, of the 606th Quartermaster Graves Registration Company.

The report of investigation included a sketch of the cemetery showing the exact location of the graves of seventeen American soldiers buried there. It is noted that the town was referred to as Castel in the report and on the sketch. Current maps and geographical information about Germany identify the town as Kastel.

COMMENTS REGARDING THE REPORT OF INVESTIGATION

Clarification is offered regarding the "approximate date of death" shown on the report of investigation as "28 Nov 44." Other army eyewitness reports clearly established Uncle Bob was killed the evening of November 24, 1944. The obvious question arises as to how his body got to the Kastel cemetery which is located about 20 to 25 miles from Butzdorf. There is a reasonable explanation for this occurrence. K Company was cut off in Butzdorf from the remainder of the 3rd Battalion, 358th Infantry the evening of November 24. It was not until sometime the next day, November 25, that L Company, reinforced by tanks of the 10th Armored Division, was able to make it into Butzdorf to allow the survivors of K and M Companies to withdraw to the battalion rear area. Butzdorf remained under heavy fire from German tanks and small arms fire throughout the day. L Company and the remainder of the 3rd Battalion withdrew from Butzdorf the evening of November 25 and the entire 358th Infantry Regiment was withdrawn and assigned to division reserve the next day. [9] It would be another few weeks before Butzdorf and the surrounding area came under control of the Allies. German troops entered and occupied Butzdorf when L Company withdrew. Sometime during the next two or three days the German soldiers picked up the bodies from the area and transported them to the German Military Cemetery in Kastel where they were buried. The sketch that accompanied the graves registration report identified at least four other members of the 358th Infantry Regiment who were also buried at the Kastel cemetery.   It is believed these men were also casualties of the action at Butzdorf and their bodies were removed and buried at the same time as Uncle Bob's body was recovered by the German troops. The Germans, like the Americans, were known to clear contested areas of the dead as quickly as the battlefield conditions permitted. The detailed records kept by the German cemetery caretaker also lends credence to these conclusions.

According to the investigative report, as soon as Uncle Bob's remains were identified, they were disinterred by graves registration personnel and moved to the U. S. Military Cemetery in St. Avold, France for reburial. The Report of Burial reflects that reburial took place on February 21, 1946. [10]

Delay in Reporting to Family and Important Omissions

Unfortunately Uncle Bob's family was never provided the detailed information contained in the graves registration report of investigation. It was several months later, in October 1946, that the family received its first official correspondence that Uncle Bob's body had been recovered. The letter from the Quartermaster General of the Army provided only the burial location, U. S Military Cemetery, St. Avold, France, plot RRR, row 5, grave 53. No other details concerning the date, location, and circumstances surrounding recovery of the remains were provided. [11]

A DECISION ON FINAL INTERMENT

It was another year before the next communication from the Quartermaster General of the Army to the family arrived. The letter addressed to Roxabel was dated October 17, 1947. This letter informed her of the congressional authorization of the disinterment and final burial of the World War II dead.

It also provided two pamphlets, "Disposition of World War II Armed Forces Dead" and "American Cemeteries," which explained the disposition, options and services made available by the government to the next of kin. Also included was a form entitled "Request for Disposition of Remains." Roxabel being the next of kin was requested to use this form in deciding upon the disposition of Uncle Bob's remains. [12] It was well over a month before Roxabel made her decision known leading one to believe she likely consulted her siblings before making the final decision. With her signature on the form dated November 29, 1947, Roxabel opted to have Uncle Bob permanently interred in the U.S. Military Cemetery, St. Avold, France—the same cemetery where he was initially buried after recovery of his remains, with the stipulation that if his remains were ever to be moved again she wanted them moved to the United States.

A SISTER'S PERSISTENT QUESTIONS

From the earliest point of receiving the news about Uncle Bob being missing in action, and then suffering through the weeks until news arrived that he had been killed in action, Roxabel had been skeptical about whether the army really knew what had happened to Uncle Bob. The ensuing delays in receiving official information about his status further served to reinforce her skepticism. At the same time Roxabel returned the form to the Quartermaster General, indicating her decision about disposition of Uncle Bob's remains, she sent a letter to the Army Adjutant General, Casualty Branch, requesting information to clear up her questions about the circumstances surrounding Uncle Bob's death: where his body was finally found, and any other material concerning her brother. She pointed out that the information she had received from the War Department was in conflict with the information obtained by her brother-in-law, Lt. Alvin T. Wiley, while he was stationed in Germany in 1945, shortly after the war. Roxabel was apparently referring to the 358th Infantry Regiment letter of June 5, 1945, sent to Alvin in response to his request for information about Uncle Bob. The information provided in that letter to Alvin stated that Uncle Bob's body was never recovered and that no burial report was ever received. Of course, this was true as of June, 1945, because Uncle Bob's body had not been recovered and no one knew what had happened to it. [13]

A RESPONSE--TOO LITTLE, TOO LATE

The letter Roxabel addressed to the Adjutant General,

requesting more information about the circumstances of Uncle Bob's death, was referred to the Quartermaster General for reply. She received a response from the office of the Quartermaster General dated February 2, 1949. It provided the following information:

> *"The official report of burial indicates that the remains of your brother were originally interred in Castel, Germany, in the vicinity where he met his death, but were later disinterred and moved to a more appropriate location where constant care and protection could be given our honored dead."* [14]

The letter also provided information that was previously received in October, 1946, about the location of Uncle Bob's remains in the U. S. Military Cemetery in St. Avold, France. Even though more details were provided the most pertinent information regarding the identification and recovery of Uncle Bob's remains was not included. Regardless, it was probably much too late to satisfy Roxabel's doubt and cynicism about her brother's death, and whether the remains recovered were actually those of Uncle Bob.

The root of the problem was the fact that the Quartermaster General did not inform the family when the body was recovered in February, 1946. As noted, they were informed in October, 1946, merely of Uncle Bob's burial location. Although the information was available in the graves registration report of investigation, no information was provided concerning when and where his remains were found. Possibly much of Roxabel's consternation and skepticism, about whether the remains were actually those of Uncle Bob, would have been avoided if the report of investigation by the Graves Registration was made available to the family.

NOTE: It was not until December, 2007, sixty-one years later, when I was able to obtain Uncle Bob's Individual Deceased Personnel File that the family first learned about the Graves Registration report of investigation that documented the initial location of Uncle Bob's remains and the circumstances regarding his burial. Speaking with familiarity of army personnel and administration policy and procedures, from forty-two plus years of service with that organization, there is no doubt in my mind that the remains recovered were those of Uncle Bob. I know that graves registration personnel went to great lengths to assure that recovered remains were accurately identified. If there was any doubt about identification, the remains were classified as unidentified. Based on my review of the detailed, well-prepared report of the graves registration team, including an imprint of Uncle Bob's ID (dog) tags, I am one hundred percent certain that it is Uncle Bob who rests along with the other thousands of heroes in the U. S. Military Cemetery, at St. Avold, France. The saddest aspect of this whole misfortune is that my mother, Roxabel, passed away in June 2007 without knowing these additional details about her brother's death.

A FINAL RESTING PLACE FOR UNCLE BOB

Over four years and three months had passed since the receipt of the awful "missing in action" telegram when the War Department made its final contact with Uncle Bob's family. That contact was by letter, dated March 25, 1949, from the department's Office of the Quartermaster General addressed to Roxabel and provided information concerning the permanent interment of Uncle Bob's remains. Marked by a white cross inscribed with his name, rank, service number and unit, Uncle Bob was laid to rest on January 11, 1949 alongside thousands of other brave men who paid the ultimate price in the service of their country. The customary military funeral services were conducted at his gravesite: Plot A, Row 22, Grave 52, U. S. Military Cemetery, St. Avold, France. [15]

American Military Cemetery (Lorraine), St. Avold, France. Captain Mac's final resting place—courtesy American Battle Monuments Commission

Peace be to your soul, Captain Mac--Uncle Bob.

Chapter 20 Endnotes:
1. "Captain's Awards are Presented to Nephews Sunday," Springfield News-Leader, 1 December 1945.
2. Mary Scott Hair, "Rosary for Remembrance," Congressional Record, 21 May 1946, A2996-A2997.

3. Letter, Hqs, 358th Infantry, 27 December 1944.
4. Documents, Official Personnel File.
5. Documents, Individual Deceased Personnel File.
6. Documents, Individual Deceased Personnel File.
7. "Graves Registration Search and Recovery Operations after World War II," Quartermaster Review, May/June 1946.
8. Documents, Individual Deceased Personnel File.
9. Bryan, 20.
10. Documents, Individual Deceased Personnel File.
11. Letter, Army Quartermaster General, 7 October 1946.
12. Letter, Army Quartermaster General, 17 October 1948.
13. Documents, Individual Deceased Personnel File.
14. Letter, Army Quartermaster General, 2 February 1949.
15. Letter, Army Quartermaster General, 25 March 1949.

Epilogue

Nothing experienced in my life's journey can exceed the joy of the birth of my children along with the countless times they have made me proud to be their father. Neither can the unconditional love, devotion, and loyalty of the perfect mate with whom I am blessed be surpassed by any worldly achievement. However, the incalculable hours spent collecting and compiling information about Uncle Bob, not to mention the actual writing of this tribute, take their place near the top of my proudest and most rewarding moments.

Along this wonderful journey to document Uncle Bob's life I have met many new friends and renewed acquaintances with many others. I will forever be indebted to so many who have shared their time and memories with me about Uncle Bob. I can never repay them for their patience and selflessness in abiding with my constant visits, telephone calls and letters. I could never have completed this tribute without them.

As noted, my greatest regret is that I did not decide to accomplish this tribute earlier. Had my journey begun even a scant few years earlier so much more anecdotal information could have been gained about Uncle Bob from relatives and friends who had close ties with him.

Over the years Uncle Bob's service has been recognized in many ways. I wrote earlier of the Easter lily that was dedicated annually in the Easter service at the Hurley Methodist Church to honor those from the community who died in World War II. The Missouri State University Library in Springfield, Missouri displays a biographical sketch of Uncle Bob in its special War Memorial Album Collection. The Hometown Heroes of the Show Me State website honors Uncle Bob as a recipient of the Distinguished Service Cross. His name is entered on the Stone County (Missouri) Memorial Scroll of Honor for his service in World War II. A book, "The Lorraine Campaign" chronicling his heroism in the Butzdorf action was presented to the library of his alma mater, Hurley High School, in a special Veterans' Day ceremony in 2000. And, of course, there is Tom Hill's "Uncle Bob" jeep that regularly honors Captain Mac's memory in exhibitions and parades. I am certain there are other tributes.

My hope is that Uncle Bob's memory will live on as well as the memory of countless others who sacrificed so much for our great country. A tribute such as this could be written for almost four hundred thousand others in World War II who paid with their lives, tens of thousands who suffered terrible debilitating physical and emotional wounds, and over two million others who answered the call to defend our way of life. May God bless each of them for what they did to preserve the precious rights and freedom we enjoy every day in the greatest country ever.

Mary Scott Hair—courtesy Stone County Historical Society.

Appendix
ROSARY FOR REMEMBRANCE

By Mary Scott Hair

Dedicated to the Memory of Capt. Robert McHolland, "Greater love hath no man than this, that a man lay down his life for his friends."

"The personal effects of an individual missing in action overseas are held by his unit for a period of time, and then sent to the Effects Quartermaster, Kansas City, MO., for disposition as designated by the soldier."

Those words are familiar words in homes all over America. They have been read and read again, so many times it is not necessary to look at the letter, on official War department paper, to read them. You can look at a blank piece of paper and see the words neatly typed thereon.

A telegram arrived, telling the family and friends of Capt. Robert McHolland, Hurley, Mo., that Bob, previously missing, was killed in action on November 24, 1944.

Then the period of waiting began—waiting for details of what happened. Waiting that seemed endless—in which no clue was too small to offer hope. His old letters, carefully kept and treasured, were once more combed for names of men in his company.

Bits of news, interesting because they express Bob's personality so forcefully, began weaving a pattern in the tapestry of life the Great Weaver finished so suddenly on that November day.

May 9, 1944—Somewhere in England.
"The war cry of this war is 'Any gum, chum-' Every English kid you see has that on his lips soon as he spots a Yank.
"I talked with a ten year old boy about school and fighting and life in general. The boy said he would quit school and go to work in a carpet factory when he reached the ripe old age of thirteen.
"I asked him who he thought the world's best fighter was—and he said he guessed Hitler was. Any way it looked that way to him."

June 26, 1944—France, Somewhere.
"I am enclosing some pictures I found on the battlefield. I did not take them from a dead German—the Krauts carry pictures of their loved ones, too. Any personal belongings such as letters and pictures are scattered like leaves, after a battle.

"I studied these pictures carefully. This one of

the little boy and his mother—there will be no swastikas for him. He will have a chance to grow up in a free world where he can think for himself, a free man.

"Not only for Jerry, Bobby, Johnny and Thomas Earl, but for any children and for all people everywhere, will our sacrifices be made—that they may live the 'Abundant Life' due them.

"I firmly believe that peace will triumph over war and that love will rule the world."

In a V-mail letter dated August 18, we received our first name clue.

"Our chaplain, Capt. Edgar Stohler, of the Salvation Army, is just about the biggest hero around here. Watch for his story in the paper."

We watched, and sure enough the account written by Edward Ball, of Associated Press, appeared in the daily paper. It told how guns on both sides stopped as three chaplains went out in a strip of marsh no-man's land to bring in the wounded. A German cameraman came out and snapped pictures of them. Within a few minutes after the chaplains reached the aid station the silence was broken by German shell fire. War was resumed once more. One of the chaplains was Capt. Edgar Stohler, of the Salvation Army.

September 27—France.
"These French kids sure are cute. Many of them

speak three or four languages. They call me 'Captaine Robaire.' And they make more noise than a full-fledged attack. You can't help loving them."

October 15—France.
"Today is Sunday. If the situation is favorable we may have some kind of service this afternoon.
"I am sending you a pressed flower. I found it in a German officer's medical manual.
"If the Lord is willing, I'll be seeing you all, some-day."

That was my last letter from Bob.

The flower was a beautiful pansy, carefully pro-tected by two folds of waxed paper, "Pansies for thoughts"—

Chaplain Stohler's letter came, finally. Just a few sentences but they told how considerate and kind Bob was to his men, how he attended religious services, and ended with this: "Bob was a dear personal friend. Will you please tell his family and friends that their loss is my loss, too."

Other bits of information came—a few letters from relatives of men in Bob's company; clip-pings from newspapers.

In September 1945, the War department notified Bob's sister, Mrs. Roxabel Wiley, of Hurley, Mo., that three awards, the Silver Star with Oak Leaf Cluster, the Bronze Star Medal and the Distinguished Service Cross would be awarded, post-humously, to her, or a member of her family.

In September, too, Bob's personal belongings arrived. First came the army foot locker containing clothing and some letters. Two other packages of clothing followed and finally his bed-roll came. There is something personal and final about a bed-roll.

One package was socks and small articles of clothing. And packed in among the handkerchiefs and socks was an old French heirloom, a rosary of Lourdes, France. No one will ever know what story the rosary would tell—if it could. But in one of Bob's letters, he wrote about a little French girl ten years old that he had befriended. The ever-grateful French people were known to give their liberators many prized keepsakes and heirlooms. And, while it is merely a supposition, it seems logical to suppose that little Marie Eugene gave this lovely string of carved wooden beads to her hero, Captain Robaire.

The beads are large, an inch in diameter, and are made of olive wood, carved in a distinct pattern. The chain between the beads is old and worn.

The heart-shaped wooden emblem between the 50 Hail Marys and the three Holy Marys says on one side, "Coeur Immacule of Marie protegez nous."

The round wooden disc at the top of the cross

has a religious carving on one side, of a kneeling girl and the Blessed Virgin. On the other side are these words, "Allezz Boire a la Fontaine et vous y laver."

The cross, also of wood, was broken. The mended place is plainly visible in the picture. The image of Christ has been removed from the cross, leaving only the "prints of the nails."

When we examined the rosary carefully and realized what a treasure it is, a quotation from the story of Bernadette, the little French Peasant girl who saw the Blessed Virgin, came to mind.

"All the women and girls of Lourdes carry a rosary upon their person. It is the authentic tool of their piety. The hands of poor, hardworking women have not the habit of stillness. A prayer with empty hands would be not prayer observance for them. But the prayer of the rosary is to them a sort of heavenly manual toil, an invisible needlework, a knitting or embroidering busily wrought of the fifty Hail Mary's and the nine other invocations of their string of beads."

Capt. Robert McHolland was a Protestant, a sincere Christian and a man's man in every respect. He was a Mason, member of Crane Lodge No. 519, and also a member of the Eastern Star. He shared the idealism of Wendell Willkie's, "One World"; he gave his life that those ideals might come into being in actual life, to the great and the small, the rich and the poor alike. His personal creed was big enough to love little children, regardless of race, creed or social standing. He was an ardent admirer of Abraham Lincoln and Honest Abe's words, "With malice toward none" could easily be said of Capt. McHolland.

Bob loved Christmas. I think it must have been his favorite time of the year. He always took part in our programs and went with us to sing carols on Christmas Eve. All of us received cards, written and mailed a day or so before his death. A hasty note scribbled on the back of one card said, "I'd give anything to be back home and go caroling with you—but those times seem so long ago."

From the grim story told by the War department, we know that Bob's last days were full of anxiety and despair, for his first consideration, always, was for the safety of his men. He died trying to save two wounded members of his company.

The words from the beautiful song, "The Rosary," come to mind again and again—"O memories that bless and burn—O barren gain, and bitter loss—" That a life so young and so promising should be sacrificed seems, at times, "A bitter loss."

But there was One who died on the Cross of Calvary, that men might live triumphant lives. And the words come again—in the whisper of wind in the leaves, in the voices of happy children at play, in the peace and quiet of the early morning— "Greater love hath no man than this, that a man lay down his life for his friends."

Front: Howard Pemberton, Jerry Wiley, Rear: Ardys Pemberton , Sheila Wiley at the Pemberton home in Storm Lake, Iowa, 2007—courtesy Sheila and Jerry Wiley.

Tom Hill, Howard Pemberton, Jerry Wiley, Fort Worth, Texas, 90th Infantry Division Mobile Exhibit, 2007—courtesy Sheila Wiley.

Captain Emmett T. Boyd, U. S. Army, Retired, and Jerry Wiley at Captain Boyd's home in Woodbine, Georgia, 2007.

Captain Emmett T. Boyd, U. S. Army, Retired—courtesy Captain Emmett Boyd.

Entry to 90th Infantry Division Mobile Exhibit, Fort Worth, Texas, 2007—courtesy Tyler Alberts, 90th Division Historian.

Tom Hill's "Uncle Bob" jeep displayed at the 90ᵗʰ Infantry Division Mobile Exhibit, Fort Worth, Texas, 2007—courtesy Tyler Alberts.

Exhibit honoring Captain Mac's K Kompany Kraut Killers (note KKKK patch on left breast of combat uniform), 90ᵗʰ Infantry Division Mobile Exhibit, Fort Worth, Texas, 2007—courtesy Tyler Alberts.

Photo of exhibit from the 90ᵗʰ Infantry Division Mobile Exhibit showing Tom Hill's tribute to Captain Mac. It includes photo of Captain Mac receiving his second Silver Star from BG James A. Van Fleet and displays the combat awards he received—courtesy Sheila Wiley.

INDEX